A VOYAGE TO WAR

A VOYAGE TO WAR

AN ENGLISHMAN'S ACCOUNT OF HONG KONG 1936–41

Taken from the original correspondence by Peter Dulley
Written and edited by Hugh Dulley

This edition first published by
Uniform
an imprint of Unicorn Publishing Group

Unicorn Publishing Group
101 Wardour Street
London W1F 0UG

All rights reserved. No part of this publication may be reproduced,
stored in a retrieval system or transmitted, in any form or by any means,
electronic, mechanical, photocopying, recording or otherwise, without prior
permission in writing from the publisher.

© Hugh Dulley, 2016
www.unicornpress.org

© Preface by Mark Whitehead
© Foreword by Tony Banham
© Images belong to the Estate of H. W. M. Dulley unless otherwise specified. Every
effort has been made to trace copyright holders and to obtain their permission for the
use of copyright material. In some instances this has not been possible.
The publisher apologises for any errors or omissions in the above list and would be
grateful if notified of any corrections that should be incorporated in future reprints or
editions of this book.

South China Morning Post pp. 198, 271, 296–298
Australian War Memorial p. 216
Imperial War Museum p. 241
The Estate of Eva Davidson p. 273
Richard Hide, the Hong Kong Escape Re-enactment Organisation (Hero) pp. 274–275
The Estate of Alan Corrigan (back cover image)

Maps drawn by Felicity Price-Smith
Interior design by Vivian Foster
Index by Elizabeth Wise

A catalogue record for this book is available from
the British Library

ISBN 978-1-910500-55-2
PDF 978-1-910500-56-9
Mobi 978-1-910500-57-6

Printed and bound in India

CONTENTS

	Preface	7
	Foreword	9
	Introduction	11
	Personal Timeline	14
	Map of Hong Kong in the 1930s	16–17
	Map of Journey to Aden and Back	18–19
	Map of the Mediterranean	20–21
	Map of the Chinese Coastline	22
1	Arriving in Hong Kong in the 1930s	23
2	A Whirlwind Romance	53
3	A Long Distance Engagement and a Trip to Shanghai	60
4	Making Plans for the Bride's Return	74
5	The Wedding and the Honeymoon in the Philippine Islands	95
6	Hong Kong	104
7	Hong Kong in Wartime	112
8	The Evacuation to the Philippine Islands	123
9	Planning the Return to Hong Kong	161
10	A Sad Departure	171
11	Preparing for the Voyage	183
12	The Voyage to Aden	202
13	Life in Aden	219
14	The Return Journey	227
15	The Last Few Months	236
16	The Japanese Threat	255
17	The Invasion	260
18	Epilogue	269

Appendix I: The Glossary 284

Appendix II: Place Names Old and New and Abbreviations 286

Appendix III: List of Names Mentioned in Letters 287

Appendix IV: Exchange Rates 295

Appendix V: Press Statement on the Evacuation – October 1940 296

Appendix VI: HWM Dulley's Ships 299

Appendix VII: The Crew of *St. Aubin* 300

Appendix VIII: The Jardine Matheson Archive 301

Appendix IX: Letters from Internees of the Japanese Camps in
    Hong Kong 303

Bibliography 314

Index 316

RHKYC 香港遊艇會

A Voyage to War – An Englishman's Account of Hong Kong 1936–41

On Sunday 7 December 1941 the Royal Hong Kong Yacht Club was hosting a regatta and preparing for lunch when news of the Japanese invasion of Hong Kong broke. Many members of the Club were killed or wounded in the subsequent fighting while those who survived became prisoners of war or, if civilians, interned.

Lieutenant Commander Dulley went missing, presumed killed in action, sometime between 7 and 25 December 1941. As a keen sailor and Olympic oarsman he had been a very active member of the Club for over 10 years, winning the Commodore's Cup twice, the Cruiser Championship, the Illingworth Cup and the Long Harbour Race as well as coming second in the Macau Race.

To this day, the Club commemorates the important role played by Peter Dulley and all those who volunteered for service with the Hong Kong Royal Naval Volunteer Reserve (HKRNVR), by running a pursuit race, in which sailors compete for the HKRNVR Memorial Vase.

We are proud to be recognising the sacrifices that these volunteers made and are honoured to have been asked to show appreciation for their efforts on our behalf in this book.

Mark Whitehead

Mark Whitehead
Commodore
Royal Hong Kong Yacht Club
May 2016

ROYAL HONG KONG YACHT CLUB 香港遊艇會
KELLETT ISLAND, HONG KONG   TEL: (852) 2832 2817   FAX: (852) 2239 0329

Foreword

There is a special poignancy in reading a story whose ending you already know. I first came across Lieutenant Commander Hugh 'Peter' Dulley's name some thirty years ago. I knew him as one of a number of men who lost their lives at a house called Postbridge. At that time I knew nothing else about him; I didn't even know where Postbridge was.

I even wrote about him, just a few words in a book I composed about the battle of Hong Kong. And then years later, when studying for my PhD about the evacuation of British women and children from Hong Kong to Australia in 1940, I came across his name again. Then I learned about his wife and as yet unborn son, and their break of journey in the Philippines where that son would be born.

Now, with this book, we have the chance to understand more about the family. Why Peter was in Hong Kong, how he met his wife, their romance and life together for a few short years before war came. And that of course is the poignancy; this was years before I was born, yet I am considerably older now than they were then. They were two young people trying to start a family at a time when much stronger forces were turning the world to war. In that experience, of course, they were far from being alone. And this just adds to the impact of their story. It speaks for thousands, in fact hundreds of thousands, of other ordinary people at that turning point in history.

So in essence it is a sad story, and yet an inspiring one. They did their best, though Peter would be killed and his wife left widowed and looking after young Hugh (the editor of this work) alone. Like many other ladies in that situation, she managed. She had little choice.

For Lieutenant Commander Dulley, and many of his comrades, December 1941 in Hong Kong marked the end. His body was never identified after the war. It may still be hidden somewhere in Wong Nai Chung Gap where he fell, though more likely he is lying in one of the many graves in Hong Kong marked only 'Known Unto God'. That was Rudyard Kipling's phrase, applied to all unknown British and Commonwealth graves ever since, originally including his own son John who was lost in the Great War.

So, in the absence of an identified memorial, this book will suffice – with a granularity of detail and personality that three words carved into stone could never reveal: Here lies Lieutenant Commander Hugh 'Peter' Dulley, in his Voyage to War.

Dr Tony Banham
Hong Kong, May 2016

To Peter and Therese

Introduction

Producing this book has been a hugely interesting and rewarding journey. I now feel that I have come to know my father (Peter) and to admire his letter writing, with all the illuminating insights into his life in Hong Kong. He took letter writing very seriously and allowed plenty of time, so that the result was a well-crafted letter. In preparing this book I had an advantage in that my mother (Therese) had told me stories about pre-war Hong Kong, and I know the Dulley and Davidson families well, both past and present.

The aim of this book was to make these letters on pre-World War 2 Hong Kong available to all who might be interested, so that they did not just lie in some archive, possibly never to be seen again. They provide a vivid picture of the social history of Hong Kong at the time and also life in the Hong Kong Royal Naval Volunteer Reserve in the lead up to the Japanese invasion. My main objective has now been achieved and I hope that the reader will be drawn into accompanying Peter on his journey.

It seems a long time ago but then the British Empire still ruled a large part of the world, those parts coloured in red in a school atlas, and many thought it would continue to do so. The invasion was to mark the beginning of the end of the British Empire. Hong Kong was a very different place to the modern, vibrant international city of today; it was even called sleepy by some. Many of the differences are well known, such as Hong Kong is no longer part of what was the British Empire, but has now reverted to being part of China, which then was a far cry from the major power it is today. It is hoped that this book will show the other differences.

As Tony Banham says in his Foreword, the Dulley's fate was sadly not unique in Hong Kong or for that matter much of the rest of the world. World War 2 had an enormous impact on all, the men going away to war and many families having to leave their homes or to suffer enemy bombing or both. We have all been fortunate in living during a period of over seventy years without another World War, so it is hard to understand the sheer scale of the trauma created at the time.

I have added some additional chapters to the letters. Chapter 1 was written to cover what is not in the letters, which were written to Therese, Peter's wife, who had lived in Hong Kong in the 1930s, so did not need a description of life there. For most this will not be the case as they were not living in Hong Kong in the 1930s or may not have been to

Hong Kong. The introductory chapter also places Peter's letters in context. Chapter 16 has been added to explain the Japanese threat to Hong Kong from 1936–41. Chapter 17 covers the invasion from Peter's point of view and Chapter 18 brings the story to a conclusion following Peter's death. Every effort has been made to ensure that these chapters and all the footnotes are historically correct, but if there are any errors, then I apologise to the reader in advance.

Chris Munn, who was then in the Hong Kong University Press, offered me one of the most important and delightful pieces of advice – 'no matter how interesting the letters are they should be halved in length'. Remarkably this was achieved by removing duplication, information that would have been of no interest to the reader, and summarising some topics in the first chapter. A few colourful remarks and some short pieces that were not really part of the main story were also cut out. The letters to Therese are the main core of the book and other letters have been deleted where they duplicated information, apart from the letters written during the voyage to Aden, which have been amalgamated to provide one text.

I have read many books on Hong Kong's history and carried out searches on the internet over the last five years. The object of the book was to publish the letters and the rest fits around them. There may be more detailed accounts of various subjects, but it was considered that what was required was an adequate explanation of the letters and life in those times, rather than an in-depth one.

The letters were written between 1936 and 1941, seventy-five to eighty years ago and naturally they reflect those times, which were very different to today. Events and comments need to be judged by early 20th-century standards and then compared with the 21st. It is on this basis that some pieces have been left in, which might otherwise have been deleted. As an observer we bring our own values to judge a situation; the values of today are very different to those of Hong Kong in the 1930s.

Of the many people I would like to thank for helping me with this enterprise, I wish to mention first my cousin, Mary Beal. She has given me a substantial amount of her time and we have had many valuable discussions. She also carried out some very useful research, drawing on a lifetime's experience as an art historian. She advised on the format of the text and footnotes and carried out the original proofreading. She transcribed all the letters to other members of the family and the letters of condolence written to Therese. She believed in Peter's letters and her support gave me confidence to complete the book.

Mary introduced me to Amelia Allsop of the Hong Kong Heritage Project and, through her, Chris Munn of the Hong Kong University Press, both of whom provided valuable advice on publishing.

I am also very grateful to Tony Banham, who wrote the definitive book on the invasion of Hong Kong, *Not the Slightest Chance: The Defence of Hong Kong, 1941*, on which I drew heavily for the chapter on the invasion. He has sent me many very helpful emails along the way and very kindly agreed to write the Foreword to this book, which I feel is perfect and really gets to the heart of the story. I would like to thank Mark Whitehead, Commodore of the Royal Hong Kong Yacht Club for writing a thoughtful Preface to the book and thereby providing a link to the Club's past members, Peter and Therese and their friends.

My thanks to the Grieve family, Elizabeth Henderson and James Grieve, whose parents were great friends of Peter and Therese in Hong Kong, for their support and loan of photos and other material. The Davidson family for their interest and encouragement. Charles Moore, my old Australian friend, who has provided me with various insights on the Far East and Australia. The many people along the way who have given me advice and support, including Owen and Sally Bryant and my local walking friends and wives. Jardines, for allowing me to search their archives at Cambridge University. The archivists at the Imperial War Museum, London, the National Archives and at the Jardine Archive for all their help.

My thanks to Lucy Duckworth and her team at Unicorn Press, particularly Vivian Foster, for all their help, advice and ideas, the end product of which has been this quality book.

My daughters Kath Hipwell and Lou Carpenter and their husbands Simon and Ben for all their support and advice on some key issues and letting me draw on their advertising, research and IT skills.

Finally I would like to thank my wife Barbara for all her encouragement, support, advice, proofreading and many other things. In addition, for her ability to interpret Peter's handwriting, using the skills she has developed over many years of reading doctors' handwriting and finally for putting up with the many hours I have spent on the book.

This book is to be published shortly before the 75th anniversary of the Japanese invasion of Hong Kong and I hope that it will in a small way help to commemorate all those who were in Hong Kong at the time of the invasion.

Hugh Dulley
August 2016

Personal Timeline

Hugh William Macpherson Dulley 1903–1941
(Known as Peter)

Date	Event
1903	Born in Wellingborough, Northamptonshire.
1915	Gadebridge Park School, near Hemel Hempstead.
1917	Westminster School, London.
1923	Worked in the City of London.
	The family brewery Messrs Wm. Dulley & Sons Ltd, Wellingborough closed.
1924	Rowed in the Paris Olympics.
1925	Worked for Gibbs & Co. mining company, Valpariso, Chile.
1927	Returned to London and worked in the City.
1930	Joined Jardine Matheson in Hong Kong.
1930	His father died at his home in Normandy, France.
1934	First home leave by the Pacific and Canadian Rockies, returning by France and the Suez Canal.
1935	Peter joined the Hong Kong Volunteer Force, which became the HKRNVR.
1935 10 November	Peter and his crew on his yacht *Monsoon* discover an unknown rock to be named 'Dulley Rock'.
1936 14 April	Became engaged to Therese Sander.
1936 23 November	Married in Hong Kong.

Date	Event
1938	Second home leave, both ways by the Suez Canal and Peter met Therese's family for the first and last time.
1939 August	Called up in the HKRNVR.
1940 June	Peter promoted to Lt.Cmdr.
1940 July	Therese evacuated to the Philippine Islands.
1940 26 July	Hugh Peter (HP) born in Baguio.
1940 December	Therese and HP return to Hong Kong.
1941 March	Therese and HP evacuated to Sydney, Australia.
1941 May	Voyage to Aden as Captain of the HMAPV *St. Aubin*.
1941 July	Arrived in Aden and left after a few weeks.
1941 September	Returned to Hong Kong.
1941 November	Appointed First Lieutenant HMS *Cornflower*.
1941 8 December	Japanese invade Hong Kong.
1941 19 December	Peter killed in action, while fighting on the Island.

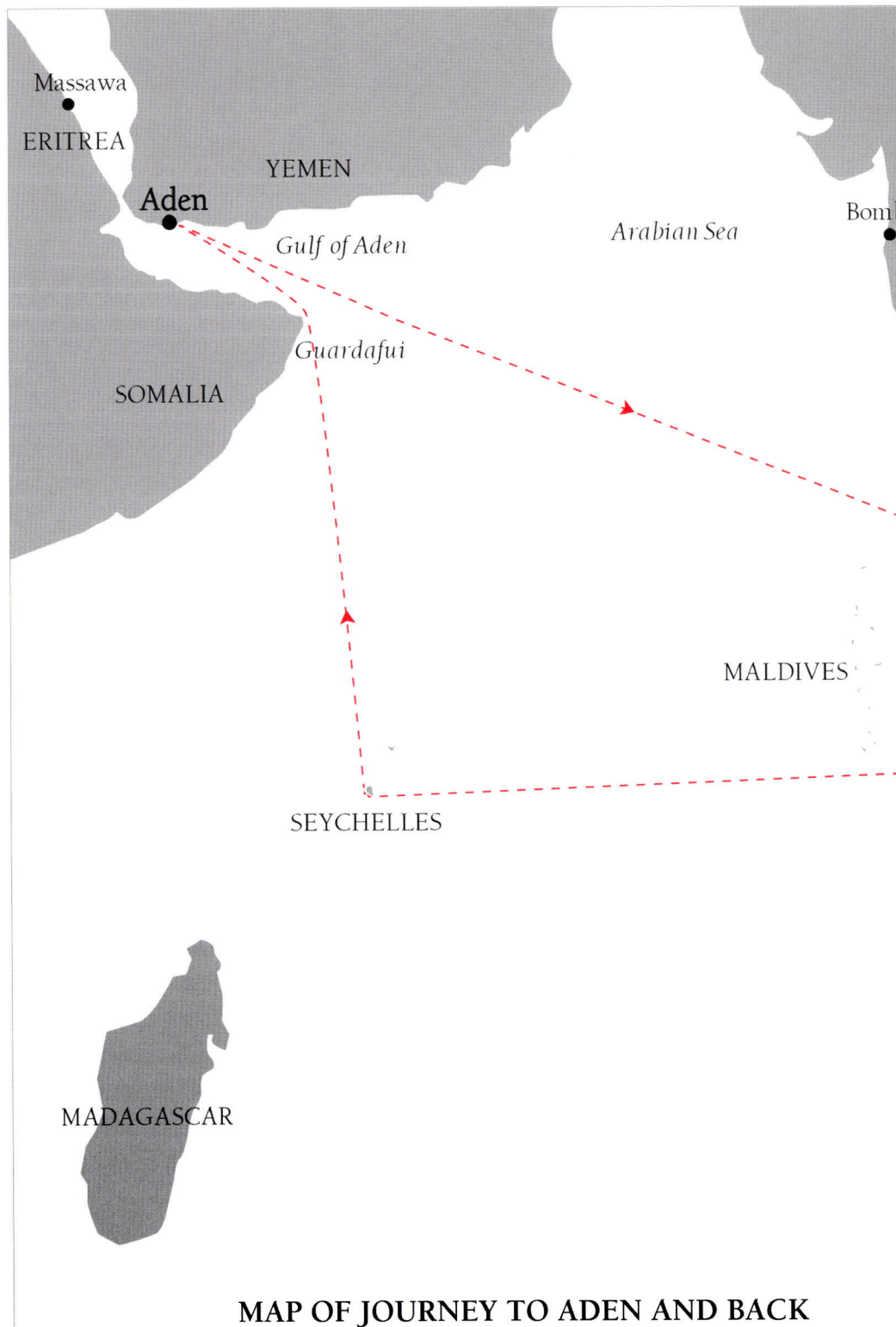

MAP OF JOURNEY TO ADEN AND BACK

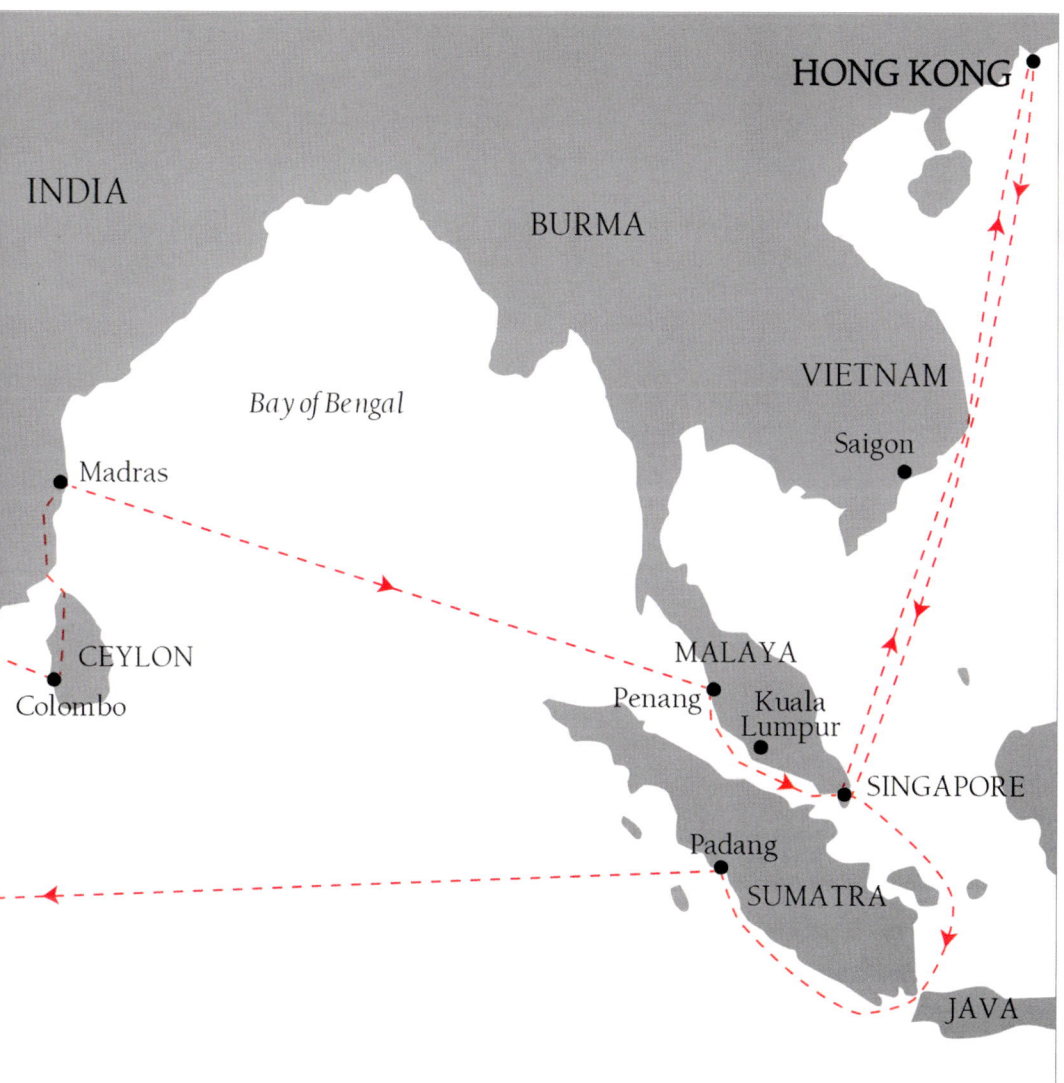

Peter stated in his letter of 13th May 1941 that the distance from Hong Kong to Aden by sea was 6,500 miles.

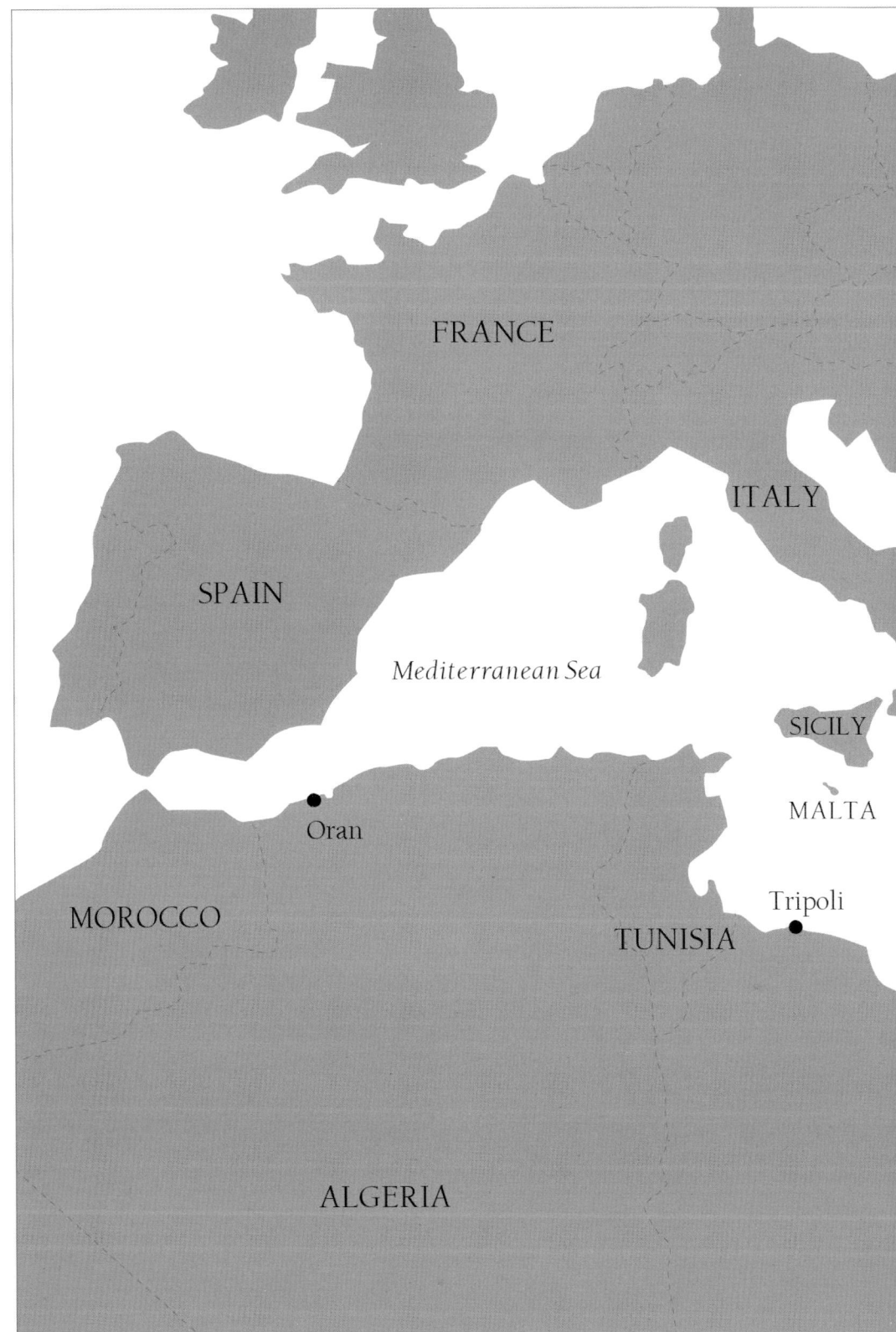

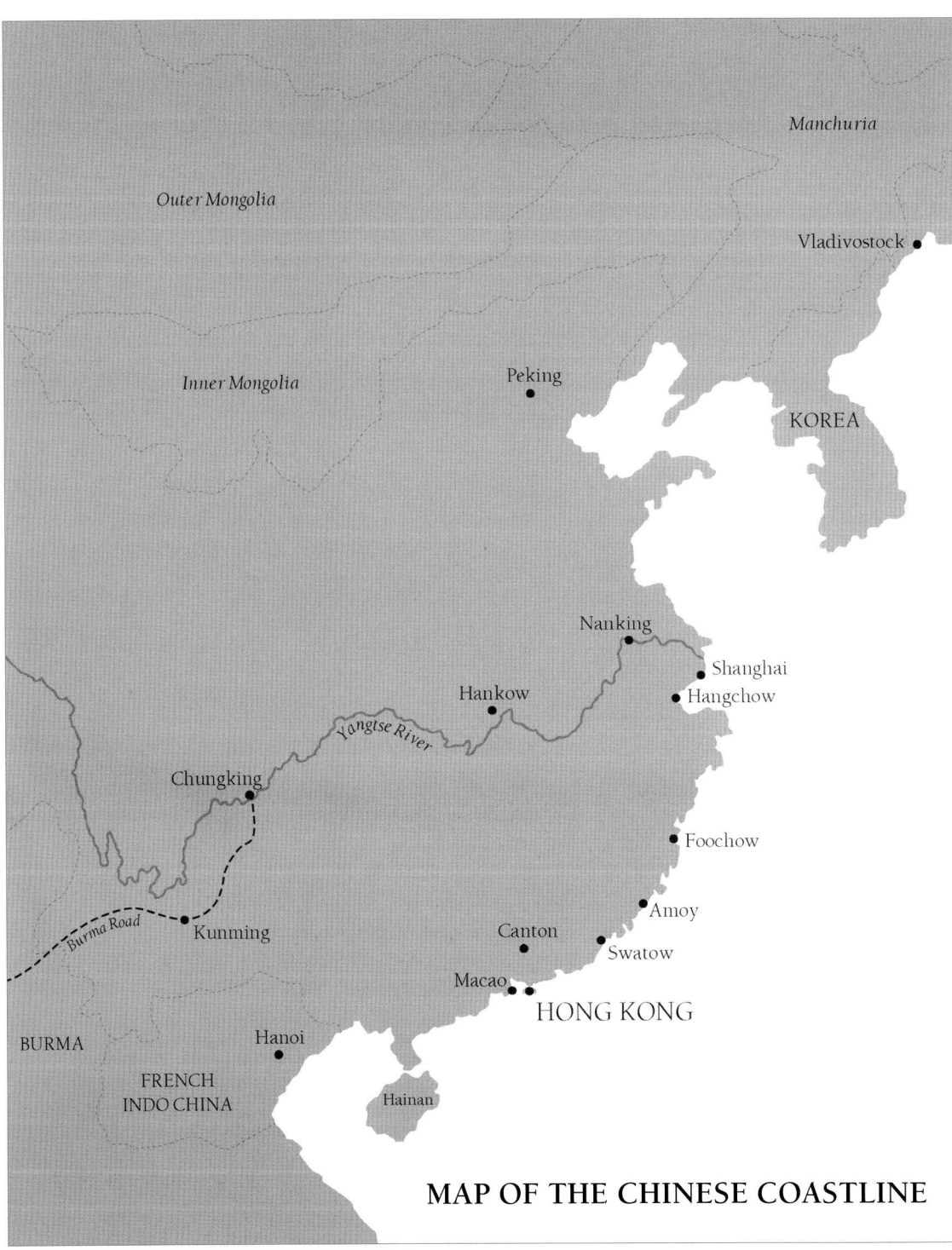

CHAPTER 1

Arriving in Hong Kong in the 1930s

'To port lay the Island itself, with the hills coming down to the sea, but there were many promontories, on some of which were attractive houses set well apart, their white walls shining in the sun, their red or green roofs setting the seal on spacious comfort. The coastline was jagged, interspersed with sparkling sandy beaches on which the deep-blue water gently lapped … We passed the fishing village of Shau KI Wan, teeming with junks and sampans … Some were busy drying fish and others doing chores aboard their vessel.'[1]

Peter Dulley[2] looked out from the deck of the *Rawalpindi* and, like many before him, felt he had arrived in a form of paradise and so it would be for the next nine years. There was no hint of the final role he would play in the year of the centenary of the founding of the Colony in 1941. Peter stood there enjoying the moment. He felt very happy about his decision to turn his back on a life in the City of London and the commute to work by train each day.

The last couple of years had been busy. He had decided after his return from Chile, where he worked for a mining company, Gibbs & Co., to go overseas again. From enquiries with friends, it was suggested he apply to Jardine Matheson in the City of London for a job overseas. He may have read of the Far East[3] and been drawn by its mystique, the opportunity for adventure and the offer of a different career and lifestyle. Companies recruited British middle class men for careers in the Far East; they came from the public schools and were imbued with the idea of service.[4] Selection depended on the interview. They particularly wanted sportsmen and those with some experience of leadership through being a school prefect or being in the Officer's Training Corps.[5]

The selection process may not have proved a hurdle; however there were demands made by companies then. It was made clear to recruits that marriage before the end of the second

---

1 Bosanquet, p. 15.
2 Peter was an adopted forename, his full name was Hugh William Macpherson Dulley.
3 A term in use then to denote distance from Great Britain.
4 Allen, p. 20.
5 Allen, p. 22.

Hong Kong Island from the Harbour

tour of service was not considered appropriate, and permission had to be sought.[6] Peter, however, married half way through his second tour but at thirty-three would have been older than many.

Then there was the clothing that had to be purchased for those warmer climes. In Hong Kong's case there was the need to have both summer white suits and warmer winter clothing; it was a time-consuming task. Tropical kit lists were provided with the names of colonial outfitters. Friends and relatives who had lived in those parts provided advice, for example to buy only formal articles of clothing at home and purchase the rest from Chinese tailors and shoemakers in the Far East.[7] The Straits Settlements *sola topee* was regarded as essential protection for Europeans in the tropical sun; however by 1937 they were scarcely worn as the users found them cumbersome.[8]

The normal means of transport to Hong Kong then was by ship. Therese Sander, Peter's future wife, took something over a month from London to Hong Kong via the Suez Canal in 1936. During the voyage her ship would need to stop possibly twice to refuel with

---

6   Allen, p. 30.
7   Allen, p. 27.
8   Allen, p. 28.

coal. There was real drama in sailing to distant places. They were often unknown, their cultures totally different and the venture took weeks. The great shipping lines were the P&O,[9] which was rather grand, the Blue Funnel, the Glen Line, the BI[10] and the Bibby Line. They took passengers to all corners of the Empire.[11]

The departure was made more memorable as passengers would be away for four years by the 1930s. The docks had an atmosphere all of their own, old brick warehouses, tall, grey steel cranes and railway lines with goods wagons lined up along the quays. The ships dominated the quayside, each with one or two long white gangways. The passengers' trunks marked 'wanted on voyage' would be awaiting them in their cabins whilst the rest would be stored in the hold. There would be final farewells to loved ones. Paper streamers would have been obtained, one end being held fast whilst the roll was thrown to the family waiting on the quay to wave them farewell. This signified the last link and as the ship moved slowly away, with much hooting, the tape was finally broken. Those on the quayside continued to wave until they were just small specks in the distance.

For newcomers sailing East, the month-long voyage would be a memorable experience.[12] By tradition, the East began at Port Said, which was a coaling port. Orders would be given that portholes should be closed and the cabin door sealed against coal dust and thieves, who were said to come aboard.[13]

Each day a good lunch was followed by a siesta, then deck tennis or a lounge in the canvas pool, which was erected over the fore hatch.[14] In the early evening people bathed and changed for dinner. The custom was to wear dinner jackets until Port Said and then a short white jacket with black trousers, which was known as the bum freezer.[15] The passengers came from similar backgrounds and there was generally a happy atmosphere on board; many becoming lifelong friends.[16] After dinner there was dancing to the band which played tunes from the scores of Cole Porter and Ivor Novello. For the non-dancers there was the option of playing bridge.[17]

---

9   Peninsula and Oriental Steam Navigation Company.
10 British India Steam Navigation Company.
11 Allen, p. 31.
12 Allen, p. 31.
13 Allen, p. 33.
14 Allen, p. 33.
15 Allen, p. 34.
16 Allen, p. 34.
17 Allen, p. 35.

There were shipboard romances encouraged by the feeling of freedom and of getting to know people quickly. There were young ladies travelling to join their parents, brides-to-be and wives, all of whom were an attraction to the male passengers.[18] Despite this idyllic description, there could be problems with sea travel, such as the choice as to where to sleep; some preferred the troubled slumber on deck in long chairs to the heat of their cabins.[19]

Joseph Conrad vividly remembered his first experience of the Far East: 'Suddenly a puff of wind, a puff faint and tepid and laden with strange odours of blossoms, of aromatic wood, comes out of the still night – the first sigh of the East on my face. That I can never forget. It was impalpable and enslaving, like a charm, like a whispered promise of mysterious delight.'[20]

Jack Dulley in 1933

18   Allen, p. 35.
19   Deakes and Stanley, p. 52.
20   Allen, p. 19. [Quote from Joseph Conrad, 'Youth'.]

ABOVE: *Agnes and Herbert Dulley visiting Peter in Chile in 1926*
BELOW: *Evelyn Dulley or Sister Marie Joseph, after she had retired*

The vegetation of Penang, the last stop before Hong Kong, was most luxuriant: coconuts, oranges, bananas and other fruits grew in abundance beside immense numbers of flowering plants and shrubs.

The exotic East was all very different to Peter's early life experiences. He was born in Wellingborough, Northamptonshire on 12 July 1903 and was christened Hugh William Macpherson Dulley. In the 1920s he became known as Peter. His father was Herbert Dulley and his mother Agnes Leonora, who came from the Macpherson family in Uddingston, Lanarkshire. Peter was the Dulley's youngest child, Evelyn the eldest, followed by Jack.[21] The extended Dulley family lived in Wellingborough and were respected citizens of the town. They ran the brewery and over a number of decades built a grand Baptist Chapel and an indoor swimming baths for the town, astutely using the hot water from the brewery process to heat the pool. Many of the male members of the family became clergymen.

When Peter and his immediate family moved to London, the children were sent off to the Blunts in Wellingborough for the holidays. The Blunts had been the coachman and parlour maid at the family house near Wellingborough. There was a strong family tie with them and Peter was obviously fond of Lizzie Blunt, as he was still in correspondence with her in his thirties. Jack and Peter went to Westminster School in central London, where Peter obtained a scholarship, thus becoming a King's Scholar. The pupils were made vividly aware of the Great War by the Headmaster who, during morning prayers, read out the names of old boys who had been killed in battle. Peter eventually became the senior cadet in the Officer Training Corps. He left school in the early twenties just when London was coming back to life. He rowed with Thames Rowing Club, went to the Chelsea Arts Balls and was selected to row in the Paris Olympics on the Seine in 1924. These Olympics were immortalised in the film and music of *Chariots of Fire*.

The other key players that appear later in the story are Therese Sander, who became Peter's wife, and Edgar and Eva Davidson, her uncle and aunt, who had lived in Hong Kong for many years. They, together with Peter and Therese's other family and friends mentioned in his letters, are recorded under Names in Appendix III.

On arrival in Hong Kong in 1930, Peter was to discover a city that was both modern and crowded like every large port, but nearby was the old China with its ancient traditions.[22]

---

21 More details are given in Appendix III, List of Names Mentioned in Letters.
22 Thorbecke, p. 4.

Thames Rowing Club Grand VII that went on to row in the 1924 Paris Olympics

Olympic blazer badge

Street scene

This oriental life was both strange and beautiful to the Europeans, in particular the Chinese dress, temples and food. There was also a wide variety of transport ranging from sedan chairs, rickshaws and sampans to the more familiar forms of travel, such as motorcars, trams, ferries and a funicular railway.

Hong Kong was born after years of conflict between the Chinese and British, which were called the Opium Wars. Settlement was reached by giving Britain sovereignty over Hong Kong Island; the British flag being raised on the Island by a naval party in 1841. Jardine Matheson and several other firms followed immediately.[23] Hong Kong was acquired by the British Government under the Treaty of Nanking in 1842; Kowloon and Stonecutters Island later in 1860; and New Territories in 1898.[24] It could be said that Hong Kong did not get off to a very good start with Lord Palmerston describing it as a barren island that would not provide much trade.[25]

---

23 Morris, p. 25.
24 Morris, p. 27.
25 Welsh, p. 1.

It had little agricultural or other value to the Chinese at the time. It did, however, provide a naval and military base for the British Empire in the Far East and a vast commercial port for its traders. With the help of the British and the Hong Kong Chinese, Hong Kong has been transformed into what it is today. There may be criticism of the Hong Kong colonial era but it is important to remember its origins and purpose were as a base and a trading centre.

The Governor of Hong Kong held a very powerful position in the Colony supported by an Executive Council, and in the 1920s one Chinese representative was admitted.[26] The business houses were represented by such dignitaries as J. J. Paterson, Chairman of Jardines in the 1930s.[27] The Legislative Council was a subsidiary body and in 1929 the number of Chinese seats was increased to three.[28] This was a very small number compared with the total Chinese population.

The Chinese were the original settlers on Hong Kong Island and came from a much older civilisation than their European counterparts: Ancient China dated from over 2,000 years before Christ.[29] In AD 1600 the Chinese Empire was the largest and most sophisticated in the world.[30] China had been far more advanced in science and other subjects and had, for instance, invented gunpowder,[31] something which was later developed by the West into a lethal explosive. Great Britain had rapidly progressed during the Industrial Revolution and before, yet China had changed very little. Great Britain had benefited from competition with the rest of Europe, while China, because of its beliefs, size and location in the Far East had been isolated from the outside world for many centuries.

By the early part of the twentieth century the Chinese Empire was crumbling.[32] The gaps were being filled by initially Chinese warlords and then Chiang Kai-shek and the Kuomintang (the Nationalist Party). By 1928 they, together with local potentates, held most of China and looked as if they might bring some kind of order.[33] However, the Communists had not been defeated and were still a threat to them. The famous Long

---

26 Morris, p. 194.
27 Bosanquet, p. 18.
28 Snow, p. 17.
29 Wikipedia 'Ancient China. The first recorded dynasty', 22 May 2014.
30 Spence, p. 7
31 Wikipedia 'Invention of Gun Powder', 22 May 2014.
32 Welsh, p. 354.
33 Welsh, p. 377.

Fishing Junk *Fishing Sampan in Rocky Island Bay*

March by the Red Army took place in 1934 from southern to northern China,[34] which led to their eventual domination. The Japanese annexed Manchuria in 1932.[35] The result was a fragmented country under pressure from three very different powers: the Nationalists, the Communists and the Japanese.

The Japanese extended their occupation of China in 1937 by taking Peking, later followed by Canton in 1938 and in the same year set up a puppet government in Nanking.[36]

Throughout this period there was a steady flow of Chinese into the Colony. The newcomers would normally take up lowly jobs, such as coolies (unskilled labourers) but it was possible for Chinese to progress in the commercial field to becoming a comprador. Robert Ho Tung, a Eurasian, earned more than the wealthiest Europeans and was subsequently knighted,[37] forming with other members of 'the gentry' a small elite group of Chinese and Eurasians who came to play a key intermediary role between the Chinese and the British.[38] In the early days of the Colony, the commercial firms and public services were staffed by Europeans. Gradually Chinese staff were taken on, helped by the opening of the Hong Kong University in 1912,[39] but change was slow and for the majority of Chinese the scope for promotion was limited.

---

34 Morris, p. 35.
35 Welsh, p. 385.
36 Morris, p. 36.
37 Snow, p. 11.
38 Snow, p. 12.
39 Welsh, p. 357.

The Europeans were a small minority but wished to maintain control of the Colony and its financial world. Between 1916 and 1923 expatriate groups pressed for constitutional reform, but the democracy they wanted was only for Europeans. The Colonial Office saw that this would be unacceptable to the Chinese and indefensible.[40] If elections were granted for European residents, the same rights would have to be given to the Chinese, which would be the end of British Hong Kong.

Language and culture were a barrier to social interaction between the Chinese and Europeans (which loosely included Americans). As a result, they relied on Chinese interpreters or the dreaded Pidgin English. Interestingly enough, there are many examples of Chinese Pidgin English but the efforts of Europeans are not so available, though no doubt equally amusing. Few British, even longstanding ones, could speak more than a few words of Cantonese, the local Chinese dialect,[41] with the result that the British made little attempt to control Chinese life.[42] Finally, there was a vast difference in income between even the average European and the majority of the Chinese who lived at poverty level; this situation was exacerbated by the continuing flood of refugees from war-torn China. The cultural differences also meant that the Chinese and Europeans did not mix socially. Unlike the Indians, the Chinese did not play cricket, polo or hunt, or show any inclination to follow British social behaviour.[43]

As well as the Chinese and the Europeans, the population included Eurasians, Parsees, Sindihs, Jews, Armenians and Americans.[44] The last pre-World War 2 census in 1931 showed a total population of 849,751, of whom 97 per cent were Chinese and the rest were European or other nationalities.[45] No census is available for 1941 but it is estimated that the total population had grown to 1,007,000 in 1937 and stood at 1,639,000 in December 1941.[46] This meant that the population had almost doubled in the ten years before World War 2. The Chinese were attracted to Hong Kong by jobs and better opportunities.[47] In spite of low wages, long hours and harsh working conditions, they were better off in

---

40 Snow, p. 4.
41 Snow, p. 4.
42 Snow, p. 4.
43 Welsh, p. 382.
44 Snow, p. 2.
45 Hong Kong Government Census 1931.
46 Tsang, p. 109.
47 Tsang, p. 110.

Hong Kong and many were able to send money home. Those who sought the safety of the British colony after the full-scale Japanese invasion of China in 1937, did not develop a loyalty to Hong Kong and this would create problems during the Japanese invasion. Owing to the large influx of Chinese refugees, by 1938 it was necessary to provide refugee camps, medicine, funds, preventative medicine and social workers.[48]

On arrival in 1930 Peter took up his duties in the Insurance Department of Jardine Matheson & Co., a Scottish firm founded in 1832.[49] This was one of Jardines' oldest activities and grew from the need for a Lloyd's type of insurance in the Far East.[50] Since the end of the nineteenth century the Keswick family had managed the firm.[51] Prior to Peter's arrival, Henry Keswick died in 1928,[52] and his second son William Johnstone Keswick, known as Tony,[53] and already in China, took over running the company. John Keswick, the third and youngest, arrived in 1929; thus the Keswick dynasty was maintained together with the help of J. J. Paterson and David Landale Junior in the 1930s.

The Jardines' office in Pedder Street was an old colonial building with a veranda all the way round, great high ceilings and fans and most of the staff worked in open-plan offices. Many of the Chinese working there wore long silk gowns to their ankles or short high-necked shirts with black silk trousers.[54] People of many races worked for Jardines, including some Portuguese. Hong Kong did not avoid the world recession and Jardines had to make economies. In the 1930s European staff were not taken on, and there was a five per cent reduction in monthly pay,[55] but by the late 1930s the economic situation in Hong Kong had improved.[56]

In spite of the poor economic situation there were some fine hotels. The top hotels and restaurants were of a high standard and there was a lively nightlife.[57] The 'Gripps', the nickname given to the Hong Kong Hotel,[58] was a social centre where dinner jackets were mandatory. Overlooking the exquisite coastline on the south of the Island was the Repulse

---

48 Snow, p. 31.
49 Keswick, p. 20.
50 Keswick, p. 181.
51 Keswick, p. 38.
52 Keswick, p. 46.
53 Keswick, p. 205.
54 Bosanquet, p. 16.
55 Keswick, p. 211.
56 Keswick, p. 215.
57 Lindsay, p. 39.
58 Snow, p. 51.

Jardines' illuminations for the Coronation in 1937

Bay Hotel, which had an old-fashioned colonial style. In Kowloon the Peninsula Hotel had international significance, being situated at the end of the Trans-Siberian railway. The hotels, in accordance with Chinese custom, served formal Chinese meals of twelve courses. The menu would include something that swam, something that flew and something that crawled. The guests, usually all men, drank brandy or whisky and made numerous toasts saying 'yum shing', meaning drink it all.[59] Clubs played a key part in the European social life and in 1940 and 1941 Peter often writes about some item of news that probably came from a visit to the Hong Kong Club. As a result of his sailing he was also a member of the Royal Hong Kong Yacht Club, which at the time had a 'whites only' policy, as did the Hong Kong Club. The Jockey Club was also very popular and the 'better off' would have a box from which to watch the racing; the well-to-do Chinese could also be members. The Chinese population generally were avid gamblers so horse racing was strongly supported.

There was a bachelor culture among the male Europeans in Hong Kong; young men would arrive single as was required by their employers and were then discouraged

The Hong Kong Club

---

59 Lindsay, p. 38.

EWO Mess, 8 The Peak

initially from marrying. The female European population was small and consisted mainly of married women, so the opportunities for finding a partner were limited. Young men would reside in company messes and with this bachelor life it was inevitable that drinking and generally 'high living' ensued.

After one weekend's sailing, Peter and a friend met another boat in a bay where they went to shelter for lunch. 'A good quota of gin with the Bank [Hong Kong Shanghai Banking Corporation] lads and so home to the Yacht Club. Griff a lot healthier than when he started, the latter not a very high standard I regret. Griff's reform, which started when we went up the Peak, did amazingly well for the first two weeks but the pace was too hot and he had a relapse, with the result that our wandering boy comes home at most odd hours.'[60]

Another example of this culture was in a cable to Peter on the announcement of his engagement to Therese:

'Congratulations, Second Samuel Chapter one verses 25 and 26.'[61]

---
60 Peter's letter to Therese, 4 June 1936.
61 Peter's letter to Therese, 21 May 1936.

EWO Party, November 1932

This reads: 'How are the mighty fallen in the midst of the battle! O Jonathan, thou wast slain in thine high places. I am distressed for thee, my brother Jonathan: very pleasant hast thou has been unto me: thy love to me has been wonderful, passing the love of women.'[62] Another bachelor friend actually phoned to check, as he did not believe the news.

Hong Kong was now moving with the times and in the 1920s it became the only British overseas possession where you could book a train ticket to London. The station was situated on the Kowloon waterfront and the train travelled from there to Canton, Peking and then via the Trans-Siberian railway to Moscow, Berlin, Paris and Calais; and from Dover in the Pullman coaches of the Golden Arrow to Victoria Station, London.[63] In the 1930s Imperial Airways [which became the British Overseas Airways Corporation in 1939[64]],

---

62 The Holy Bible AD 1611.
63 Morris, p. 15.
64 Wikipedia 'Imperial Airways', 25 May 2014.

The morning beer on 'Luana' (Peter on the left)

Sundowners on 'U & I' – Peter and Roger Grieve by the hatch

followed KLM and started a service to the East.[65] Flying boats even offered some of the comforts of airship travel but not a through flight, as there were many changes and overnight stops, not all of which were comfortable. Flying at that time required cloudless skies and low wind speeds.[66] Planes would only take twelve passengers and flying was only made possible by Imperial Airways, Air France, KLM and Pan Am being heavily subsidised.[67] Hong Kong's first air link was of course to London. In 1936 the first scheduled flight arrived at Kai Tak to the east of Kowloon. The plane was an Imperial Airways de Havilland 86 biplane and was escorted by nine aircraft from HMS *Hermes*. It was the start of a weekly service to Penang where passengers could join the flying boat service from Australia to Britain. It took ten days to get home via Karachi, Bahrain, Alexandria, Brindisi and Marseilles. Pan American flying boats then followed from San Francisco.[68]

Even though there were major developments in flying, there was no international telephone system, just a local telephone exchange.[69] By 1939 there was a telephone for one in ten of the inhabitants, who dialled H for the Island and K for Kowloon. For urgent international communications cables or wires could be used. Electricity had been provided by the China Light and Power Co., part of the Kadoorie empire, from an early date.[70] There was also a refrigeration plant supplying ice, which, like almost anything else, could be delivered by coolies to the elite houses on the Peak. This provided employment of an arduous kind in view of the climb, for the poor Chinese – both men and women.

From shortly after the founding of Hong Kong there were rowing regattas and later sailing, and the two nautical clubs merged in 1894 to be renamed the Royal Hong Kong Yacht Club, having obtained royal approval.[71] The clubhouse made a number of moves including using Deepwater Bay,[72] before a new Yacht Club was finally built more centrally on Kellett Island and was officially opened in October 1940.[73] Yachting was beginning to become a popular sport,[74] and Peter and his great friend, Roger Grieve, loved the outdoor

---

65   Keay, p. 125.
66   Keay, p. 125.
67   Keay, p. 126.
68   Morris, p. 155.
69   Morris, p. 157.
70   Morris, p. 178.
71   Chambers, p. 12.
72   Chambers, p. 59.
73   Chambers, p. 64.
74   Lavery, p. 10.

'Monsoon' in 1935

Wins: *1932/3 Commodore's Cup; 1933/4 Cruiser Championship, Commodore's Cup, Illingworth Cup, Long Harbour Race*
Came second: *1932/3 Macao Race; 1934/5 Lantau Night Race; Illingworth Cup*

Village near Duck Rocks

Near Hebe Haven, Chinese New Year, 1938

active life of sailing and also rowing. The Royal Hong Kong Yacht Club provided both these facilities. They had bought a small cruising yacht called *Monsoon*[75] in 1931. The great benefit of sailing in Hong Kong was that as the north side of the Island and Kowloon were densely populated, it provided the opportunity for getting away from it all to unspoilt and beautiful islands. The boat was 5.18 tons, wooden, and built for cruising with four berths. It was also advisable to have a boat boy to help with the general maintenance of the boat, act as crew and to provide security. When on board, the boat boy, Ah Kung, slept in the bows with the sails and the anchor chain. He was *Monsoon*'s boat boy for seven years until he was called up as a rating[76] in the Hong Kong Royal Naval Volunteer Reserve (HKRNVR) in 1939. The Bank Holiday weekends were very popular for sailing trips and Sundowners played an important role. The yachts would congregate at a predetermined spot and drinks would be served to the passengers and crew from the cockpit hatch.

Peter obviously took to sailing, as he and his crew won many races between the years 1932 and 1934. In December 1932 the annual Hong Kong–Macao race for the Potts Challenge Cup was held, however the lack of wind and a strong tide turned it into an endurance race. So much so that at one stage several boats were unaccounted for and planes from the aircraft carrier *Hermes* were sent out to search for them.[77] The race was won by *U and I* in 35 hours 16 minutes, followed by *Monsoon* in 41 hours 27 minutes. However, in the 1935 race *Monsoon* struck an unchartered rock on the return leg shortly before reaching Hong Kong. As far as is known no great damage was done but because it was Peter's boat, his friends insisted that the rock should be named Dulley Rock. The rock was recorded on Admiralty Chart No. 3681 at Lat. 22° 21' N Long. 113° 52' E. It was formally christened at the Royal Hong Kong Yacht Club annual dinner dance at the Peninsula Hotel on 17 April 1936.

By 1936 Peter was sailing most weekends and he and Therese sailed regularly once they were married. However, in his war-time letters there is no mention of sailing and he subsequently sold his beloved *Monsoon*. This was no doubt because his patrols in the HKRNVR lasted the best part of a week and, because of the uncertainty of when he would be called out, he was not able to arrange for others to join him. The eventual sale of *Monsoon* may also have been influenced by the possibility of a Japanese invasion.

---

75 A 4-ton Auxillary Gunter Sloop.
76 The lowest rank in the Navy, the equivalent of a private in the Army.
77 Chambers, p. 53.

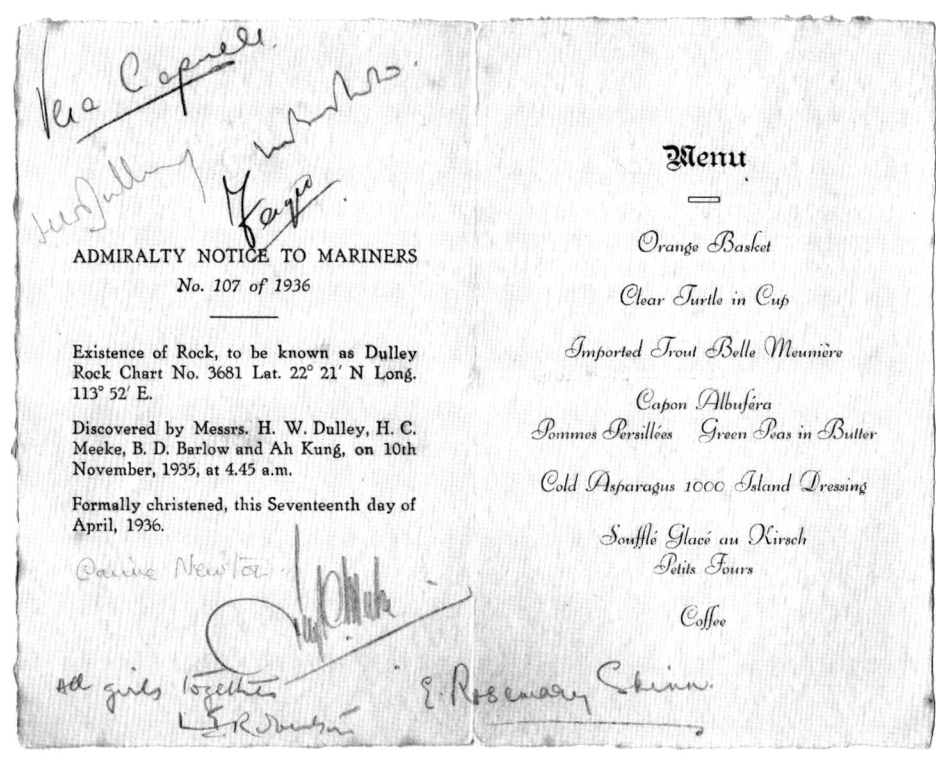

RHKYC Dinner Menu

After he arrived in Hong Kong, Peter took part in the Interport Regattas – in Hong Kong in 1930 and in Manila in 1933. The following year he and Roger Grieve won '4th Submarine Flotilla Cup', and for their efforts they were presented with two heavy Chinese pewter tankards. In the year before the Japanese invasion he went back to rowing in what he called an 'old man's four'.

As the Royal Navy will play a large part in the story, particularly the Royal Naval Dockyard, it is appropriate to provide a very short history of the Navy in Hong Kong. The Royal Navy began setting up store sheds as early as 1841 and subsequently used ships moored in the harbour for specific purposes, for example a hospital.[78] Later that year the dockyard site at Harcourt Road was acquired.[79] The dockyard in Victoria Harbour was

---

78 Melson, p. 6.
79 Welsh, p. 136.

exposed to attack from the Mainland, so a second naval base was built in the southwest of the Island at Aberdeen.[80] A permanent China Squadron was established in 1844, which tackled pirates and enforced trading rights.[81] The gunboats had a major role in these duties.

HMS *Tamar* arrived in Hong Kong in 1897 to take over the role as Receiving Ship and was subsequently moored along the west wall of the dockyard basin. She was built at Millwall, London, launched in 1863, was barque rigged and had a steam engine.[82] The foundation stone for the new dockyard, situated near to the Star Ferry terminal on the Island, was laid in 1902 and the bulk of the work had been completed by 1908.[83] *Tamar* was used as office accommodation and a home for many officers and men, and also acted as the Commodore's accommodation at certain times of the year. The ship hosted a variety of social functions, including plays and musical entertainments. She served the Navy for seventy years only to be scuttled in December 1941 to prevent her use by the Japanese.[84]

The Royal Navy's China Station heyday was between the two World Wars. The fleet was based in Hong Kong and consisted of the 5th Cruiser Squadron, the flagship, the 4th Submarine Flotilla of twelve boats, the Yang-Tse flotilla of ten gunboats,[85] the West River Flotilla of five boats, the 8th Destroyer Flotilla of nine ships and often an aircraft carrier, such as HMS *Hermes*.[86]

The concept of naval volunteers had existed before but the new Royal Navy Volunteer Reserve (RNVR) was first formed in Great Britain in 1903. Many of the reservists served on the Western Front in World War 1 in the Royal Naval Division.[87] The RNVR later became known as the Wavy Navy, because the officer's gold stripes were wavy, while the Royal Navy had straight stripes. In 1934 the Hong Kong Naval Volunteer Force was founded and took part in the annual King's Birthday Parade, looking resplendent in all white uniforms and white pith helmets. Peter was one of the founder members and they trained on HMS *Barnet,* an old motorised fishing boat. A large number of the Yacht Club members joined RNVR along with 'many Chinese boat boys enrolled as ratings'.[88] A year later on 2 December 1936 Peter was promoted from Sub Lieutenant to Lieutenant. The HKRNVR, the Hong Kong Volunteer

80 Lindsay, p. 36.
81 Melson, p. 8.
82 Melson, p. 10.
83 Harland, p. 27.
84 Harland, p. 6.
85 Used to protect British interests against local warlords and pirates.
86 Melson, p. 55.
87 Lavery, p. 17.
88 Chambers, p. 54.

Hong Kong Naval Volunteer Force, King's Birthday Parade, June 1934

Defence Corps and the Royal Air Force volunteers were all formed to provide support to the regular services for the defence of Hong Kong.

In 1841 the Army also acquired land for building gun batteries and a hospital on the higher locations of the Peak.[89] Despite failure to implement recommendations for improving the defences of Hong Kong in 1881, the garrison was later strengthened by the addition of three more Indian regiments, additional heavy guns and quick firing pieces.[90] The lease of the New Territories improved the defence of Hong Kong by ensuring no gun batteries could be built in Kowloon overlooking the Island. By 1941 there were a number of barracks on the Island and in Kowloon.[91]

Despite the many advantages of Hong Kong, there were some disadvantages too. Families had to accept a long separation, as those working in the Far East could only return to England every four years. It was also the practice to send children to boarding school

---
89 Welsh, p. 136.
90 Welsh, p. 295.
91 Welsh, p. 321.

Hong Kong Naval Volunteer Force on HMS 'Barnet', October 1935
(Later to become the HKRNVR)

in England but it would not have been feasible for them to return in the holidays, necessitating a stay with a relative or guardian. Some of these issues are outlined by Eva Davidson[92] in a letter to Therese on her return to England in 1938.[93]

'Jack [Eva's son] met me at the Docks (had been waiting for me there for two hours) and we had a wonderful five days together in London. He was so pleased to see me – and it is so good to get in touch with him again after the longest separation we have ever had. I am conscious that he is 'Sizing me up' quietly in his mind, and making up his mind gradually, *how* far he will let me share his life – below the surface and bit-by-bit we are discovering each other. I endeavour not to hurry the process, or let my grey hair stand too perceptibly on end – I have christened him my 'little Benito Muss'[94] as I maintain he has much of the forceful temperament of Italy's dictator – actually he is a dear lad and if Peter

---

92 Eva Davidson was Therese's aunt, who had lived many years in Hong Kong – a fuller description is given later in the chapter.
93 Eva Davidson's letter to Therese dated 2 May 1938.
94 Named after the Italian dictator Mussolini; this was, however, before Italy declared war on Great Britain.

finds him 'a bit pleased with himself and inclined to lay down the law, he will I know make allowances for a boy, who has had to look after himself from a very young age.'[95]

Another example of the problem of separation occurred in 1930 when Peter's father died; Peter had visited him in Normandy, France the year before. Having just started work in Hong Kong he would not have been granted leave for the necessary two and a half months return journey and in any event travelling by ship would have meant he arrived too late for the funeral.

Peter's letters will take the reader back to the days of letter writing, when there was no other means of communication over long distances apart from very brief cables, which still had to be delivered to the address at the other end, possibly by bicycle. Peter considered that there were certain requirements for a good letter: peace and quiet to compose the letter, a proper desk to write at, suitable quality paper and a fountain pen.

Prior to airmail, all mail had to go by sea and would have taken about a month to get to England. So if the writer asked a question in a letter, the earliest an answer could be received was two months: that clearly had its problems for the sender. The expansion of flying in the mid-1930s made airmail an economic proposition. For those who had experienced the sea mail, the advent of airmail was something to celebrate. Eva Davidson wrote: 'Isn't airmail wonderful now, I had two lovely ones from UE[96] last week. He sounds well and happy.'[97] There were, however, problems at the outset. In a letter, Peter states: 'There is the Rangoon direct airmail service leaving here every Friday, also on Tuesdays there is supposed to be a sea mail to Singapore which connects with the Air Route there. Recently they have given up advertising all mails except the direct airmail, so there is nothing to tell you whether the Tuesday mail is running or not.[98] With all these typhoons the clipper [airmail] departs quite regularly tomorrow, and it is always tomorrow.'[99]

Wires and cables also had problems. Peter's cable to Therese: 'I am glad that you got my birthday cable eventually; the difficulty is that they can give you no idea when cables will arrive. All I could elicit was that if I paid double the full rate, it would go "fairly quickly" so I allowed three days to spare and sent it services rate.'[100] Peter sent a cable to Nancy,

---

95 At boarding school.
96 UE was an abbreviation used by the family for Uncle Edgar (Davidson), fuller details are given later in the chapter.
97 E. Davidson's letter of 2 May 1938 to Therese.
98 Peter's letter to Therese, 5 May 1941.
99 Peter's letter to Therese, 14 July 1940.
100 Peter's letter to Therese, 21 May 1941.

his mother-in-law, to tell her of the birth of their son. In it he said Therese was very fit, but this was changed to very sick![101]

Dinner parties were a frequent social event and would be cooked and served by the hostess's Chinese servants. Drinking was a significant feature in Hong Kong life, and because of the problems of wine 'travelling', the main drinks were whisky and gin. Sometimes a dinner party would be followed by a dance elsewhere or a visit to the cinema. Cocktail parties were also very popular and for the ladies coffee mornings and light lunches. The Dulleys organised a house-warming cocktail party in November 1939, i.e. shortly after the outbreak of war. Therese's notes show that seventy-three people attended. Many are mentioned in Peter's letters, including Major Charles Boxer,[102] an army intelligence officer, and his wife. Between them all they drank twenty-one bottles of whisky and gin, averaging out at the equivalent of one third of a bottle per head. Therese also records that there were not enough sausages but a large amount of the Red Caviar was left over.[103]

Leisure activities were important to the white residents of Hong Kong. In addition to sailing and rowing there were a number of golf courses. Peter began playing golf again when he and Therese were on honeymoon in the Philippine Islands. They

Kowloon Wharf

---

101 Peter's letter to Therese, 18 August 1940.
102 Major Boxer played a significant role at the time of the invasion.
103 Therese's notebook.

then played regularly at Fanling and even in the war years Peter was able to play at Fanling, Deep Water Bay and Sheko with his friends and Edgar Davidson. Peter and Therese were keen walkers and would moor their boat in a bay and then go exploring, latterly using their handbook *Rambles in Hong Kong* by G. S. P. Heywood, published by the South China Post in 1938. Therese also played tennis and badminton. Apart from dining out there was the cinema, variety and amateur dramatics. Indoor activities included bridge, whist, mah-jong and listening to the wireless,[104] courtesy of The Empire Broadcasting Station of the Far East based in Hong Kong, or the gramophone, reading and finally jigsaw puzzles.

With Therese's diary we can follow her social life in January 1936, which is probably not atypical of how a young lady passed her time:

2nd Lunched with Mrs Murdoch – dull, left early.
3rd Lunch party at home.
4th Lunch Mrs Scott at Sheko – met Sir J. Nicholson.
7th Lunch Mrs Roberts. Cocktail party at home; quite amusing.
8th Badminton. Cocktail dance on HMS *Tamar*. Dinner and film with Peter.

Some subsequent entries:
Dinner at Flagstaff House. Dull. Played games.
Our tennis party was held at the Peak Club. Dinner and games. Went on to the Gs [The Gripps?[105]], ate sausage and mash at deadly hour.

In view of the death of King George V on 20 January 1936, various dances were cancelled during the state mourning. Another entry in Therese's diary states, 'Saw off the *Empress of Japan*, rather an experience, a wonderful ship.'[106] The arrival and departure of large passenger ships in Hong Kong would have been an occasion, particularly the former as it was possible to see who was arriving in the Colony. The *Empress* was one of a series of passenger ships named 'Empress' and operated by Canadian Pacific Railways. In 1941 Therese would later be evacuated to the Philippine Islands on the *Empress of Japan*.

---

104 Therese listened to the Hong Kong station on the Medium Wave and Manila and rather surprisingly Germany on the Short Wave.
105 The Hong Kong Hotel.
106 Therese's Diary, 14 January 1936.

Therese's uncle and aunt, Edgar and Eva Davidson, had lived in Hong Kong for many years and came from large, well-to-do families. Edgar's father was a senior partner in a large firm of accountants in Liverpool. He had been to Sedbergh, a public school on the edge of the Lake District, with his three brothers and then the University of Cambridge before becoming a solicitor. He ultimately became a senior partner in Hastings & Co. in Hong Kong. Eva came from Clifton in Bristol and, because of her reliance on servants then and when she moved to Hong Kong, it was always said that she was not able to boil an egg. As their Christian names both began with an E, they became known in the family as the E's or UE or AE.

Therese Sander, their niece, came to visit them in 1935, with her uncle, Gerald Davidson, who was an architect and designed various buildings in Hong Kong. It is said there were some raised eyebrows on the ship out when he explained that the young lady with him was his niece. Therese met Peter at a New Year's Eve party at the Peak Club in December 1935 and by 14 April 1936 they were engaged. Therese was the daughter of Agnes Helen Sander and was born in 1913. Her mother was known as Nancy to the family, her father was Max Zander, a German lecturer in Hull. At the time of World War 1 Nancy changed her name from Zander to Sander to hide the German link. Max was interned in England during World War 1 and then returned to Germany without Nancy or the girls.

Therese left for England on 1 May 1936. She was returning to see her family, meet Peter's for the first time and to prepare herself for a life in Hong Kong. It would be six months before the couple were reunited, so their correspondence served as a way of getting to know better each other's thoughts and views and to plan the wedding and their future together. The wedding was unusual by today's standards as it took place thousands of miles from England and the bride and bridegroom's families. The only relatives who attended the wedding were the bride's uncle and aunt. The organisation of the wedding largely fell to bride's aunt and to a lesser extent the bridegroom, who consulted the bride by letter, so it could take weeks to obtain a reply.

Once they became engaged, Peter had a meeting with Edgar Davidson, acting in *loco parentis*, and gave him an account of his prospects. It may sound very formal and old fashioned but Therese would be dependent on him financially once married. He also wrote to Nancy seeking her approval. As can be imagined it was all a whirlwind of planning before she left. They had all chosen to write to Nancy, so she would have been totally unaware of her daughter's engagement as Therese left Hong Kong.

Going to Hong Kong was an adventure; it was after all for four years, with the need to buy tropical kit and the romantic journey out on a liner. It is hoped that this introduction will provide a background to the letters that follow. They give a first hand account of Hong Kong in the period from 1936 to 1941, covering the build up to the Japanese invasion. The majority were written to Therese when she was evacuated first to the Philippines and then to Australia. There is limited background detail in them as Therese had lived in Hong Kong for four years and therefore knew it and the way of life. There is also little detail in letters to the family. So this chapter has aimed to fill in these gaps and provide a backcloth to the story that follows.

CHAPTER 2

A Whirlwind Romance

January to April 1936

Therese was twenty-two years old and had arrived in Hong Kong in the autumn of 1935, staying with her Uncle Edgar and her Aunt Eva at 191 The Peak. She writes to her mother, Nancy, to whom she was very close, about her excitement of being in Hong Kong and of meeting Peter.

Therese to Nancy   3 January

The New Year dance at the Peak Club was very good. We went in a large party. Uncle Edgar [UE] as a sheik, Aunt Eva [AE] in her Venetian costume and I in my little Spanish peasant outfit, which looked quite sweet. I wore the big bow in my hair. There were a lot of very nice people there. I met a sweet lad (I say lad but actually he is 32), who asked me to go sailing with him the next day, needless to say I accepted. I enjoyed it very much. We started at about 11 am and did not get back till about 6 pm. It is a very nice little yacht and will take four people besides the Chinese boy. It has a cabin and a motor, so if the wind drops, one does not become becalmed! We motored out of the harbour and then sailed around to some of the outlying islands, there was not very much wind, but just enough. It really was perfectly beautiful, especially at sunset. We anchored in a little bay for lunch and then landed on a wee island, where we sat and sunned ourselves. Peter and Roger Grieve, the co-owner, use the boat a lot for racing. Peter has been sailing about for about three years, but still I gather makes mistakes, much to the amusement of the Chinese boat boy [Ah Kung], who knows absolutely all there is to know about sailing.

   I enclose some photos. They were taken in the E's little garden. You get some idea of how high up [on the Peak] we are and what a beautiful view we have, by the background. Someone here has told me it is a very bad light here for taking views.

   AE is giving a bridge luncheon this afternoon, so I am going to escape after lunch and go down to the town to catch the mail. We were out for lunch yesterday and are to be out again tomorrow. In fact, all told, except for today, I don't think I have had a lunch at home all this week.

A later photo of Peter and Therese at the Hong Kong Bank junior mess fancy dress in 1937

Every day is booked up with something, except one. We are going to dine at Flag Staff House on Friday, very swish. I expect we will have to dine at Government House sometime soon and if I know anything, it will be a bit dull. I must fill up this page, at the risk of boring you, as I can't bear to waste space. We have been absolutely living on turkey this week, as everyone is trying to use up their [Christmas] turkeys. Turkey boiled, roast, stewed, fricasseed, in gelatine etc. etc. ad lib. I am sick of the sight of it, I am also getting very weary of mince pies. Thank goodness everyone seems to have finished their plum puddings!

Three months later Therese again writes to her mother.

Therese to Nancy   15 April

The absolutely unexpected has happened. I have got engaged to be married. At the moment of writing I am feeling completely stunned. I can't sort of realise it. The brave man is Peter Dulley. He proposed to me last night and I have never had such a surprise in my life. I had not the faintest idea he felt seriously about me, although I knew my heart was not by any means intact. We are neither of us head over heels in love, but we think we can make a success of it. My dear, I am afraid that this is all very badly put, I wish I could express myself better, but I am in such a state of feeling that I don't seem to be able to write properly, or put my feelings onto paper. How I wish you were here to talk to; AE has been an absolute dear, but no one can take your place. You'll love Peter, you could not help it, he is a most lovable person, and I am tremendously flattered that he should feel as he does about me. I still feel as if I can't believe it and that I will wake up and find that it is all a lovely dream. One thing does distress me and that is that it will mean my living out here. I know how you feel, and yet I am sure that you would not wish me to spoil this great chance of happiness, for you, knowing how very unselfish you have always been. The present plans are, that I give up Shanghai [which was to meet her cousin Peggy Killery], stay on here for another two weeks, and then go straight home on the *Empress of Japan* (with Peggy of course). I would then spend the summer at home and return here in the winter to get married. It all sounds very hectic, but we are not in favour of a long engagement and I don't imagine you would be either. I could perhaps travel back with Peggy as she returns in the winter, about November. I realise £. s. d [Sterling before decimalisation] is bound to come into the question and that you are not at all in the position for more heavy expense at present, but I hope we will be able to find a solution. All I have I am willing to spend, and perhaps if necessary, UG [Uncle Gerald] would give a loan. After all, when it is all over, you will have me off your hands for good. Peter is not opulent but has enough to marry on, and I presume you would be able, at any rate in time, to give me a small allowance.

Continued   16 April

I am beginning to feel slightly calmer and more myself. Thank goodness one does not get engaged every day!! But I still feel as if I can't believe it. Peter went and saw UE this morning and I gather his prospects are very good, far better than he led me to believe, bless him. He is coming up here tonight to see the family. UE and AE are giving a cocktail party, where they will have to spring the news on people. I have got out of it and so has Peter as I feel that it would be rather an ordeal. So Peter and I will have a quiet hour to ourselves, which we have not had since he proposed, and which I feel is badly needed, there seems to be so much for us to talk about. Then we are dining 'en famile' and going on to an amateur dramatic show in town. I suppose I ought to try and give you a description of him: he is a little taller than I [Therese was a tall women] and dark, he is not exactly good looking, but he has a very attractive face, at least I think so. He is not the strong silent type, quite the <u>reverse</u>, which is as it should be, I always felt that I should marry a talker. He has seen a good deal of life and has taken some hard bumps. He was mining in South America for a time and life out there is anything but easy. He then lost his job, through no fault of his own, and was rather stranded at home for a while until this job in Jardines Insurance cropped up, which he has been in now for quite a while and is doing well.

    AE has written you a long and very nice letter, she has read it to me. She puts things so well, far better than I do, and I feel that you will feel really in touch with things when you read it. UE is also writing to you on more business lines, so by the time you have read all our letters you will know about all there is to know. I am afraid that the news will not be all pleasure to you, my dear, and I am sorry. Don't worry about me, as there is really nothing to worry about. I think I can safely say that I have achieved my greatest ambition for life, and now I only hope that I can make a success of it. I am not doing anything mad, or reckless, Peter really is a good sort and is spoken of very highly.

Ah Kung

Therese to Nancy   21 April

Here I am again, feeling very thrilled with myself and life in general. At first I felt as if I could not somehow realise things, but now I am gradually coming to and just loving it. Peter and I are more in love now, after a week's engagement, than we were at the beginning, which I feel ought to be a very good sign. We have of course seen a lot of each other and Peter seems to get keener each time we meet, which is very delightful, especially as I do not have exactly a great excess of ego!!

I am hoping you will wire congratulations as I do so want to feel in touch with you. It is awful to think that at the time of writing you still don't know anything and are fondly thinking I am in Shanghai. There is one thing, my dear, I am quite <u>certain</u> that he is the right man. I don't think I could possibly have found anyone nicer or more considerate. We have of course had some intimate discussions on various subjects connected with marriage and he has been so awfully nice. It may sound silly and lovesick, but Peter really is a cut above the average, if it convinces you at all, I am not by any means the only one who thinks so. He has written to you and showed me the letter yesterday, for my approval. He found it rather difficult to know what to say, as he said that he did not want to be formal. On the other hand it is difficult to be chatty

Peter with a pipe and a drink

and familiar to a person one does not know and also he was afraid that you might think it rather cheeky on his part.

I cannot remember whether I said anything about the financial side of things last time. The long and the short of it is that we can marry and live quite comfortably on what Peter earns. He refuses to take any interest in what I may have, as he firmly (and quite rightly up to a point) thinks that a husband should be able to keep his wife. All the same, I presume that I will be able to have a little money of my own, as I think that it is nice for a wife not to be entirely dependent on her spouse. AE thinks so too and so I am sure you do, considering what you have been through, poor dear.[1] Peter of course knows all about my father and does not care a hoot. He did not even appear to be particularly interested and he very sweetly said that it was me he was marrying not the family. I want to send you some photos of him, but at present I have only got one which is not very good and as I am very anxious not to give you a false impression, I am going to try and get some nicer ones to send. I took a lot during the weekend and Peter has some to enclose in this letter.

You will be amused to hear that our engagement seems to have given the Colony quite a thrill, I almost feel famous. I have never been made such a fuss over before; I can't think why people are so nice, considering that I don't even belong here. Peter says it is the combination of his aloof and apparent complete bachelordom and my sweetness; personally I rather doubt the sweetness. All of his bachelor friends are completely bowled over, they are so surprised. The announcement of the engagement came out in the Hong Kong papers today, rather a thrill. We have also sent one to *The Times*.

The weather has been beautiful all week. I do hope it keeps up over the weekend, as sailing is so lovely just now; an absolutely perfect pastime for an engaged couple. The whole coast is so beautiful. I hope I will learn quite a lot about sailing in time. The more I see of Hong Kong the more I love it and, except for parting from you, the thought of living out here suits me down to the ground. I long to hear from you, my dear, but heaven knows when I will, not for ages unless you wire. I do hope you do. I think about you a lot.

---

1 Therese is referring to her mother's separation from her German husband after World War 1.

CHAPTER 3

A Long Distance Engagement and a Trip to Shanghai

May to July 1936

Letters from Peter in Hong Kong to Therese on her journey back to England in 1936. They were initially addressed to the ports Therese called at and then to her home in England. She travelled via Vancouver and Montreal and would have taken the rail journey through the Rockies. During this period he also wrote a letter to Lizzie Blunt, who had looked after him in childhood.

To Therese   11 May

You have now been away nearly a fortnight and I have thought about you and missed you a lot. I had your letter from S'hai, which was most welcome and consoling, do not be afraid of writing and saying exactly what you want to say, it is the only real way of communicating between two people, who want to be, and should be, extremely intimate. I am very glad that you feel our marriage is going to be a real success. I have been sure all along, as far as it is possible to be sure of anything in this wicked world.

Of the news there is not a great deal. Fergie, Griff[1] and I moved into the Hancock's house the day you left and are now comfortably installed there. Griff and I have gone on a very definite reform and for the past ten days running I have been to bed between ten and eleven. The HK Hotel has been ruled out of my curriculum and I intend to live a Godly, Sober and Economic life this summer. My various chits for April gave me a fairly handsome jar, when they came rolling in, but still one is only engaged once (or hopes to be) so what the hell girls, what the hell.

Last weekend the Naval Volunteers had to do their annual shoot on the Stonecutters' ranges on Sunday, so Meeke and I sailed off on Saturday and returned to Stonecutters on Sunday morning, along with Barlow, who is now running *Norseman*, Gaswork Nic's erstwhile yacht. General form with rifles and revolvers was surprisingly high, seeing that we only shoot once a year. Barlow came out on top with 88, Berlyn from some

---
1 Two of Peter's great friends.

submarine, who is one of the crack shots of the Colony, only registered 81, and I was third with 78, to my intense surprise, seeing that it was only the second time in my life I have shot on an open range as against a miniature range. Meeke took a pretty 25 out of 25 on the 200 yards range, but fell down on some of the other targets. I have not yet seen my full scores for revolver, but I fancy I was fairly near the top, although I missed one or two easy shots I should have got. Cmdr and Mrs Barnard joined us at Stonecutters at about 12.30, when we had finished shooting and we sailed off for Gin Drinker's Bay for a bottle and lunch.

Incidentally talking about marriage and giving in marriage, do you remember Rosemary Skinner who was at the Yacht Club party? Fergie and I are to dine with the family next week and Fergie is afraid Mrs S has marked down his body as being a suitable husband for her Rosemary. Fergie is very upset and nervous about it, but the only consolation I gave him was 'wade in and win big boy, you might do a lot worse'. I thought she was a bright and amusing wench.

Since starting this letter I have received ones from my mother and brother with congratulations on the good news. They seem quite cheered that little brother is off at last. Jack tells me that my mother's reaction to earlier references to yourself was 'Therese sounds far too suitable, so Peter cannot possibly be interested.' Don't pass these whisperings back to Mamma, but it sounds a bull point for you, as my mother will start off with the right impression, one which you will have no difficulty in confirming. I feel sure that my mother will take to you and feel duly relieved that her wandering son has found such a charming fiancée to keep him out of mischief and to share his declining years.

Your Uncle and Aunt [Edgar and Eva Davidson] came in for a drink the other evening and they and I chatted pretty hard about not a great deal. I have not yet managed to do anything about entertaining them properly since we have not got set up in our new abode and further wish to enjoy a surfeit of the quiet life before launching forth into the giddy social whirl. We had intended to have a dinner party for some of the older generation on the King's Birthday[2] and so onto Gov. Ho. after. That solves the problem of entertaining them after dinner. Probably your Uncle and Aunt, the Halls, the Murdochs and the Skinners if Fergie is not too afraid. I appear to have made my piece with Mrs Mudie since I am bidden to dine there on Friday.

---

2   Edward VIII.

I looked into the question of writing to you en route but unfortunately it could not be done after you had left. However, I sent you a letter to Montreal, to wish you happy returns and I hope you got it alright. I would address this one to meet you on arrival at Glasgow or wherever it is, but I feel that it is safer to send it to Bough Beech [Therese's home]. I have also sent a copy of the photo of myself that you wanted, but I forwarded it by ordinary mail so it will arrive after this.

To Therese   21 May

I was glad to hear you met your cousin [Peggy Killery] alright and that she bore no grudge [because of Therese's delayed departure following her engagement]. As regards Tony Keswick's [Head of Jardines, Shanghai] remarks re myself to your cousin, it is all very bright and fine to have the Taipans calling you a Star young man, but it is not of much value when they will not supplement their remarks by a suitable hand out of £. s. d.

Do not for a moment think you weary me with harangues on matrimony in your letters. After all we are going to get married, so we might just as well air our respective views, so that any necessary mutual readjustment of our ideas may be the easier. I agree with you that you should certainly expect something above a home and furniture. That is the Chinese idea since to them marriage is purely a business transaction for which the woman receives the material benefits of a home and food; the man, in return, has bought a lifelong lease on a concubine by providing these material benefits and nothing more than this is called for or expected.[3]

On Sunday I had to eat an Archducal tiffin with the Patersons, preceded by a bathe at Castle Peak. Mrs J. J. [Paterson] made some very smooth remarks about my good fortune in having such a beautiful fiancée, quite sincere too I fancy. She also gave some deep advice on the subject of a successful marriage and how the trick is done. However, I will not repeat these, but try them on and see how they work.

In a letter from my mother this week, she said she had arranged to meet yours quite shortly, so some of the ice will be broken before you get back. My mother goes to Aix-les-Bains [France] for a month until 15 June.

---

3 The wife was not considered equal to her husband then. Mao Zedong, while governor in Jiangsie Soviet in 1927, made a new marriage law that forbade arranged marriages and stopped all purchase and sale in marriage contracts. Change was inevitably slow. Spence, p. 376.

To Therese   28 May

I heard from my brother by this week's airmail that your mother and Agnes [Therese's sister] had been to tea with my fond Mamma before she left for France. He also said that various people had been asking about wedding presents. Something useful around the house but we should try and avoid any bulky articles as the freight out would make them more of a liability than an asset.

Here in Hong Kong we plod on in our not very eventful style. Last week I went to the cinema and after dinner at the HK Hotel with your Uncle and Aunt and Mrs Hall. A most enjoyable evening, your Aunt and I talked ten to the dozen and Mrs H [Hall] made me dance far more energetically than is my wont. I was not allowed to get tucked away in corners of the floor and maintain a show of dancing with the minimum of movement, but had to scurry about the floor, knocking people about as I went: most nerve wracking. Mrs H tells me incidentally that I am younger in manner than I was when she met me in 1930.

Last weekend I had to take to sea on Sunday in the Barnet, a North Sea trawler owned by the Navy. On Saturday I went out for the afternoon with the Barnhams and Miss Cavanagh, J. J. Paterson's Secretary [Jardines]. Mrs B is rather bright and amusing in her party way. She seemed to think that we were mutually very trusting to allow a separation of six or seven months between getting engaged and married, but it occurs to me that if the desire to marry and make a home is not strong enough to stand six month's separation, it is certainly not the type of bond on which to found a life partnership.

Your mother, when writing to me, said that she was going to give you a dress allowance and the question is how is she going to do it? If capital corresponding to the income your mother intends to give you were invested in your name in various Govt. securities, then the income would come to you free of Income Tax. I do not want to interfere, but am merely passing on the tip, which I know from our company business.

And what of the lovely Therese? Do you still think of me periodically and not feel too appalled at the prospect of supervising my wellbeing for life? I think about you for considerable periods each day, and say good morning to your photos, which sit on the dressing table. You have taken hold of me, my dear, in a way which becomes steadily stronger as the days go by and strange to say I like it.

Photo of Therese taken by Peter, early 1936

To Therese   4 June

I was hoping to hear from Honolulu today [Therese arrived in England on 31 May], but I do not know if the mail in question is yet in, so suppose I must possess my soul in patience and assume you still love me, and, my dear, strange though it may seem, I still love you.

One item of news which is of practical interest to you, a day or so ago Hall [Peter's boss in Jardines] asked me if we would like to have his house next summer while he and Mrs H are away. I provisionally said yes, but naturally wished to ask you about it before confirming definitely. It would be for a period of six months, there will be no rent, as Insurance Companies [Jardines] own the house. We will have to keep on all the servants, but when Fergie and I lived there last summer, Hall provided their wages and threw in $50 per month as an allowance against the rather heavy expenses in the form of gas, electricity etc. As a result we did ourselves fairly proud on about $150 each per month, large parties, lots of drink and what have you.

If you agree to taking over the Hall's house, it will split your eighteen months or so here until we go on leave in 1938, into roughly three periods of six months, two winters and a summer at the Hall's. That has the disadvantage that we cannot do anything about settling down until we come back in 1938, but things looked rather that way anyhow. My idea for when you were out first, was something in the nature of a furnished flat at Garden Terrace; the rents are reasonably low, $115 or thereabouts and Meeke tells me they run theirs for $400 to $500 per month. That means that we should not average more than $450, with a charming chatelaine to supervise leakages, and so should be able to keep up the yacht alright with careful and discreet living. How does the idea strike you? You must always bear in mind that going on leave tends to run one into expense greater than one's pay, so we will need to be economical out here if we are going to have any money to spend on leave. I only get six months' pay, so with the present mingy point of view as regards salaries, I am not likely to draw more than £400 [salary of £800 pa] for while we are away from here.

Incidentally I am off to Shanghai for a fortnight on 26 June and back here on the 10 July. I do not know exactly what the idea is, partly educational and partly to get to know the people.[4] Nothing appears to be fixed as yet for what happens when Hall

---

4 It may be a coincidence but the invite comes only a short time after Peggy Killery spoke to Tony Keswick.

retires, so possibly Tony Keswick wants to give me the once over in Shanghai. I met him down here in 1934, but I was on leave most of the time he was Taipan in Hong Kong, so I did not see much of him.

To Therese   11 June

I heard this week from my mother, who I gather intends to organise a cocktail party in the middle of July as a simple method of introducing you to the family and relatives. I am afraid it will be a bit of an ordeal for you in some ways, but I think you will find them all fairly friendly and open hearted.

My sister Evelyn very much wants to meet you. I would be grateful if you could look her up in the convent in Bayswater. Despite sixteen years in a convent she is still remarkably human and worldly. Also had a letter from Lizzie Blunt, who used to be our parlour maid when we lived at Ecton in Northamptonshire. She remembers me from about the age of four and very much wants to meet you.

The house is going strong, but our first month's bill worked out a great deal higher than we had anticipated. I wanted to live quietly this summer and save up some money, so we have started a close check on the drinks and cigarettes.

I hope the summer will not seem too long, since being engaged by correspondence is not a very satisfactory proposition and I want to see you back here again in the flesh, so that I can talk to you, look at you, admire you, kiss you and generally make a fuss of you.

The next letter is to Lizzie Blunt, who was a 'mother figure' to him. His tone changes completely and the content is markedly different, as he discusses the political situation in Asia.

To Lizzie Blunt   13 June

Trade is a bit depressed here but not so bad as last year when this absurd American silver buying[5] programme knocked us all sideways in China. The political outlook is

---

5   The silver purchase programme, initiated by President Franklin Roosevelt in late 1933 in response to a pressure group. China was still on the silver standard and it caused wartime inflation and post-war hyper-inflation. The silver purchase programme also contributed to the ultimate triumph of the Communists. Milton Freeman 'Franklin D. Roosevelt, Silver, and China.' Chicago Journals – Journal of Political Economy – Vol. 100. No. 1. Feb. 1992. 21 October 2014. http://www.jstor.org/discover/10.2307/2138806?uid=3738032&uid=2&uid=4&sid=21104988290473

most disturbed and obscure; Japan is eating large slices out of North China[6] and shows no inclination towards stopping. The Chinese have no proper army, the ones you read about in the papers being only private bandit armies. They have no patriotism and they are not natural fighters[7] so they cannot resist the Japanese by force. The Chinese down this way and around Canton do not admit that Nanking is the capital of China, so Canton rules itself. At the moment it looks as if there is going to be civil war between Canton and Nanking, but there will probably not be much fighting as these things in China are always based on how much of the local taxes the various warlords, who really govern China, can put into their pockets. Where will it all end? Lord knows, but how China manages to continue, with an almost complete lack of government and an amazing amount of bribery and corruption, is an absolute miracle.

As regards myself, I fit in very well out here although some people say the climate is not good. The summer is not really hot, as heat goes in the tropics; we have a temperature of 85 degrees to 94 degrees (usually 87 degrees) [Fahrenheit] from May to October but it is very humid, so the sweat pours off you even wearing the thinnest of white clothes. However, there is a hill on the island [The Peak] about 1,800 feet high and most of us live up there at about the 1,300 feet level where it is distinctly cooler.

I still sail a lot and hope I will be able to afford to keep the yacht on when I am married; the place is ideal for cruising with lots of islands and bays all around for about thirty miles East and West. It is not advisable to go further than that as we are still old fashioned enough to have pirates, their chief lair being Bias Bay just outside British waters. I spend most of my weekends out sailing and am thoroughly enjoying it.

To Therese   18 June

So you have found out that all mail steamer ports are much alike. To find the differences and what you might call the real spirit and soul of a town, port or city, you must live in it and amongst its people for at least a year. If you pass through ports in a ship, you just go ashore as a tourist, go to the same hotel, drink the same drinks, do the same things, go for the same motor drives and altogether achieve a marvellous effect of sameness. That is the reason why you find all ports the same,

---

6   The Japanese annexed Manchuria in 1932, As a result of the subsequent criticism from the League of Nations, they withdrew from the League in 1933. Welsh, p. 406.
7   The ancient teaching of Confucius taught peace not war.

although at least they are not necessarily so. I was glad to hear Hong Kong came out well from your recent survey of the world, but then you were at an advantage because when you arrived here last autumn you were coming to the place as a temporary home and were not a passer through.

To Therese   25 June

I am afraid this will be a rotten letter, as I feel both hurried and harried. I am off to S'hai in the *Empress of Japan*[8] tomorrow. There seems to be a lot of things to do and not enough time in which to do them. It takes a long time for me to write a decent letter and I have not got it.

I was much touched at your labour of love over my birthday, to wit the pullover, and I need one badly. I am sure with your able and fond care it will turn out very well. I was glad you are to get a day up at Henley [Regatta]; if fine it is a grand show and it is one of the very few big sporting meetings which is still really amateur. Wimbledon is certainly not. Write and tell me about it as I will be most interested.

Last Saturday I took your Aunt and Uncle sailing for the afternoon out to Junk Bay. It was a perfect day, but Mrs Hall, at the Club where we lunched first, was full of dire forebodings and by the time we got off your Aunt looked like one of the Early Christian martyrs. However, to her intense surprise she finished up definitely liking it and sailed the boat home herself. In fact she wants to come again. I shocked her rather badly when she found the drinking water was out of the tap and insists that you be allowed no water which has not been boiled and filtered. She appeared to think that I was going to try to poison you straight off in one act, but I replied live and let live and that within reason you could drink what you liked.

On Tuesday it was a holiday for the King's[9] birthday and Ah Kung[10] had to go on a parade at 4.30 pm. Young Potts, recently out from home, who was to come out with me, got ill so I finished up by sailing the boat single-handed out to Gin Drinker's Bay and back. It was the first time I had sailed single-handed and I learnt quite a bit; no mishaps fortunately but I put on the motor to pick up the moorings in Causeway Bay.

---

8 Used subsequently for the evacuation of women and children, including Therese, to the Philippine Islands in 1940.
9 King Edward VIII – 20 January to 11 December 1936.
10 Peter's boat boy.

At 5.30 on Tuesday there was a most successful review and march past at Happy Valley. I did not have to go on parade as we were represented by a party of Chinese Ratings under two officers, so I watched from the Hall's race box. In the evening [your] Uncle and Aunt, the Murdochs, the Alec Potts and Vera Crapnell came to dinner and we went down to the reception at Govt. House after. Last night I went over to Kowloon, after going for a row, then dinner with the Norwegian, Knudsen, who is in our regular four. This evening, after dinner, I have to bowl at the Club for the Naval Volunteers against the Land Volunteers, so I fancy a rest will be indicated in the *Japan*.

To Therese   29 June   Shanghai Club c/o JM & Co. Ltd, S'hai

Here I am in the great city of sin, having arrived here in the *Empress of Japan* yesterday morning after a pleasant but not very eventful trip. We had fine weather and sun all the way up, but it was sticky directly one got out of the breeze. S'hai is as expected, hot as hell and my shirt has not been dry since I arrived. Yesterday was a heavy thundery 96 degrees and one perspires continually even when sitting under a fan. My first impressions of the town are not, I fancy, quite as bad as yours, but they are by no means good and I am glad that we are never very likely to be sent here.

I am staying at a mess out in the French Concession run by three bachelors, to whom I was introduced by Gompertz who, until recently, was living there. They seem to be quite pleasant fellows, one each from Jardines, the Mercantile and the Hong Kong Bank. Last night two of them took me to the Paramount and the Del Monte, two of the local haunts of vice, but I did not respond to my erstwhile tendencies and the thoughts of meeting a Russian Princess.[11]

I will write again before I leave here, but in this damp and heavy heat I really feel I cannot do prodigies of energy in the form of correspondence.

To Therese   3 July   c/o JM & Co. Ltd, S'hai

The first two days here were Stonkers for heat 96 degrees of temperature and 95–100 per cent humidity, so I am afraid that my last letter was not exactly the model type of correspondence from a prospective perfect husband, but I hope you will make allowances. Today is cool and pleasant; I take up my pen to endeavour to express the

---

11 Shanghai had some very attractive escorts; mostly white Russians who claimed to be princesses, and some were. Keay, p. 145.

feelings, which are so much more easily conveyed by the physical touch than by the spoken word. I love you, my dearest and I think I always will, not possibly because you are Therese, but because you have such a sweet and lovable nature. I knew that all along and I was very foolish not to propose sooner. (Incidentally, would you have accepted me if I had proposed to you after say a week?) But there was some odd inner complex inside me, restraining me from doing so.

I do not yet know whether from a business point of view my trip up here has been a success, but I have hopes. I went around the Private Office on arrival (Tony Keswick etc.) and on being asked what I was up for, I was rather stumped and had to stall. People have been most pleasant to me and I have so far been out to dinner every night except the first and look like being so for the rest. Last night I got on a toot with a couple of men from the office and we explored a number of the dance halls and dives of this city of sin, but the thought of you was a restraining influence, most salutary in its effect and most surprising in its novelty.

The place, where I am staying is Route Ferguson, out in the Western and the more countrified part of the settlement. I took a walk around for several miles yesterday afternoon and the development is really rather priceless. Up until ten years or so ago all this very large area was out and out country, with a few Chinese villages, cultivation, hideous smells, garbage heaps etc. Now that it is being opened up you have European bungalows and American style eight and ten-storey apartment houses arising out of the country, with all the previous Chinese village houses sitting right alongside them. The effect is the maddest thing I have seen.

Continued   4 July

Saturday and the weekend is now with us. Two more evenings of cinemas and racketing round cabarets have passed and I am glad that I do not live here, since spending all my evenings in cabarets would not appeal to me as a permanency. The weather has been averagely mouldy, periodical rain, and the earlier heat has now given way to a distinct cold, so much so that the white clothes, which are all I have up here, seem distinctly unsuitable and I have had to borrow a pullover.

To Therese   9 July   SS *Corfu*

First let me deal with the all your various queries, otherwise they will probably not get done. I was very glad to hear you had definitely booked a passage to come out here. I think it is most desirable and almost essential that you should travel with a chaperone. That may sound a bit heavy, but I have seen too much of girls and wives going off the rails when they suddenly get out in the tropics on board a ship; and is it worth taking the risk? I know you are full of common sense and able to look after yourself, but I am rather against people being put into difficult circumstances unnecessarily.[12]

One of the legacies of a misspent youth is a fairly accurate knowledge of the difficulties besetting a girl travelling alone, the people who sit around waiting to take advantage of her and the way in which it is done. Hence I would strongly recommend acquiring a chaperone before you start. I will look up your ship and get your Aunt to scour around for someone in case you do not know of anyone.

I heard from my mother by the same mail as yours and I gather that you have been approved of, so you may congratulate yourself on passing a fairly stiff exam. She says, 'We were both [she and Jack] very favourably impressed and that I am to be considered lucky,' and I can assure you that my mother would not be favourably impressed by many of my friends, so much so that in various cases I have not worried to effect a meeting.

I left S'hai on Tuesday. General impression of S'hai not too good; I think the trouble is that they have none of the uplifting influence of the beauty of nature in the scenery around. The effect is to throw people back very much on their own resources and most of them have not got away. Hence the rather dubious stimulant of cabarets and the rather hectic life people lead, which is a reaction to boredom and nerves on edge. I only saw Tony Keswick for a few moments to say What Ho and Goodbye; I was to have gone in a party with Eric Pollock the No 3, but it had been raining a bit and the Hunjao [Hongqiao] Golf Course, the rendezvous, was under water. JM & Co. is very much a survival of the fittest proposition at present; the rough drift is promotion for young men to senior jobs at about half the salary those jobs were paying ten years ago. The young men have got to be definitely on the spot and know their stuff, whereas a number of older ones, at present on higher salaries have

---

12 This issue is also addressed in *A Century of Sea Travel*. The *City of London* was known as the bride's boat and on its cold weather trips to Calcutta she carried a number of young women pledged to marriage. These could be hazardous journeys and, if the engagement was broken due a shipboard romance, it was known as a 'Colombo Desertion'. Deakes and Stanley, p. 36.

been passed over and it is probably only a matter of time before they are out. The trouble is business has been too easy in the past and we have been carrying too many passengers; business is now distinctly difficult and it is a fresh start with younger men who were not brought up in the passenger tradition, while life for passengers, who have not so far been fired, looks distinctly bleak. That is what you are marrying into, my dear, and at times I wonder if it is wise. I reckon I am one of the ones who know their stuff and my job should be as safe as one can expect in these difficult days, but if things get any worse it is not a very bright prospect for all of us. On the other hand if they get better I should be sitting pretty.

I think my trip to S'hai was a success on the whole, although I cannot point to any very positive results and further I was probably PERSONA NON GRATA, when I went up there. However, it stirs the mind up a bit to see how things are done in other ports and it is sound propaganda to have oneself admitted as one of the people who should move around a bit and get general information on things.[13]

We arrive in Hong Kong tomorrow and I will not be sorry to be once again settled down to my normal life, although I have enjoyed the trip and it has been a pleasant break. Life will be a bit hectic on arrival as there will probably be nearly a fortnight's work waiting for me.

Later on 2 November Peter wrote to Lizzie Blunt, saying:
It was quite interesting seeing Shanghai, but I am very glad I do not live there. Very much the big city and dead flat for hundreds of miles around, with the result that there is the complete absence of any kind of scenic beauty whatsoever. This place [Hong Kong] is hilly with precipitous slopes going right down into the sea and scores of islands and bays all around, with the result that it is extremely pretty.

---

13 Peter was responsible for accounts in Hong Kong and would have benefited from seeing the Shanghai systems.

View of the Peak and Mt. Austen from the Harbour

CHAPTER 4

Making Plans for the Bride's Return
July to October 1936

Peter wrote to Therese and in his letters covered all the things that engaged couples need to plan for i.e. the wedding, honeymoon and where they would live, but with the difference that this was Hong Kong in the 1930s. Where on the Peak should they live? The only feasible place for a honeymoon was the Philippine Islands. Therese also needed to visit Peter's relations. There was also the complication that the wedding was being planned by airmail letter and that four people were involved – Peter, Therese, Nancy and AE. The latter was conscious of what was expected in Hong Kong and that considered members of the establishment should be invited. In addition, there is news of life in Hong Kong – sailing, socialising and the HKRNVR.

To Therese   16 July
Your sister wrote a very charming letter welcoming me to the family. It seems a pity I have to wait so long to meet your mother and sister, but I feel we will have a great to do when we really get down to it. [Peter was to meet them for the first and only time two years later in 1938.]

If we go to Baguio[1] we have to go by ship to Manila and so on by car or rail or a mixture of both. Manila in the winter is like HK in the summer, whites all the year around for men, but Baguio is up in the hills at about 4,000 feet and the nights are colder, needing fires and warmer clothes.

I am glad you are going to see Evelyn. Personally I do not think going to a convent an ordeal, chiefly I suppose because my ideas on religion are fairly flippant, but you never know how it may strike others.

To Therese   23 July
The airmail is late this week on account of a typhoon which entered the coast around Tonkin, so I have no letter from you, which is most distressing.

---

1   In the Philippine Islands [Philippines].

I had dinner with your Uncle and Aunt last Thursday and we discussed all sorts of things but mainly little Therese. I have no doubt she will have written to you all sorts of bits of information and advice but the main thing which emerged from the discussion was a suggestion of Mrs Hall's, to wit that we should be married at the Peak Church and have the reception at the Peak Club. Mrs H, of course, is trying chiefly to boost the Peak Club, but nevertheless the idea sounds eminently sensible to me. The expense would be about half.

I fancy your Aunt would dearly love us to live on the Peak, but my point of view is that if the firm expect their younger married staff to live on the Peak, then they must pay Peak salaries. When we are married I will be drawing $880 per month and a Peak house, the unfurnished rent of which would be about $180/200 and would cost at least $600 per month to run. This would leave very little margin and certainly mean saying goodbye to *Monsoon*. The Garden Terrace flats are about $115 per month, smaller and cheaper to furnish, and the Barhams tell me they run theirs all in for $400, so they sound a far more attractive proposition to me.

You have made a distinct hit with the family, my dear, and my sister writes 'Mum and Jack came along the other day after meeting Therese, both of them very pleased. It seems in fact a general chorus of approbation.' Well done, I am only sorry I was not there to hold your hand over the awkward moments. I heard from my Aunt Helen and she was full of eulogies on the strength of the photos I had sent her and reports from my mother.

I swept mines on Sunday morning in a North Sea Trawler, the *Barnet*, owned by the Navy. We used heavier gear for the first time. It all has to be landed by tackles as it is too heavy to be lifted by hand and to our intense surprise we got it overboard correctly the first time without casualties to any of the crew.

Fergie and Griff are off on Thursday for six weeks of debauchery and sin in Japan, which they grace by the name of a holiday. Gompertz, who you have not met, is coming to live with me and will provide company and transport. His father used to be a Puisne Judge[2] here and I was at school in the same house with his son.[3] I live pretty quietly,

---

2 A Puisne Judge is a regular member of a court, as opposed to head of the court or ex officio member. The term almost exclusively used in common law jurisdictions in the UK and what were some of its colonies such as Hong Kong. https://en.wikipedia.org/wiki/Puisne_judge
3 That was a house called 'College', which was for all the scholarship boys.

with one eye on the Shekel situation and June ran off well with a profit of $145. May not so good, as I had an expensive repair on the yacht, while April was positively disastrous due to a lot of whoopee making with a young woman named Sander. However, I hope to accumulate a mild surplus before you return, which will assist in the matter of getting married to said young woman.

To Therese   30 July

I was glad to hear that your famous cocktail party had gone off successfully, also the stay with my mother. I fancy you have scored a bull's eye there because my mother, writing after your visit, even said, 'We got to know each other distinctly better and I still consider that you are very lucky.' So do I and I will compliment Mum on her sagacity.

You must not bother yourself about my mother worrying. It is all wrong and she wears herself to death with it, but she always has done and always will. You would think an unearned income and a service flat [just off Kensington High Street] should produce a certain amount of leisure and peace. But not my mamma!! No, no, she is always in a terrible rush.

I was glad to hear you got on well with Jack; actually I have got a bit out of touch with him in ways, as I went to S. America in January 1925 and since then I have only seen him for the four months, when I was home in 1934. You seem to have picked up the idea that you are marrying a very bright young man. I do not know where and how you did so, but even if somewhat incorrect it seems a sound line, so see you always treat me with due and proper respect. Poor old Jack has had a rather rotten break, with getting TB in Calcutta.

On Tuesday I went to a cocktail party at the General's on an invitation to the Naval Volunteers. Vast quantities of people and I fell in with bad men, army sailing crowd of no inconsiderable thirst. We adjourned to the Hong Kong Hotel. I regret to say we all became monumentally inebriated, so today leaves one in a somewhat mossy feeling. You definitely have to take this party question in hand and lead me away at the right moment. I do not go to many parties, but this bulldog spirit of sticking it out to the end does keep one up rather late and involves an unnecessary amount of drinking.

The coming weekend is the August Bank Holiday one and I had tried to organise a cruise up to Mirs Bay, but there is one typhoon about 300 miles off coming this way and another following it at a distance, so prospects do not look so hot. I was to have gone with the Sheldons in *Luana* but the No. 1 Signal[4] is up and they are in a bit of a flat spin as to whether to go out.

I quite understand what you say about leaving your mother and realise that it will be a difficult parting for both of you, more especially for her. But it is usually inevitable in the history of any family and each generation has to take it as it comes. However, you will be seeing her again in 1938 and possibly after that, when we get settled down here she might, as you suggest, like to come out here for a winter.

To Therese   6 August
On the question of you travelling alone, I know you are perfectly able to take care of yourself, but in general theory I am against people being exposed to unnecessary temptations of any sort. I will speak to your Aunt about it and see if she knows of anyone travelling. Veronica Evans (Mrs Don Evans) is travelling on the P&O, which arrives on the 11 November, so it is a pity I did not know before otherwise you might have booked on that, the *Naldena* I think.

During the last few weeks the official Chinese Govt. from Nanking have taken over the administration of the Kwangtung Province [Guangdong], of which Canton is the capital. There is great talk of a vast programme of reform, social, economic and political, and if they only do one half of what they promise, it will go a long way towards making the province far more prosperous. How far we will share in this remains to be seen, but there are plenty of signs over the last five years of a rejuvenation of China, which would not previously have been possible. There is hope of prosperity out here, but it has not yet materialised and then there is always the wretched Japanese to be coped with.

On Friday the typhoon stopped about 220 miles SSE of us and the gale warning signals went up. Still on Saturday and still not a breath of air, but on Saturday night we had a colossal thunderstorm with 8¾ inches of rain and a total of 13 over the weekend, or about one quarter of the English yearly rainfall.

To Therese   20 August
I am glad you think the Peak Church/Club idea a sound one as it seems to me to be

---
4   The typhoon-warning signal.

far more in keeping with our not very pretentious respective outlooks. Guests are the catch; I gave your Aunt a list of about fifteen to twenty people, which will see me off, but as regards her list she has got the convention bee in her bonnet and says she must ask so-and-so, altogether totalling about 130. Some of the people give me an acute pain in the neck and if it was my funeral I would put a codicil in my will to restrain them from being allowed to attend, but I did not tell your good Aunt so. The difficulty is that with the crowd of people she has asked, lots of whom you and I scarcely know, I should really increase my list considerably so as keep things a bit in harmony. Personally, if I do get an invitation to any impending wedding, I always regard that as a bull point [good thing] but everyone does not look at it that way.

Re the *Antenor*, I have heard that a Mrs STUART-SMITH has changed her booking to that ship. I do not know her very well, her husband distinctly better in fact, but she seems to know some distant connections of mine in England, so I thought you might link up with her if you do not find anyone else. Her husband is a stockbroker here and has written to tell her to look out for you. I fancy you would get on alright, she is a pleasant sort, one child I think, sex unknown, her age about twenty-seven.

The chief news of the week was our typhoon of Sunday night; I do not know if it was reported in the home papers, but if not I am sending various press cuttings via Suez, which may be of interest. If it was reported it was probably done in a pretty lurid way and I hope you did not have any unjustified qualms on my behalf, since to be perfectly candid I slept through most of the worst part.

I went sailing for the weekend with Major Dixon, Mrs D not being able to come out on account of sickness of one of the kids. There was little wind on Saturday, so we only got as far as Joss House Bay (*left*). Sunday morning early, one of the police launches passed us flying the No. 1 or warning signal; we came in to Junk Bay for lunch and were back in Causeway Bay by 4.15 pm, the signal for a NW gale having gone up at 2.30 pm Sunday.

I was back to dinner in the house and afterwards it started to blow up pretty fresh; I took a last look outside at about 11.30 pm, by which time the wind had started to come up pretty squally, and I then started to turn in. All the windows were firmly shut

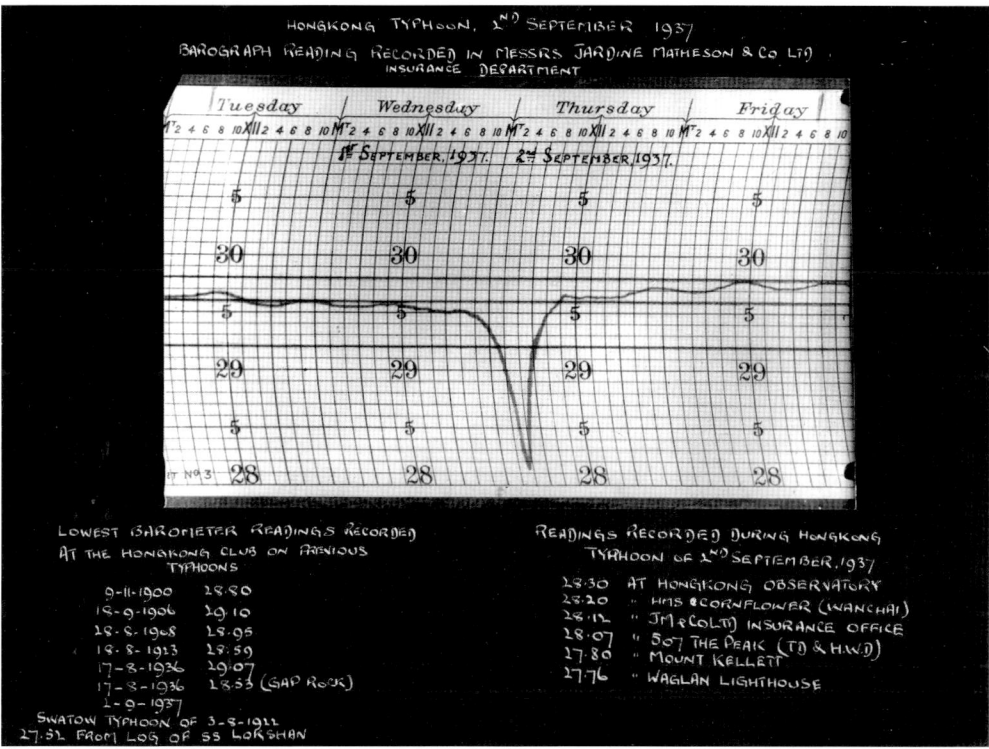

A chart of the typhoon in 1937

with the typhoon bars on them, but by the time I had got into bed 'it was blowing a four penny one' and I started to feel the windows could not possibly stand the strain. Up I got and shut all the wooden jalousies [on the inside of the widows] of the enclosed veranda, the second line of defence of a house here, and by the time I had finished it was all I could do to shut them, since with only one pain of outside glass broken there was half a gale blowing through the house. Gompertz and I kept at it until we had got everything bolted, barred and made fast, all doors shut, and then we had a drink and I did the rather unconventional thing of going to bed and sleep.

My recollections of hard winds and gales at home are those of a high whistling note round a building, but this was a deep roar of thunder and every time a squall hit the house you could feel the whole building shudder and hear the China etc. rattle on the mantle shelf, even with two sets of closed windows to protect them. The squalls came about three a minute for five hours, so we had plenty of it. Honestly, unless you had heard it you would not have believed the forces of nature could be capable of such an awe-inspiring display. The wind got up to 131 mph on the heaviest squall (above 90 mph you cannot stand up) and remained at hurricane force from about midnight until 6.30 am, by which time it had veered from East to South and taken off a bit.

On Monday morning everything was chaos. Gompertz and I motored down the old road at about 9.00 am and it was more like a hurdle race than a motor drive. Trees down everywhere, pieces of rock just blown off the cliffs, and the trees that stood looked as if some giant animal had been browsing off the branches.

The ABS Steamer the *Sunwing* was blown ashore in Junk Bay with both anchors down and steaming full into it; she was twisted in pieces and the bows finished up some 200 yards from the rest of the ship. *The Talma* (B&I) [sic], also in Junk Bay, lost both her anchors and took the very outside chance of falling back through Lyemun;[5] she was swept through the pass broadside on, sending SOS signals and with her sternpost hitting a rock, but eventually got into Kowloon Bay and managed to weather it.

The good ship *Monsoon* met with a mishap in Causeway Bay, as *Irene* dragged back onto her and snapped *Monsoon*'s bowsprit,[6] so with no forestay the mast just snapped. Unfortunately *Irene* is owned by a Shyster Swede, who has already been slung out of the Yacht Club for not paying his bills, so there is no prospect of compensation and he even tried to make out it was *Monsoon* who had dragged.

All the people who said they wished to see a typhoon have now changed their minds and feel that one is enough. I had dinner with your Aunt and Uncle on Monday and they were none the worse for the typhoon.

To Therese   27 August
I was glad that your Aunt Eva had received such a pleasant impression of her prospective in-law, and it strikes me as solid and beneficial propaganda to relay it onto your mother. I was interested to hear about Agnes's devoted admirer; arriving in time to wash up breakfast things on Sunday is a definite test and if Agnes has any decided weakness in this direction, I should say she might do worse than grab him.

Your orgies of cooking sound most suitably domesticated and definitely a mark

---

5 Lyeemun Pass, between Devil's Peak and Lyeemun Bay on the Island. The ship was being blown NW into Kowloon Bay.
6 Spar in the bows used to extend ship's sail.

SS 'Hong Peng' Quarry Bay, 1937

on your side. I am sufficiently un-modern to feel that a girl should be able to cook at least efficiently, even if she will not necessarily have to practise her art when married.

I have got a bit of staff work going as regards a honeymoon for us. After an intense search around the shipping offices, I have found that the least expensive fare to Manila is the JCJL (Dutch Line) and that with their ships you can do a round trip in a fortnight, provisionally for the 24 November to the 8 December, which would give us eight days at Baguio, the hill station in the Philippines, two days at sea and one day at Manila/Baguio each way. I think it is about the best place to go at that time of year and they say that the Country Club at Baguio, for which I will arrange to get us put up, is delightful. As regards clothes, when you arrive here on 7 November, we will be just about out of whites, but only just. Going to Manila it will be tropical one day out of Hong Kong, tropical in Manila, but at Baguio, which is about 4,500 feet up it will be hot during the day and cold (with fires) at night.

Last weekend was a bit of a flop as I had no yacht. Hop Kee, a boat builder from the Kowloon side, was putting in a new mast, but on Friday evening when I went over to see it, it looked such a rotten piece of wood, that I told him to take it out and start afresh. Actually I said to do so on Monday, but out of spite I suppose, he whipped it out on Saturday morning. I met the Dixons round at his yard on Friday and went back to the house for a drink, eventually staying for dinner, and I regret to say becoming somewhat

Quayside scene and in the background the 'An Lee' blown onto the quay in the 1937 typhoon.

Causeway Bay

inebriated. Their hospitality is rather pressing and their ideas of size of drinks definitely out of line with mine.

And what of Therese and Peter? The latter is in rather a state of animated suspense and the cause for it is the former. Having got over a stage of horror and surprise at realising the momentous thing I had done in asking you to marry me, I have for a while past settled down safely and happily to the contemplation of prospective marriage. I have now got a bit more advanced in that state and am extremely anxious to start the adventure forthwith; for once in my life I am feeling impatient.

To Therese   3 September

No letter from you this week as the Horsa,[7] which was carrying the airmail from England, came down in the wilds of Persia [Iran] and the mail will not get here until next week. So I must bite on the bullet and assume you still love me, but I will be relieved if I get two letters next Tuesday confirming this happy state of affairs still exists. I strongly fancy I still love you but will let you know for certain on 7 November, when it can be done with full honours and not in this somewhat anaemic correspondence style.

Last week end I had *Monsoon* back in commission with her second new mast installed and it seemed to stand the strain alright, although there was not a vast deal of wind to test it. I went out with one Baker from PWD [Public Works Department] and we went round to Hebe Haven in Port Shelter, where we met Dreyer (the Great Dane) on *Cigale* with attendant Russian women. Andersen, another Dane, was with him and when one of the women was introduced as Mrs Andersen, I chortled and thought how discreet to hide the lady's honour like that. Imagine my surprise when I got back to *Monsoon* after sinking two of their colossal gins, and Baker told me she really was Mrs A.

There was not much wind on Sunday, so we started off straight for home, instead of sailing round Rocky Harbour, and picked up Merrit Cootes in an 'A' boat[8] for tiffin

---

7   The Horsa was a Handley Page 42E and was designed for the long-range Eastern routes and used by Imperial Airways (Forerunner of BOAC and then BA). It was a large unequal-span biplane, all-metal except for the fabric coverings of the wings, tail surfaces and rear fuselage. It carried eighteen and later twenty-four passengers. http://en.wikipedia.org/wiki/Handley_Page_H.P.42. 15 April 2015.
8   Anker Class, flush deck cutter, designed by the Norwegian, John Anker. https://en.wikipedia.org/wiki/Johan_Anker. 7 February 2016.

at Clearwater Bay. He is a junior American Vice Consul and distinguished himself last summer by sinking an 'A' boat in a squall, but he does not seem to have lost his taste for that type of sailing.

Not much news here and each week seems to be rather the same as another. The nights are starting to get cooler and I hope they keep it up. Your Uncle and Aunt are coming to dinner tonight for a run over arrangements and if we are not as good as married after your Aunt E has stage-managed me for a couple of hours, then my estimate of her capabilities are all wrong. Actually I think she is rather enjoying the whole affair and having a little 'niecey' to marry off is just tickling her to death. Hall continues to register poor health and is not able to settle down to work in the way he used to. Actually I think he has rather worn out his constitution with a hectic youth and an outflow of nervous energy spreading over many years and I doubt if he will ever get better from his present troubles. As a result I personally will not be very surprised if he does not come back from leave in 1937, or at least only for a very short while to clean up, but do not air my views about this as it is rather dangerous to suggest these things.

It seems funny to think I will only write to you twice again in England. I will try to rack my brains for bad experiences of the distant past and give you lots of sound advice for deportment on the way out. Interpreted into plainer language, it means look out after Suez, avoid boat decks, moonlight motor drives and other people's cabins. Everyone goes a bit mad on a ship, but that is only an interlude in life, whereas you and I are life itself. Be careful and good, my dearest, as you are far too attractive to be roaming about the world by yourself.

To Therese   11 September
I am very glad to hear Agnes and Robert seem to have found the big thing, but I do not know that I agree with all your ideas about seeing each other a lot before marriage and knowing each other so well. Is it apt to make it all rather stale? After all the engaged state is really rather an unnatural one, at least if it is protracted beyond a period of six to nine months; you are nearly married but not quite so, with the result you get all the difficulties of convention and none of the freedom of marriage. In our case we know very little of each other in cold, hard experience and are just backing our intuitions and the soundness of common sense on either side. I feel sure we are right, but it is

the very fact that we are backing intuition against certainty, which makes it all such an adventure.

On the subject of being engaged from the other end of the world, I agree with you without any reservations whatsoever, it is decidedly unsatisfactory. But anyway, there are less than two months before we are together again.

Last weekend was a two and a half day affair apropos Monday being taken as a holiday and Meeke and I had planned to go cruising up to Mirs Bay. A typhoon was passing 180 miles south of us on Friday/Saturday and they did not lower the No. 1 signal until 5.00 pm Saturday; however, from Saturday until Monday we had twelve inches of rain, so the weekend was spent mainly in the house, failing to write letters, reading books and going to the cinema.

To Therese   17 September

I thoroughly agree, Aunt E's conventional social tendencies must be checked, even if it is poor little compliant me who has to do it. She has got the Peak Social bug at the back of her mind. 'Who must we ask?' After all it is our show and convention demands that your poor unfortunate mother has to pay for it all, so why should you be forced to have the notable bores of the Colony, who you will probably not know, or want to know, later. I am going out sailing with your Uncle and Aunt on Sunday, so I will try a mixture of social indiscretion and lack of tact. Incidentally, the Peak Church has no music whatsoever but I suppose it is possible to import temporarily a harmonium or a radio gramophone, the latter to be trained to give the appropriate sounds at critical moments, which, possibly rather wooden and hard boiled, would probably be more effective than an indifferently played harmonium.

Well this is my last letter to you in England. I will be able to write to you at all ports by air or other mail, on the way out, and so will you to me.

You say that a husband is a bit of a convenience as regards the uncertainties of a double cabin, when travelling on board ship. You talk about being seen off [departure for Hong Kong] and I feel here a word of warning is indicated. At home it is appalling and I refuse to have it happen except at a railway station, when the train moves out on time and the wait is then curtailed to say fifteen minutes. On ships, NO, it is too long and drawn out, upsetting and unsatisfactory. Out here it is not nearly so bad. Usually you are going on leave or to another port and everyone will see you again in due course, and besides that they are used to parting and only really come on board to drink at your expense. Hence everyone knows more clearly where they are and vague and unidentified sentiment does not come into it to the same extent.

Last weekend was fine for a change and I sailed round to Deepwater Bay with Gompertz in order to inspect the prospective site for the Yacht Club at Deepwater. On Saturday night we fell in with bad men, to wit Meeke and Roger Grieve in *Cormorant*, and Beck, Mrs B & a Major Davies in *Norseman*. Net result a handsome libation of gin was poured.

Gompertz left me last Thursday and Griff and Fergie got back on Friday. They had a most health-giving four weeks up in Hokkaido, but the health so obtained was too much for them when they got back to the wicked cities. First at Shanghai and, since they have been back here, they have been on a solid toot all the while and breakfast this morning was not a festive meal.

I have tried to lure out the King girls on two occasions, but all to no avail. I felt it was the matey thing to do, if they are to be your bridesmaids, but it looks a little as if Mrs K has said to them 'I have seen men like that before.'

I will write you next at Marseille and hope you will have a calm trip round to there. I am afraid you will be feeling rather sad, at any rate for the first part of the voyage, as you will have left behind everyone you know and love and you will be feeling rather lonely on a strange ship. However, it will not be for long and soon you will be out here so that I can make a fuss of you. Remember all I said about young girls in the tropics, alone on board ship; it is not all hooey and eyewash, but a cold hard result of observation and experience. I hope you find Mrs Stuart Smith pleasant.

To Therese   24 September

No news from you on this week's airmail and I hope that does not mean that anything is amiss.

On Sunday I took your Aunt and Uncle out in *Monsoon* and it was a perfect day with ideal conditions. She thoroughly enjoyed herself and is on the way to becoming an enthusiastic yachtswoman. Actually she is rather funny over it all and exactly resembles the Willoughby family who are our relatives, they used to have a rooted objection to boats and water until my mother took Daphne Morgan (aged about fourteen) on a lake at Ranelagh and then the family took to the river 'en masse'. Your Aunt has for twenty years had a rooted objection to sailing, based entirely on the fact she has never tried it, and now when she does and likes it the whole show is rather amusing.

On Saturday I sailed with the Barnards, who are now back from Wei-Lai-Wei. They are a most pleasant couple and I think enjoyed their afternoon. We went out to Junk Bay, bathed, had tea and drinks first in *Monsoon* and then in *Cormorant*, Roger Grieve's boat. The party adjourned to *Luana* for dinner with Mrs Sheldon, where we had an abundance of good food. Somnolence then set in and I started a minority movement to stay there for the night, but Barnard had to be back early and Frances Bouillin had not got leave from the hospital, so we rallied about 9.45 pm and had a race back to the Yacht Club for the three yachts at a dollar a boat. Altogether a most enjoyable afternoon.

The weather is starting to cool off very definitely and I am using a thick blanket at night; there are signs of the NE Monsoon settling in already, but I fancy the wind will turn South again and we will have some warm, sticky stuff before the summer eventually goes. By the time you arrive here, the weather should be nearly perfect, warm midday and cold at night, so I hope it greets you by living up to its usual standard.

And what of Therese? I am sending this letter to Marseilles on the assumption that you boarded the *Antenor* at Liverpool, since it would be too late to catch you before you left. I hope there are some pleasant people on board. Aunt E said Mrs de Martin was possibly travelling. What of Mrs Stuart Smith? Have you hit up with her yet? She arrived out here to marry him late in 1932.

Peter, Frances Bouillon, Bish and TC

I am looking forward terribly to your arrival, my dear, and am starting to get fidgety already with six weeks still to go, so if I am a bit difficult when you eventually arrive, you will know it is due to boxed up excitement. I feel we have before us the possibility of great happiness for the two of us; it is all waiting there for us to take and I am impatient to start.

To Therese   1 October

Arrangements here are progressing steadily and I have bought a set of furniture for $500. It belongs to the naval couple and most of the pieces were new eighteen months or so ago. Your Aunt E told me it seemed a very fair bet. Your collecting instincts (if any?) will have to wait until 1939 for the major exercise, when we will possibly need to supplement things if we take a house.

Hall has written to a friend of his in Manila with a view to getting fixed up at the Country Club at Baguio, which is rather pleasant; private cottages all around the grounds and a central club house for meals. You need not distress yourself about your golf, as mine is not so hot, and I regard the game as a most agreeable amusement not a religious rite. We are to sail on 24 November and return to Hong Kong on the 6 December.

Dr Black says AE is in a very rundown state of health. She seems perfectly cheerful and I stayed for dinner on Monday night when she was looking bright as well. We went into the question of invitations and I quite see it would be extremely difficult to have sixty people. We have cut it down to 120 and it has got to be that or a private affair with about ten only. You see your Uncle has been here thirty years and is head of a legal firm, so it is inevitable that he asks the Chief Justice, the Attorney General and so forth, irrespective of whether we like them or not. Also there is the other side of it, to wit, if you have a fair sized wedding to which all these people are asked, it gives you a far better send off socially in your taking up residence in the Colony as a young wife. I am at rather a turning point as far as things social here are concerned; to date I have mixed mainly with a youngish bachelor crowd, not given a damn for the older generation and refused to call on them. However, if I am going to succeed in JM & Co. and get on above the average, which seems a fair possibility but by no means a certainty, it is not exactly judicious to start one's married life by upsetting a considerable proportion of the older generation of the Colony. I do not mean to suggest that I hope to obtain advancement by crawling round to all sorts of people, but from the opposite point of view I do not intend to obstruct it by needlessly annoying them.

You say you are getting excited about starting and longing to be back here and you are not alone in that. I, too, am already getting excited about your return and want to do all the things you want done to you.

Therese left England for Hong Kong on 3 October.

To Therese   8 October

I wrote to you on the 24 September to Marseilles and the 1 October to Port Said, so I hope they both caught up with you alright.

I love you and I am quite sure, as yet I do not love you as much as I feel I eventually will, but that is due to our not really knowing each other well enough yet. But I know you well enough to realise that I am perfectly and implicitly sure that we can make a grand success out of our marriage between the two of us. You give me a sense of serenity and security, which without you I lack badly. Without you it is merely a matter of time before I make an ass of myself and get in some awkward jam, but with you there is safety, decency, marriage and happiness stretching out before me.

The Blunts are a great couple, she used to be our parlour maid when we lived in Northamptonshire and he worked originally in the Brewery at Wellingborough and later as gardener to my father's cousin, so they know the family fairly well. Yes, I think they are extremely happy and devoted to each other and they have been married twenty-five years now.

Last Saturday I sailed with Mrs Dixon, who is to race *Monsoon* in the Opening Cruise on the 16 October. I went back to dinner with them at Kowloon, where they had a party for Tommy Fairburn, who was down from Canton with a team to race against the Yacht Club. We went on to the hotel dance after. As the Dixon's idea of hospitality is distinctly convivial we had a bit of a thick night. On Sunday I went out mine sweeping in *Barnet* and it was filthy; buckets of rain and no proper tackle with which to handle the gear, so by the time we got the sweep out we were all soaked to the skin and very disgruntled. We then got it in, had tiffin and came back as quick as we could.

I hope the trip in the *Antenor* is going along OK and that you have remembered my advice in moments of crisis.

Therese relaxing on deck on her return to Hong Kong

To Therese   15 October

I received yours of the 30 September today, written just before you left London, also one from my mother with a postscript to say she had just seen you off at Euston and I was very glad to get them and to hear you were really on your way.

You need have no qualms about being seasick on your first night as a bride; I do not recollect how far I had got in telling you about the wedding arrangements, but here is the rough drift of things. We get married on the 23 November, as late in the afternoon as is convenient, so as to enable people to attend the wedding and the reception without too much stress to their arrangements, and so out to Repulse Bay for the night. Off at 10.00 am on the 24th in the *TJINEGRA* for Manila arriving on the 26th at daylight. Up to Baguio that day, arriving there late in the evening. Six days at Baguio, where I am fixing for us to put up as members of the Country Club through the kind offices of F.C. Hall. So to Manila, where we will probably have to spend a night and then back to HK in the *TJISALAK* arriving on the 6 December. I know quite a crowd of people in Manila, so we will be likely to have a pretty hectic night there, but they are all very good scouts, even if a bit thirsty.

I was glad to hear of the wedding present you have duly chosen, and I hope you really like it and that it is what you wanted. You need not worry about the cost, I want you to have something really nice and, if fortune smiles on me out here, I hope to be able to give you lots of the sort of things you want. But on broader lines, definitely when we are married, and to all intent and purposes we are now, we will be on a half joint account basis as regards money and finance, so the money spent was as much yours as mine.

Last weekend was a Saturday/Sunday two-day affair,[9] Saturday, 10 October being a holiday here since according to the Gregorian Calendar it is the anniversary of the founding of the Chinese Republic. I sailed for the two days with one Baker and we went round to Port Shelter in company with *Norseman*. Mrs Beck laid fairly low and did not repeat her boast of some six weeks ago that gin had no effect upon her; it was grievously wrong then as Sunday proved to her cost and I feel she is learning prudence. I have just had a new suit of sails made for *Monsoon* and I had them out stretching, but could not use them on Sunday as it was blowing a bit fresh and it does not do to reef unstretched sails, otherwise they do not stretch true. I am having the

---

9   They must have normally worked on Saturdays. It was still quite common to work some Saturday mornings in England up until the 1970s.

yacht all pansied up before you arrive, so I hope she will be looking nice and fresh. Incidentally you arrive here on a Saturday, so keep some suitable clothes near the top in case you would like to sail over the weekend. Medium weight as it will be warmish (65/75 degrees) midday and fresh in the evening.

Now I will give you a choice little bit of that commodity which is dear to every woman's heart, to wit, scandal. Do the names Mrs P & R convey anything to you? She is a gunner's wife, a buxom baby if ever there was one, and he is tall, dark haired and fresh faced, also a gunner, they were at Repulse Bay together on the veranda when we were there the night before you sailed. Things apparently came to a head a short while ago, how I do not know, and P beat up Mrs P to such an extent that she had to retire to Kowloon Hospital. The ostensible reason was her immoral association with R, and admittedly from the little I saw they had been making the pace pretty hot. I think R is an extremely nice fellow and would like to feel he had always remembered he was a gentleman, but somehow I feel it was not in human nature. The upshot is that Mrs P goes home, P to Singapore and R to Colombo; so another triangle drama is temporarily torn apart.

I saw Mrs J. J. Paterson and she said that she wanted to give a dinner party for us, which is very kind of her. Wednesday, 18 November has been fixed as the provisional date and I gather she wants to have your Uncle and Aunt, the King girls, the ushers and all the various other characters in our act.

The furniture question came to a head with a resounding crack the other day, when Mrs Clutterbuck rang me up saying they were leaving the flat that afternoon. However, I fixed with Dr Phoon to have it put in our flat and have got the Flannagan's boy to keep an eye on it, so I hope not too much will be pinched. I have also engaged a Cook Boy, Amah and Coolie, so with the flat furniture and servants, all it needs is Therese to make it complete.

I had a letter from Aunt Helen this week, five pages on either side, all about you, and I assure you, you scored heavily there as I expected you would. The general and universal opinion from family and friends is complete approbation, so you have got over a sticky and difficult bit of country with flying colours.

To Therese   21 October
I saw Stuart Smith in the Club yesterday and he told me he was off to Penang today

The Repulse Bay Hotel

to meet his lady, so you will presumably meet him shortly after you receive this letter.

The preparations for the wedding go on steadily; the invitations have been printed and go out next week; I have applied for a licence and will get all the legal side of things fixed up. Your Aunt is better and I hope she will not fuss and tire herself out with trying to do too much; so far as you can, you will have to do all the work when you arrive and I will feel sure you will not mind doing it.

We fixed at 4.30 pm and the reception at the Peak Club at 5.15, on the idea that a late hour would make it more convenient for people to attend. I do not know if I told you I had fixed for Fergie to be best man and Griffiths, Meeke, Gompertz and Bill Berry as ushers.

Last week we started cruiser racing and Mrs Barnard sailed *Monsoon* for me in the Ladies Cruiser Race on Saturday, but without great skill; if she had got in fifteen seconds sooner she would have been second, but as it was she was fifth. On Sunday we had a sweepstake race round, in which I got in third out of fourteen; it was a glorious day. I had the new sails up on Saturday and Sunday and they are coming out very nicely indeed; in fact they look just about the goods, so blow the cost. If all goes well it looks as if *Monsoon* may once again join the ranks of the prizewinners after an absence from these august circles for two seasons. In 1933/4 we had a cracking season and I won four out of seven cups, including the Cruiser Championship over a series of six races. That, too, was when the cruisers and four tonners all sailed together as one clan, so the average entry for a race was anywhere from fifteen to twenty yachts. Since then, however, the glory seems to have departed and I do not know whether it was a result of not racing so keenly or the poor suit of sails. But now with the new suit it looks as if we are well back in the running again. So I hope I will be able to give you some amusement over the winter.

To Therese   25 October

There is only a fortnight and two days before you eventually arrive and I am getting all worked up about it. I suggest that we start on the arrears straight away. Just take a careful look at Holt's Wharf for the boyfriend when you arrive.

I have not yet had any news from you on your way out, but I hope you have had a good trip, amusing company and good weather; it is still nearly a fortnight before you arrive, so I hope to have a letter before you get here, but letter or no letter I will be all teed up on the quayside waiting for you.

On Friday night at 12.00 am Merritt Cootes, one of the American Vice Consuls, an excellent scout, sailed for the land of his father's and I regret to say that in the process of seeing him aboard his ship, I became slightly inebriated. That left Saturday one of the not so hot festivals, but we survived. On Friday, after I wrote to you last, I had a letter from Rosemary Skinner asking us to join a dinner dance party at the Peninsula on the 10 November so I have accepted provisionally.

Therese arrived in Hong Kong on 7 November.

CHAPTER 5

The Wedding and the Honeymoon in the Philippine Islands
November to December 1936

Therese writes to tell her mother, Nancy, all her wedding news and about their honeymoon in the Philippine Islands, including their adventurous return. Peter's letters to Lizzie Blunt concentrate more on the local political situation.

Peter to Lizzie Blunt   2 November

Things have moved quite a bit politically since I last wrote to you, and in the right direction. The former independent Government of the South West of China, situated at Canton, have given into the National Government at Nanking under Chiang Kai Shek, who is now the Mussolini of China and rules about all the Japanese have left. About ten years ago China was in complete chaos, with private bandit armies each working their own patch of territory and extorting taxes from the farmers, whereas now the major part of these armies have been cleaned up and there are distinct signs of sound, well ordered government and a unified China. Things usually move slowly here and the achievements of the last ten years are an absolute record for speed, since it has taken previous dynasties about 200 years usually to obtain control over all the twenty-three provinces.

The present tendency towards a unified China and better government holds out tremendous possibilities for future prosperity in this part of the world, if only they can keep it going at the present pace and not drop back in to the previous disordered chaos. But then, of course, you always have the Japanese and they are a perfect blight in this part of the world. A strong and unified China is about the last thing Japan wants, since there are some 500 million Chinese against sixty million Japs; if the Chinese become a modern nation, in the way the Japanese have during the last eighty years, they will wipe the floor with the Japs and they know it too and are in their heart-of-hearts afraid. Altogether this looks like being a very interesting part of the world during the next fifty years or so, but I hope all sides manage to keep the peace, because in the event of war we would be too much in the front row of the stalls for it to be exactly comfortable.

Therese to Nancy   19 November

This is the last letter I will write to you as Therese Sander. I just can't realise it yet, there has been so much rushing around since I first arrived here that I have hardly had time to properly realise the real cause or foundation of the rushing. I know how much you must be thinking of me, my dear, I am on the brink of the biggest thing in my life and I would give a lot to have you with me. One's mother seems to understand one in a way that no one else quite does. Now when I am feeling, naturally, rather churned up and nervous, I would just love to have a long talk with you and in the end feel just twice the woman for it.

AE gave a dinner party for us on Monday; just a quiet affair for the bridal party. One of the key girls is unfortunately ill, but we hope she will be OK again by the 23rd. Mr No. 1 Jardines gave a huge dinner party in our honour, all most grand and important and we went down to the town after and danced. I must admit I had quite a little glow when the whole table rose to drink our health, Peter and I sitting at opposite ends of a huge table looking bashful.

Presents keep arriving all the time and I have got some very nice ones; how I wish you and Agnes were here to join in the thrill of each new parcel. AE gets a terrific kick out of it all almost more than I do. I have had rather an inrush of decanters, mostly from Peter's friends, but I dare say they will be all quite easily filled! I have also had some luncheon sets, some small silver bits and pieces, flower vases, lamps, Pyrex dishes, Chinese hors d'oeuvres dishes and various other odds and ends. I have got Peter's present in the form of two suitcases, he badly needed these and he seems very pleased. I have got really good ones and they should last him for many years to come. As we are likely to cover the world a good deal in our time, they seemed rather an appropriate gift. We have got the bridesmaids evening bags, which they said they wanted. My bouquet is to be white chrysanthemums, as the only white flowers available, but I gather that well done they can make charming bouquets. The bridesmaids are to have pink gladioli made into tight bunches with silver handles and pink ribbons, I think they will be rather sweet. I have seen the flat since I last wrote,

Peter and Therese's wedding at the Peak Church

it is very nice indeed; the bedrooms, dining room, sitting room, bathroom, kitchen, all very compact and nice and easy to run, also the furniture looks quite up to date without being extreme. We cook on gas and the bath water has a geyser![1]

I have checked up on all the furniture Peter got from the naval people. He took absolutely everything, so we should have most things, which saves me a lot of fuss and bother and I can get things organised to my liking at my leisure. I have taken the linen to the French convent where they are going to do the initialling.

Peter is going to a party tomorrow night. I believe he has asked sixteen in all, a somewhat weighty number for a dinner party in an average size house, but he seems quite bright and cheerful about it and what cutlery that they do not have, they will either beg, borrow or steal. I expect it will be a somewhat hectic 'DO' all together as Peter's friends are none of them exactly docile and domesticated. Incidentally, he has taken a lot of snaps of me which I will send to you as soon as he has had them printed. I have also taken some of him, but as I am not too gifted with his camera I am not promising anything. I was so glad to hear from your last letter that you are nearly yourself again. I can well realise you're feeling a bit out of touch with me, one so soon does.

Well dearest, I seem to have exhausted most of my news. I am afraid this is a rather scrappy letter, but I have so much to tell you that I don't seem to know where to begin and my brain rushes from one item to another at the rate one would talk, and my poor little pen scrambles along behind not too legibly. Needless to say I will think of you on the 23rd. I am going to be photographed in the house before the service, as you suggested, *especially for you* and then have all the usual groups taken at the reception, when you will see Peter, probably looking at his smuggest. I say again, as I said at the beginning , I simply can't realise that I will be Mrs Dulley when I next write to you.

Au revoir my dearest, I will think a lot of you, and know that you will be with me in spirit on the great day. I know it means almost as much to you as it does to me and it gives me a nice warm feeling full of confidence when I think of it.

Therese to Nancy   December
Here am I in my humble abode snatching a breather to write to you. There is as yet very little provision for writing in anything approaching comfort, there is no desk or table in the sitting room or the dining room in the dark, so the frugal knee is still

---
[1] A gas hot water heater: they were liable to go off with a large bang when lit.

View of Hong Kong from half way up the Peak

doing its bit.² Re my letters, I am so sorry there has been such a long gap, I can only presume that you never got it, it must have been in the plane that came down. I am so glad about Agnes and Robert,³ please give them my love and tell her that I will write a suitable letter of congratulations and sisterly advice!?

I have such a lot to tell you that I just don't know where to begin. In the first place I am well and happy. I know you will want to know that most of all. The honeymoon was a success and we did not quarrel once. Peter bloomed and played golf like a champion doing Bogeys and Birdies, and thinking that anything over a five was bad. Baguio is an attractive place but nothing very special, it is more like Europe than the Far East and reminded me a little of the Austrian Tyrol in many parts. We spent a day and night in Manila on the way out and were suitably grilled in the heat. The main fault to both Baguio and Manila was the people, the Yanks of the worst variety.

---

2 They had just moved into their flat.
3 Therese's sister and boyfriend's engagement.

My main bit of news about Baguio is the return journey. If I had more time I could really make quite a good adventure about it. We left the hotel at about 8.15 am, down to the station at what seemed little more than the cold light of dawn, and caught the 10.00 am train for Manila due in 4.00 pm. Little did we know! Peter bought a paper and we read that there was a typhoon in the offing and that it might touch Manila. We did not think much about it, our main sorrow being that there was no luncheon car on the train, and the station being distinctly native, we did not get much lunch apart from a couple of sandwiches at about 2.00 [pm]. The train stopped out in the open and then proceeded to return to the last station, a little place with nothing to be got anywhere and there we stayed from 3.00 till 9.00 with no food, no papers, nothing, the rain coming down in sheets, the cause of it all being that the next bridge had been damaged by floods. Eventually we made a transfer to another train by going as far as the broken bridge, crossing it on foot, a rather tricky job, and joining the new train on the other side, which took us to another little station. Then they calmly announced that the next bridge was also damaged so we must stop the night right there, so tired and dinnerless, we tramped out into the uninviting little village still in tropical rain and got supper at the most unattractive hotel; we even drank native gin! Once one gets off the hills the country is rather like South America as depicted on the films and the villages are just like the sort of places one sees in cowboy films. We returned to the train and then slept in distinct discomfort, at least Peter slept like a log, most irritating when one is lying awake feeling uncomfortable and generally out of love with life. However, we survived, and next day went on by car, and picked up another train, which really did get us to Manila only just in time to catch the boat. We had planned to spend the night in Manila and go on a bit of a toot with some of Peter's male friends, rather pathetic when you think how we spent the night. The voyage back was distinctly rough all the way and I am quite sure I would never have survived it if it had not been for Jack's little pills. Peter nearly gave up the ghost too and descended to the level of having a pill; we also found gin a most encouraging help. It was a small boat with only about twenty passengers and a lot of cargo and she pitched about with the greatest enthusiasm.

Returning to the present, the flat is just about liveable in and no more at present, but I am gradually collecting the necessities of life and hope soon to have it quite cosy. The boy is an absolute pet and most helpful in every way; I am struggling with masses of accounts and trying to keep some idea of all I spend. I have not had much to do with the Amah and Coolie but they seem all right. The furniture and curtains are quite nice, and I hope with a few cushions, rugs etc. to get things looking quite sweet.

The Boy seems to cook quite well but I have not yet found out his limits. He seems very anxious to learn, so I hope in time, between us, we will manage the food question quite well. We have got a little balcony looking right out over the town and harbour, a really lovely view both night and day.

Peter to Lizzie Blunt   30 December

I feel very guilty for not having written earlier to thank you and Blunt for the charming wedding present. After much deliberation we bought a tiered pewter cake stand with Chinese dragons and what have you, engraved and roaming about it; it looks very fine indeed and it was just what Therese wanted for giving tea parties. Thank you both very much for your very kind thought; we will always think of you when we use the cake stand and that will be often.

Therese arrived here looking fit and well and we had an extremely happy fortnight together before the great day on the 23 November. It was a great pity that it [the wedding] could not have been at home among all our relatives and friends, but that is just one of the disadvantages of living abroad and you have got to accept it. Our wedding day was a perfect example of our best autumn weather, just like an English summer, bright sun and warm, but cool enough to be wearing thick clothes and not white drill.

The wedding was at the Peak Church, a small building much after the English country village style of church. Therese's uncle, Mr Davidson, gave her away, Mrs Davidson was the matron of honour and Mr & Mrs Paterson (the No. 1 of my firm) represented my side of the family. Everything went off very well. There were about 130 people at the reception and everyone seemed to enjoy themselves.

It would not be until nearly two years after the wedding, in June 1938, Peter and Therese went to England on leave. Peter was then able to meet Therese's mother and sister and family for the first time.

After their honeymoon Therese had to take over the management of their flat. As the mistress she was responsible for the staff. She would say what meals were required and when they would be out, and would manage the general household maintenance. In 1938 they sub-let the flat for a rent of $115 per month and the following is based on the information given to the tenant:[4]

The No. 1 Boy or Cook Boy was paid $28 per month. He was responsible for providing all the food, which meant going to the shops and market each day to buy produce. The choice of menu would be directed by the mistress.

The Amah was paid $16 per month plus $4 living out allowance. She was responsible for cleaning: there would have been none of the present day equipment and cleaning materials to assist her. As the Amah was paid to sleep out, it implies that the men lived in, perhaps they just slept on the floor in the kitchen.

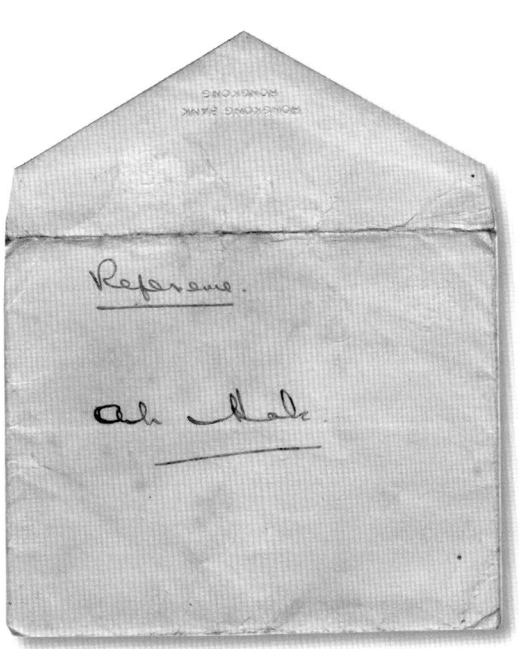

An example of a reference for an Amah

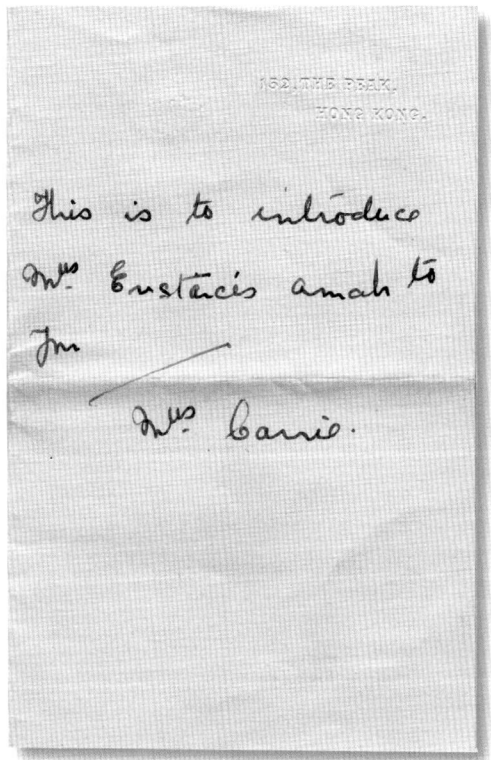

---

4 Peter's letter to Dr Stout, 29 March 1938.

The Coolie was paid $14 per month plus $1 for cleaning the car and exercising the dog. His duties would have been assisting the Cook Boy and Amah, washing up, running errands and helping the Cook Boy carry produce back from the market.

The staff possibly had time off in the afternoon in between lunch and dinner. At weekends food would have to be available, but maybe this was prepared in advance and just some of the servants were there but none on Sunday. However, when Peter and Therese were not in for meals, some of the servants could take time off. When they were away, then maybe all the servants could be off except one of the men for security.

CHAPTER 6

Hong Kong
1937 to 1939

The Dulleys lived happily on the Peak in the intervening years. Peter continued his career with Jardines and they enjoyed sailing, golf and their social life. They went on their long planned holiday to England in June 1938 and travelled via the Suez Canal. Their holiday included sailing on the Norfolk Broads with all Therese's immediate family and a trip to Scotland to meet some of Peter's Macpherson side of the family at Spital Towers, a very large house near Uddingston, Lanarkshire. They returned to Hong Kong at the end of the year, having bought an Austin 10 car. They travelled down through France before picking up their boat home in Marseilles. That was to be the last time Peter was to see England and in less than a year Great Britain and France would be at war with Germany. The letters start just before their holiday.

Agnes Dulley to Therese   17 March 1938   London SW5

You say I hear so regularly from Peter, it seems scarcely worthwhile you writing. I think it is really rather wonderful of him, as so often I notice that when men marry they seem to think that their's [wife] should do all the letter writing, even to their own people. I have, however, not had any letter from him this week.

    I am so glad to think that it is almost certain that you are both coming back this summer and it will be a great pleasure to me. I do trust that it will all come off according to plan, but here at present we all seem to be sitting on the edge of a precipice[1] and wondering at what moment we are going to be pushed over it. It seems just too awful to think that we may be plunged into a war, which would probably be much worse than the last.

---

1 Some years earlier Germany had introduced conscription and started a programme of rearmament. In March, Austria had been annexed and Czechoslovakia was later threatened. In November the pogrom, known as the Kristallnacht, was unleashed on the Jews in Germany.

Therese relaxing on the Norfolk Broads

Peter and Jack (Davidson) on the Broads holiday, 1938

Meanwhile Eva was staying with Nancy[2] before they were all due to meet up for a boating holiday on the Norfolk Broads.

Eva Davidson to Therese   2 May 1938   Tonbridge

I don't wonder that you were pleased about the car! I must say I think you were amazingly lucky to get $1,400 for it [in Hong Kong] – it just shows the demand for small cars – of course yours always looked very nice – but when I remember how many ups and downs you went through, you could not call that car the answer to a Motorist's Prayer could you!

The voyage seems weeks behind us now. It was very cool and fairly uneventful. A man died and was buried in the Red Sea, leaving a very plucky young wife and two children (four years and four months) to come along and meet his family in London. I was terribly sorry for her. In the Bay of Biscay we had sixteen hours of horrible weather, during which I lay in my bunk and wondered <u>why</u> Fate had ordained that I should care for and marry your uncle, instead of some nice placid London stockbroker with a peaceful home in Woking! These reflections vanished in the English Channel, where the weather was mill-pond calm and sunny, but bitterly cold. Apparently England had her first summer in March – realised her miscalculation, and quietly returned to winter in April and winter it still is!

The NE winds dried up my skin till I wanted to scratch myself *everywhere!* I have bought bottles of Lait Larola and Glymiel[3] etc. and am gradually calming down. Gerald took us to a most amusing play; we saw the famous Walt Disney's *Snow White and the Seven Dwarfs*. On Good Friday we went to Westminster Abbey.

I am staying another week [in Tonbridge] and loving every minute of it. We seem to have so much to talk over. She is living for your return.

Peter and Therese's Christmas card to Lizzie Blunt   December 1938

With very best wishes to you both for Christmas and 1939. This photo was taken a year ago at a fancy dress dance. Hong Kong is as sleepy as ever and you would not imagine there were any Japanese for 10,000 miles. All the scares are in the London papers, not here.[4]

---

2   Nancy was Therese's mother.
3   This was glycerine based, similar to Vaseline.
4   In November Japanese troops landed at the western end of the Hong Kong border, as a result there were a large number of refugees entering Hong Kong. By the beginning of December, all was quiet as the Japanese had moved back twenty miles to Cheungmatau. *The Times*, 28 November and 2 December 1938.

Nancy, Agnes (Sander) and Robert and Therese in a punt near Henley-on-Thames in 1938

The E's and Therese at Port Said after shopping at Simons Arts

Peter to Lizzie Blunt   6 July 1939

I feel very guilty about not answering your letter of the 5 April before this, but my busy time of the year in the office is February/June and I am afraid that my correspondence always gets behind then.

We persevere, both extremely fit and well and I am bearing up to the summer with my usual flow of intense perspiration. Therese is much more demure and dignified. We have been allotted a bungalow on the Peak and we are to have it for good; when we go on leave, someone else takes it over temporarily, but when we come back it reverts to us. It is all most convenient as Mrs Sander is due here early in November with her brother and sister, Mr & Mrs Davidson, who are returning from home leave. Mrs Sander will be here for the winter, but whether she will stay on when the weather starts to warm up I really do not know.

Hong Kong perseveres in spite of the war.[5] If the naked truth be told we are doing rather well out of it, and all this talk in the papers about British trade in China being killed by the Japanese is so much eyewash. Admittedly they are trying to terminate the foreign (non Asiatic) trade but to date their success has not been very great.

The war affects Hong Kong very little; we are still cut off from Canton, the capital of South China, which is some one hundred miles from here up the Pearl River. The Japanese occupy the city and ships are not allowed up to Canton; as a result the population is down from 1,000,000 to 500,000 – the place is a semi-desert. How the Japs can make the war pay for itself if they first capture a town and then stifle its trade, I fail to see. But their military clique, who run the country, are a shortsighted, overbearing, ignorant crowd.

They have now been at war with China for nearly two years. In theory they occupy large slices of the country, but in practice they have garrisons in the large towns in those slices, while it is not safe for them to be out in the country districts or they would be mopped up by guerrillas. Fighting stopped in Shanghai eighteen months ago, officially, but a friend of mine who lives in the Japanese portion of the settlement in S'hai, tells me that you regularly see lorry loads of wounded Jap soldiers being brought in. It does not sound so much like the glorious Japanese victories which they report so regularly in the Jap papers.

---

5   The undeclared war between China and Japan.

The Chinese are undoubtedly giving them a lot of trouble with the guerrilla tactics but it is doubtful whether this will be enough to finish them off. It looks like a war of attrition and the side that cracks first will lose. I still back the Chinese to win, but it is impossible to say how long this futile bloodshed will go on.

I don't think the Japanese efforts in Tientsin are really serious, although most unpleasant for the people there. I feel it is done more with a view to 'gaining space' and for propaganda purposes in Japan, also to try to create a diversion in Asia to assist Hitler's and Mussolini's plans in Europe. The British Empire can hit Japan very much harder economically than she can hit us, and I feel it is a pity we do not do so.

And last, but far from least, many happy returns of the 13th. May your shadow never grow shorter and may you always remain two days younger than me. I have sent a small present by parcel mail, but only on one condition, namely that you let me know if there was any import duty so that I can refund it.

CHAPTER 7

Hong Kong in Wartime
September 1939 to April 1940

Britain declared war against Germany on 3 September 1939. The following day Nancy was sent a letter cancelling her planned voyage to Hong Kong. She retained the letter and the thought of what might have been until her death.

McGregor, Gow & Holland Ltd. To Mrs A Sander   4 September 1939

Glenearn   30 September
With reference to your booking we regret to advise that the sailing of the above vessel has been cancelled, and we wait your advice as to your future movements.

You will appreciate that, at the moment, it is very difficult to say what alternative arrangements we shall be able to make but we will keep you advised in this respect.

Peter, as a member of the HKRNVR, was called up immediately in 1939 and was made a Captain of a succession of boats, which patrolled the coast of Hong Kong and the adjacent islands. Later, in June 1940, he was promoted to the rank of Lieutenant Commander. At the outset it all seemed quite light-hearted, a photo by Therese of the 'Lieutenant' in a dingy with his ship HMPS 'Perla' in the background and a jaunty photo of the Captain on the bridge in a casual open-necked shirt and a pair of slacks. There were also Christmas cards with photos of his ships HMPS 'Perla' in 1939 and HMAPV 'St. Aubin' in 1940. There was, however, no card in December 1941, when the whole climate in the Far East had changed and there was a distinct possibility of the Japanese invading Hong Kong.

The HKRNVR was expanded in order to relieve the Royal Navy in Hong Kong. At the outbreak of war, HKRNVR duties were to man patrols, to observe, report and, if practical, to fight any approaching enemy, detecting enemy mine-layers, minesweeping, maintaining the mine watching and indicator loop stations[1] and providing the majority of officers for the local motor torpedo boat flotilla. It was planned to send a small batch of officers home for general service in the Royal Navy.[2]

---
1   These were mines laid across the harbour approaches. The system would detect an enemy vessel crossing the mines and they would be detonated from the shore. Collingwood–Selby, p. 192.
2   South China Post cutting not dated, but would have been around 20 September 1940.

Hong Kong Naval Volunteer Force, 1937

This was all part of a major transition in the whole of the Royal Navy.³ It expanded its temporary naval officers, who were known as the Royal Naval Volunteer Reserves (RNVR), sevenfold during World War 2. Traditionally the Navy believed that a boy needed to start training to be an officer at the age of thirteen, as in Nelson's day, so that he had many years of hands-on experience and naval training before taking charge.⁴ To help compensate for the much shorter training many RNVR officers were recruited from weekend sailors, particularly in Hong Kong, where they commanded smaller ships and in the end often had to rely on their wits and luck.⁵

Returning to the local situation, China and Japan were at war. The Japanese military aggression towards China dated back to 1932. There was no declared war and it was known as the 'Manchurian incident'. It was not something Europeans were directly involved in, which had promoted an acceptance of the situation. That year Europeans in Shanghai were spectators,

---

3 Lavery, p. 7.
4 Lavery, p. 7.
5 'Learn as you go' the title of a chapter in a book on the RNVR covering young officers lack of experience at the start of the war. J L Kerr and W Granville, p. 163.

Peter in mufti on the bridge of a naval tug in 1939

HMPS 'Perla'

standing on verandas, drink in hand, watching the battle from the security of the International Settlement.[6] *In 1933 the Japanese occupied Manchuria and in 1937 Peking, followed shortly by Nanking. Then in 1937 the Japanese extended their control of Shanghai. In 1938 the Japanese/Chinese war came nearer to Hong Kong with the Japanese occupation of Canton and the Chinese Nationalist Government in Nanking being forced to move to Chunking.*

With the war in Europe came the need for security and thus censorship. Consequently Peter's wartime letters do not make reference to military defences in Hong Kong[7] such as the HKRNVR patrol destinations and the names of ships. Thus adding to the impression of pre-war Hong Kong. There is also no mention of all the troops thronging through the streets, bars and restaurants in Hong Kong. By the time of the invasion the garrison numbered 14,000 and would have been housed in barracks or billeted out on the Island and in Kowloon, while the volunteers would have lived with family or friends. Fanling Golf Club was on the border, in the New Territories, but when Peter visits

---
6 Keay, p. 152.
7 There are some early exceptions, maybe due to his limited interest in the censorship rules.

HKRNVR Parade in 1939. New recruits in mufti

it for a game of golf there is no comment on all the border defences there. There is little reference to the 'war' in China and nothing is said about the Royal Navy in Hong Kong and its involvement.[8] All Peter's envelopes were stamped, signed and dated by the censor, and sometimes by Peter himself when there was no one else to censor his letters. It obviously meant letters were not private and the writer would no doubt have often known who the censor would be before committing pen to paper. The Australians and others also exercised civil censorship on incoming and outgoing mail.

Peter and Therese were living in their house, 168 The Peak, and the main difference for them is that Peter was primarily in the HKRNVR with occasional visits to Jardines. Peter, as ever, is keeping up his correspondence.

Peter to Jack [his brother]   30 March   Hong Kong
Many thanks for your letter of 1 February, which has only just arrived owing to the length of time now taken by the Suez mails. I agree with all you say about the war, especially with the remark about the socialists' dream of Heaven, which strikes me as particularly apt. Will all this regulation and regimentation last on after the war? I am afraid there will be a strong tendency in that direction; when you get a body of 'little men' who have been placed temporarily in charge of the reordering of the lives of people, it takes a long time and a lot of drive to eradicate them from their position of authority.

---

8   Covered by Brice, Martin in *The Royal Navy and the Sino-Japanese Incident 1937–41*.

I agree with you about being fed up with the war. So are we all, except for a few young and enthusiastic lads who find it a grand joke and for certain others of the rather inferior type who suddenly find themselves elevated well beyond their natural station or what their capabilities justify. But the fact remains, however fed up you maybe, that there is no prospect of real peace and an ordered existence for this world until the type of aggressive tendency exemplified by the Hitler regime has been purged out of the human race. A thumping defeat for Germany is the first objective, while the second, infinitely more difficult, is to arrange a peace which will prevent the rise of a further Hitler and/or Kaiser, but at the same time not leave a basis of resentment amongst the German people which will inevitably goad them on towards having another crack at the domination of Europe.

My idea, however impractical it may sound, is to start a model Nazi colony on an uninhabited island, give them all the amenities to make modern civilisation possible, and populate it with Hitler and say 50,000 Germans, selected from the sub-Hitlers, Gestapo, Black and Brown shirts. No one may leave the Colony but anyone may join it. Give them plenty of firearms and you won't have much trouble, as they are sure to kill each other fairly early in the day. It can be advertised as the perfect Nazi State, but the weakness of course, from their point of view, will be that there will be no subject peoples on which to inflict the Nazi regime, only model Nazis, that is why they will soon kill each other; a sort of concentration camp of bullies with a free for all to decide who is to run the camp. I think it would be most interesting and if accurately and fairly reported in the press of the outer world, would have the effect of discountenancing the Nazi-style of government forever and a day.

The remainder of Germany, after being thus purged, would be split back into its separate states with a loose federal government and the more liberal elements in the country, or at present more likely exiles outside it, would govern with an army of occupation to see that there was no funny business. This latter would of course be most unpopular, so you would have to mitigate it by refinancing Germany and making sure that the material lot of the people was better under the Army of Occupation than under the Nazi regime. This process would have to go on until the new and more liberal regime was firmly established, probably about thirty years.

I was glad to hear that Jacqueline Miranda [Jack's daughter] was doing well, also that you are by now such an adept nurse and can just juggle with nappies. You will have heard by now, I presume, that we are laying the foundations of a family, expected next July, about the 12th. We are both very happy about it and I think it will be a great boon to Therese, as she rather lacks a real interest out here. I doubt that I will start to emulate your feats as a father, but maybe I will blossom forth from a somewhat dubious start.

I forget when I wrote last, around Christmas I fancy. Since then I have been through various changes in the Naval Volunteers. I was in charge of the Governor's launch *Britannia* until early February, but was very glad to finish up in her because we invariably went out on the longest beat of the lot, and to the spot where the minefield has come rather badly unstuck. Lots of floating mines, which are alright by day but not so good at night if it is a dark one. Most of the ones that come up now are no longer safe, so they go off with a discouraging thump when they hit the rocks and I am very glad to be away from that beat.

I was in charge of a 50-ton tug, *Edith* by name, for several weeks, then had a fortnight's leave to help closing the first set of [Jardine] Insurance Company books.

On restarting again I took over a 468-ton tug, the *St. Aubin*, which has just been chartered from Shanghai. We are in the process of refitting at the moment and I have not yet handled her, as she started her refit on arrival from Shanghai. She is a proper seagoing salvage tug and very much the type of thing we want for the work here. The change, however, from a 4-ton yacht to a 468-ton tug is a bit startling and she is also single screw [propeller] to make it a bit more complicated.

We have settled down into our new abode and are very comfortable here. Therese naturally finds the volunteering business not so good as she is inevitably left a lot on her own. Up to now we have been doing only about twenty-seven to thirty hours at sea out of every forty-eight hours; we are to do four days out and four days in, which I assure you is most unpopular with milady. Incidentally, my 1st Lieutenant in the *St. Aubin* is one Ralph, of the Union of Canton, who was in Calcutta and in the Light Horse at approximately the same time as yourself.

I read NW Passage[9] which you sent me for Christmas and thoroughly enjoyed it; I think it is an excellent yarn. I am sorry to hear both from Mum and from yourself that she is really not at all well, but what can one do. If she has this bee in her bonnet

---

9 *North West Passage* by Kenneth Roberts, 1936.

HMAPV 'St. Aubin'

about cleaning the flat and works herself until she is tired out, then she is not likely to feel too fit. It all seems plain and obvious to you and me but to her apparently not so.

To Lizzie Blunt   24 April
Many thanks for your letter of the 27 July of last year, which I have been disgracefully long in answering. My only excuse is that I was mobilised with the local Naval Volunteer Reserve just before the war started, since when I have been pretty busy here trying to learn to be a sailor and to do a certain amount of work in the office at the same time.

Quite a lot seems to have happened to us in the last year. We had a bit of a scene here in the last week of August when it looked as if the Japs were about to attack Hong Kong. They had almost 20,000 troops just over the border and I feel reasonably assured that an attack, or at least a threatened one, on Hong Kong, Shanghai and Tientsin, was the Japanese contribution towards the Rome–Berlin–Tokyo axis[10] in order to trap Britain out of the impending European war. However, the Russo–German pact caught the Japs completely on the wrong foot and they gave up all idea of an attack. By now they are certainly not winning in China, probably losing in a war which has degenerated into a stalemate; further they are starting to realise it and would like to get out of China if only they could do so without losing face, so I feel that we may feel reasonably secure against any further attentions from them.

However, when the war started the Navy got very hearty and converted Hong Kong into a young Scapa Flow, with minefields, submarine nets and so forth, and the local RNVR were called out in full force to patrol the waters of the Colony. I was one of the original members of the local force when it was formed in 1934, and was promoted to Lieutenant several years ago, so I was hauled out at the start. I now patrol the raging main in an odd little thing, with a mainly Chinese crew and what I don't know about night watches and tropical dawns is not worth knowing. I never want to see another.

I am afraid it is not much fun for Therese, as I am usually out every other night, which leaves her alone in the house by herself with only the Chinese servants. But there is a war on and there is no use grousing. I do not fancy I am likely to be moved from HK, as there is a tendency in the Colonies to keep civilians in their own Colony, where they can assist with the defence and so relieve the Regulars.

We moved up to the house where we are at present, No. 168 The Peak (*opposite page*), at the end of last October and hope to make it a permanent house for the rest of our spell in HK. It is a quaint five-room bungalow, old for here but not too dilapidated, with quite a pleasant flat garden. Most of the gardens on the Peak are terraced out of the steep hillside rather like the Hanging Gardens of Babylon, so you are frightfully select if you have a flat one. Most things grow here; you have tomatoes and lettuces in December/January, the local flower show is February and so on. Altogether we are very happy and contented with our little house and garden and only ask for peace and prosperity so that we can grow fat, old and lazy, talking about all the things we are going to do, but never seem to succeed in doing.

---

10 In 1936 Germany had entered an Anti-Comintern Pact with Japan. At the same time Germany provided military support for the Nationalists in the Spanish Civil War. The Italian Fascist Government sent a corps of volunteers to fight the Nationalist cause in Spain, bringing these two countries closer together. Beevor, p. 6. This was not the more formal later Axis pact.

168 The Peak

Now for the big surprise, which I have kept for the end – a little Dulley is expected about the middle of July. We are both very glad as we had always wanted to have a family. Therese is very fit and well, prospective maternity not having affected her even as much as having a slight cold. I do not fancy I will be such a model and adoring parent as Jack appears to be, but no doubt I will improve with practise.

Mrs Sander was unable to come out here last autumn apropos of the war, but we hope she will make the trip in the coming autumn. The submarine scene[11] seems to have died down and the prospect of massed air raids on England looks decidedly less. After the start of the Norwegian show,[12] the BEF landed about a week ago as I write. I have decided to be distinctly optimistic about the prospects. I think the Germans have made their first silly mistake which they are likely to follow up with several others, and that their powers of resistance are considerably lower than we have tended to estimate. Wishful thinking, possibly, but I reckon there will be signs of a break up in Germany in the summer and that the war will finish in the autumn.

---

11 Japan had not entered the war at this stage and Europe was still in the 'Phoney' war.
12 The British Expeditionary Force's landing proved to be a failure and they had to withdraw. The Germans first silly mistake is likely to refer to Hitler's decision to invade Norway. Although there were some advantages, it opened up another front, which no doubt was Peter's point. Some of the German military had been against it at the beginning, and the army argued throughout the war that it held down too many troops. Beevor, p. 73 and p. 76.

CHAPTER 8

The Evacuation to the Philippine Islands
July to October 1940

By 1940 there existed along the French frontier, the Phoney War. This was soon to be ended by the German invasion of the Low Countries in May 1940, taking the French by surprise. Back in England Neville Chamberlain had resigned as prime minister to be succeeded by Winston Churchill. Then in Europe the German Blitzkrieg caused the collapse of the French Army. British and French troops were evacuated from Dunkirk; this major exercise was completed on 3 June. France formally surrendered on 22 June; part of the understanding was that Vichy France would police itself and its colonies and the Germans took French military equipment. This was to leave unanswered questions for the French colonies and the French fleet as to what their position was in the war. The same month, Mussolini said that Italy would enter the war. In the skies over England all was peace but that would change in August.

Back in the Far East the Japanese were fighting the Chinese near the Hong Kong border. Many Chinese were killed and the injured were brought in Red Cross trucks to schools that had been converted to hospitals in Kowloon.[1] As a result of this threat the Hong Kong government decided to order the evacuation of women and children. Therese, in her diary, says that they heard about the evacuation on Saturday, 29 June. She was evacuated on Monday, 1 July and reached Baguio in the Philippine Islands very late on the Wednesday, 3 July. She was among a large group of women and children and was in the eighth month of her pregnancy. After her arrival she wrote three letters to Peter in her first four days there and one to her mother. HP was born on 26 July in the hospital Notre Dame de Lourdes. Later her diary states that 'the last batch of evacuees left Baguio' for Australia on 4 August. Therese herself was 'up for the first time' on 8 August. She left hospital for Camp John Hay, a Red Cross camp, with a nurse on the 17th. A week later an Amah took over from the nurse for about two months and Therese employed a 'wash girl' as well.

Even after nearly a year of war in Europe, Hong Kong may have appeared at peace, but

---

1 Lindsay, p. 40.

now there were signs that were not always immediately apparent, like the reduced number of European women and children in the Colony and empty houses. Others would have been more obvious such as the predominance of military uniforms and the improvement to the defences. There were also increasing numbers of Chinese refugees fleeing from war-torn China. However, the Colony's European population had not been seriously affected by the war, unlike the Chinese.

For the Dulleys, the war had meant the loss of their servants. In peacetime they had employed four servants; the first to go was Ah Kung who would have been called up as a rating in the HKRNVR in 1939. After the evacuation Peter moved out of 168 The Peak and the Amah was taken on by another lady but the number one boy, Chan, and the coolie initially transferred to Geer, the new occupant of the house. This scenario would have been repeated across the Colony as European women and children were evacuated and properties were taken over or closed. As Peter pointed out there was a reduction in the number of jobs for servants while the Chinese population in Hong Kong was continuing to increase. The situation became so bad that refugee camps had to be set up.[2]

Peter knew the Far East well from his nine years working with Jardines; this had given him the ability to analyse situations, including the threat of a Japanese invasion. However, despite this there were other factors influencing his letters apart from censorship. What he says has been filtered by his desire to protect Therese by giving her an optimistic slant on the news, which does not feature in his letters to others, and of course his own personal optimism, a powerful combination.

There is a sentence in a letter to Nancy on 5 July 1940 after Therese's evacuation, which conclusively supports this:

> 'This show [the evacuation] is for the duration of the war and Lord knows how long that will be, although I would not pass that onto Therese as I am afraid she is feeling it all rather badly.'

The letters in this chapter are written by Peter while in Hong Kong to Therese and other members of the family following her evacuation to the Philippine Islands.

My Darling Therese   3 July
I scarcely know how to start writing to you as I have never had to do so since we were engaged, and those letters were rather a flop.

---

2 Snow, p. 31.

Monday was a sad and bitter day and I have a feeling of resentment inside me against a world system, which allows such things and makes them necessary. However, it is to the future we must look, my love, and do our best to realise that the misfortunes of the present are only temporary.

I hope you did not have too bad a trip down to Manila and that it was not too rough apropos the typhoon. Hall has apparently written to one Heybrook of Wise & Co. [agents] to ask him to do what he can for you. I fancy I met them both in 1933 when I was down in Manila rowing. Gerry is also writing to one Stewart, also Wise & Co., to see what he can do for you.

We bought a proper pill on Monday night, just after you had gone. I was doing a night on *St. Aubin*, and had just consumed a couple to cheer me up, when a No. 1 Typhoon[3] signal went up. Answer: clear the basin. The Commander of the dockyard ratted on us and not only did Steve and I have to get ourselves out, but we each had to take a tug in tow. I managed to find Wilson and get some food, but we did not get going until 10.00 pm with *Minnie Moller* in tow. It was rather a nightmare; the dynamo would not work so we had three torches and candles in the navigation lights, the latter constantly going out. I had very little idea how *St. Aubin* would kick so it all took rather a while. However, we eventually got *Minnie* to her buoy by Killett Island but then the crew dropped a lot of anchor chain over the side by mistake, so they eventually had to make fast on the other cable. We got anchored in Kowloon Bay at 2.00 am and I did the first watch, so I finished one of the bitterest days of all time at 4.00 am.

We were not allowed back until 4.00 pm Tuesday and again had to tow in *Minnie Moller*, so I provided the dockyard with a second exhibition of how not to do it. I think it was a bit hard sending us out towing on a dark night on our first trip. I did Tuesday night as duty officer and have just got back to the house at 5.30 pm Wednesday for the first time since we left on Monday. Constant rain and fog and it was a very sad return. Chan [their cook] was enquiring after you and Pip [their dog] and was genuinely upset.

I am just off to the E's for dinner; she tells me she has a lot to talk about!! She got your letter OK and I gather she is not going to Manila, but I will add her news before I post this.

---

3 This was the Standby Signal. www.hko.gov.hk/informtc/tcsignal_history.htm. 12 July 2015.

Bobby Geer is quite a likely starter for taking over the house, but nothing definite yet. I saw Hall again today, he talked about reducing the rent, but everything is still so vague and I have had no time to get onto things. The Union man, Ramage, is off because his family are on the way out and he feels he cannot commit himself.

I hated your going and feel very lost. In fact, if I did not take a strong pull at myself I could spend most of the day crying; but it isn't any good, it won't help and I am supposed to be an Lt. Cmdr. RNVR, so I am one of those steely lads who bite cast iron and are prepared for anything. I hope all goes well with you and send my love and encouragement, the latter the secret sign of the Dulley's, the thumbs up.

Continued   4 July

I had dinner with the E's last night. She is definitely fixed with a job[4] at Matilda [Hospital][5] and has the consent of Montgomery and Selwyn Clerk.[6] She thought your letter to her most sensible and has been holding you up as the shining example to Mary Roberts, who is approximately in hysterics over evacuating privately to Australia with a governess and an Amah.

Miss you very badly and wish it had not all to be.

To Nancy   5 July

I am afraid that this is a rather sad letter to write to you, but fortunately there is no call for it to be disquieting as well. You will have gathered from my cable of the 30 June that Therese was being evacuated to Manila and she received yours just before she sailed on the 1st.

There were rumours about on Friday evening when we were on the way out to the Shek O Club to play a bit of golf and dine with friends; the definite orders were out for service wives on Saturday morning. Therese packed on Sunday and was off in a CPR Liner[7] on Monday. They arrived at Manila on Wednesday morning and I had a wire today to say she was at the Pines Hotel, Baguio, along with Mrs Shewan, a serious but

---

4   She decided to be with Edgar, who because of his position in the Colony intended to stay. Under the evacuation regulations everyone remaining in the Colony was required to have a job in support of the war effort, which included AE.
5   The hospital was set up in 1906 for the poor and helpless, but patients had to be white and not Chinese. Welsh, p. 380.
6   Selwyn Selwyn-Clarke was Hong Kong Director of Medical Services from 1937–43.
7   Canadian Pacific Railways was the largest transportation company in the world pre-war.

extremely capable woman, who has recently gone out of her way to be friendly to us.

It was a sad parting and if one wished to, one could positively bathe in bathos and self-pity. Our marriage has been such a success, the start was a bit shaky by all means, but over the last year or so we have been steadily coming closer together. All we wish is to be allowed to be happy to keep our home together, to have a family and for me to do my best to advance our fortunes. But with this war it was not to be, and this evacuation has torn it properly. However, it is no good moping over one's present troubles, one must look to the future and do one's best to make it a righteous and happy one instead of a Nazi bedlam run wild in a starving world.

Therese had a reasonably comfortable cabin[8] for her trip down, actually a two-bed cabin (+ 1 camp bed) shared with two other women she knew and two small boys. I don't know if they parked the small boys out somewhere, but she was hoping they would. There was a typhoon hanging about and I am afraid they must have got a bit of dirty weather, but I feel it should not have been too bad. Baguio is where we spent our honeymoon, but we stayed at the Country Club; the Pines is the chief hotel there and we dropped in one evening for a drink to have a look at it. I am afraid it will not be too good weather at this time of the year, lots of rain and mist.

I am completely in the dark about arrangements until I hear from Therese, but suggested to her that she will definitely have to stay in the Philippines for about two months, junior being due about 28 July. The bulk of the people are going on to Australia as soon as they can be taken, but I do not see that that is a proposition for her, and it seems far preferable to have her confinement in the P.I. [Philippine Islands].

I wired the McAvoys, a couple I know quite well in Manila, to do what they could for her, but apparently they missed her on arrival. Therese knows several people down there through my connections. Before they left, it all seemed so unreal and we were gaily saying they would be back in a fortnight but of course they won't.

If she [Therese] goes on to Australia, I have connections in Sydney apropos the Firm, and I feel they will look after her well. Incidentally you need not worry about the money side of things, I have started her off with about £600; Manila pesos being the only difficulty as they prohibited foreign exchange and one is limited

---

8   One figure for the total women and children evacuated is 3,414. The service families numbering 1,640 were the first to leave and travelled on the *Empress of Japan* (whose name was changed subsequently) built for 1,173 passengers. http://gwulo.com/node/17063. 22 August 2015.

in the amount you can buy. I do not know how I will be able to pay for her doctors and hospital expenses as they will be due in Manila pesos, but possibly the Lord will provide.

As regards things here, I have approximately fixed for Bobby Geer, in Jardines, to take over 168, as a bachelor mess. That is a great relief as so many houses will have to be closed down; with this arrangement we can leave the bulk of our goods and chattels in the house and keep on the servants, who would have no other means of support. I will live mainly on my new tug, which will shortly be going to sea, and the E's have most kindly offered me the use of their spare room for odd nights ashore.

We now come to the next burning point, what is all this evacuation about, and I doubt if I can answer it? People here seem to feel it is rather unnecessary. I gather we are going to tell the Japs to go to hell over the Burma Road[9] question and anything else which may crop up, so clear the decks first and tell them that if they want to fight we are quite ready to start; absolutely the right policy. They will get the shock of their lives, will fume and rant, but I would lay ten to one they will do nothing beyond a nuisance value blockade of Hong Kong. The troops, some 1,000 strong, they have on the border are a mangy scraggy lot, fed up with their years of unsuccessful war, whose only ambition is to get back to their homes in Japan. If they try any funny business here I fancy we can give them all they have asked for and a bit to spare.[10]

All the best to yourself, Agnes and Robert and there is absolutely no cause to worry about Therese and myself.

P.S. Aunt Eva is staying on with UE and under the circumstances I think it is better. It would have been very nice for Therese to have her, but it would not have done either of the E's any good at all.

To Therese   7 July
Well, I have been a grass widower for nearly a week now and I don't like it. Going back to 168 is mournful in the extreme and makes me want to cry, especially when I see your unused bed and some of your stuff lying about. But Naval Officers are supposed to be tough laddies so I cannot be down. I miss you terribly, lovely, as I

---

9 A recently constructed road in Burma, which was used for the transit of goods to Hong Kong and China.
10 In part no doubt written to reduce Nancy's worries.

knew I would, and I am afraid it is a heavy-hearted, sad little man writing to you. I took Pip for a long walk yesterday to tire him and myself out, and as we passed the Peak Church[11] there was no one to hold my hand. This place is too full of happy memories of you and they are always catching me unawares. I have spent quite a bit of time today sorting things out at 168 and it has not induced too joyful a streak. However, the weather has turned fine and sunny these last few days so there will be a chance to get things dried out a bit before they are packed up.

It now seems more than probable that Bobby Geer will take over the house. I will have all our gear packed up and sent round to the E's if they can house it; otherwise bits of it will go to the Dairy Farm.[12] As far as I am concerned, I am going to follow the suggested idea of living in *St. Aubin* and using the E's spare room. AE says she will not have me paying anything so I will make it up in bottles of hooch.

191 The Peak, the E's home

---

11 Where Peter and Therese were married.
12 The Dairy Farm Co-op. Milk Co. Ltd. founded to provide fresh milk for European children. Later expanded to provide many other services including storage. Welsh, p. 279

The E's came into dinner on Friday and I am afraid all the farewells of the civilian evacuation[13] had been too much for her. She had a cold and a slight temperature and had been in bed all day. I am afraid poor dear, she was on the edge of tears, so I served her two very healthy whisky waters, the second of which rendered her slightly hilarious, but I felt it was the best thing to do under the circumstances.

I had your cable[14] from Baguio on Friday, also one from Dennis McAvoy to the same effect, and was so glad to hear you had got fixed up at the Pines at Baguio. I am afraid there will probably be too much rain and mist at this time of year, but I hope it will not be too bad. Until two days ago, we have been sticking true to type here, to wit thirty inches of rain above the average now i.e. seventy against forty. The mails from home seem to have got badly held up apropos of the changeover and I have not had anything for weeks, nor has anyone else apparently. With all this French flap[15] on it seems to be doubtful the airmail will be able to get to Penang, as they don't like to land at Fort Bay and in French Indo China.

Everything remains perfectly quiet here and will, I think, continue to do so. Some of the wealthy Chinese are sheering off. Eu Tong Sen[16] was away to Manila a day or so ago with his sons, but left his wives behind. Apparently he was only worried about the prospects of rape if things went wrong here, so he left a chit to Sir Atholl MacGregor,[17] asking him to look after them in case of trouble. Answer from Sir A: 'You do your own dirty work.'

Big batches of civilians went off on Friday and I fancy there is a large sized hate brewing as to who has gone, who has not, and why. I went to the cinema last night and there were plenty of women about. Mrs NL, her daughter, Marjorie Fortescue, the entire King family (four in all) and many more. Dear Tina has apparently got to go, her Evacuation Committee having fallen down on her and she having no other ostensible job for which to remain. Wrong of course, as she is a most capable managing soul, entirely devoid of any suggestion of flap or sense of humour, who would be excellent in a crisis. I had lunch with Gomp at the Gloucester [hotel]

---

13 Which would have included their female friends; some no doubt of many years standing.
14 Which must have been signalling her safe arrival.
15 The occupation of Indo-China by the Japanese. Beevor, p. 248.
16 Eu Tong Sen was a millionaire businessman who owned three gothic style castles on Hong Kong Island. Snow, p. 6.
17 Sir Atholl MacGregor KC was Chief Justice of Hong Kong from 1933 to 1945.

on Friday, the day the civilians went, and all sorts of odd women in assorted uniforms. I fancy many of them were just as surprised as I, and I fancy many had only the vaguest idea of the name of the unit to which they belonged.

My tug is now beginning to show keen signs of completion. Steve and I had a grand day on Friday, each of us with sixty-two demand notes for stores and with four barrows out around the yard, bringing ironmongery home in a big way and looking like tinkers going to a fair. Now you are away, I will be thankful when we get to sea. Life is a bit empty at the moment and leisure does not suit me, there is too much time to brood. When we get to sea there will be lots to do and I am far better off with some job I can get my teeth into. Being rather a stodge, as I have often told you, it will take me quite a bit of time to get back into bachelor ways.

Well lovely, I am weary and must go to bed. I hope you are comfortable at the Pines and that you have agreeable people around you, over and above Mrs Shewan. I suggest that you insist that you stay on at P.I. for at least a month after your confinement; by that time the whole flap will be over and if you have to go on to Australia, which I sincerely hope not, you will be able to do it at your leisure and I will try to organise an Amah from here to go down with you. As regards money, don't bust yourself, the Lord will provide.

To Jack   8 July

I was sorry you feel gloomy as to the outcome of the war; I as always am the optimist but with the French collapse it will naturally be longer. If we really put our backs into it I am convinced we can do it. I write just after the Naval Battle of Oran[18] and just before the much-advertised attack on Britain. I felt the latter should most certainly be a failure and as it will have to be done on such a large scale, say a million men at least, it should be a gigantic failure. The Germans will then have the unhappy knowledge that they cannot win and will face a winter of famine conditions all over Europe with that unhappy knowledge.

In order for us to win, however, we have got to beat the German Army in the field and in order to do that we will need to make a gigantic effort raising and equipping an

---

18 The Battle of Oran took place in July 1940 on the coast of French North Africa. Part of the French fleet were in harbour and refused to surrender to the Royal Navy after attempted negotiation and a deadline; they were shelled. The result was the loss of 1,297 French sailors' lives. Beevor, pp. 124/5.

army and an air force. To do this will require a year, if we really go at it hammer and tongs, which we will need to do, and we should then be able to undertake a continental campaign and have a crack at a somewhat disgruntled and very hungry Germany.

Here not so good. As you will have seen from the papers they have evacuated the women and children and Therese went off to Manila on the 1 July with the first batch. It was a sad parting, as we have never been separated before. We were all saying that they would be back in a month but I fear not; having got 4,000 women and children[19] out of the place they will stay out for the rest of the war.

Everything is quite quiet here and I very much doubt if we will have any trouble with the Japs. However, if we do, we can kill far more of their troops than they can of ours, although losses from civilian bombing might be pretty heavy.

Incidentally I have risen to the giddy heights of being a Lieutenant Commander in the Naval Volunteers; I hope it is justified. I gather that our new and larger tugs are the longest ships in the Navy commanded by volunteer officers, so if we manage to handle them efficiently it should be OK, but we will need a lot of practice before we get to that stage. The first time we moved them was a week ago, when we had to go out of a small crowded basin in the dark with another tug towed alongside. I do not mind admitting it was a nightmare.

I will not be able to write to Mum this week, so can you pass on the drift of it to her. I hope she is out of London safely in the country somewhere.[20]

To Therese   11 July

I am afraid you had a pretty mouldy trip one way and another, but I suppose these things are almost inevitable when one starts to move people in the mass without opportunity for suitable previous organisation. I think you were quite right to plump for the Pines and in order to set your mind at rest I wired you to that effect today.

Now, first the business side of things. If you are being done comfortably, if not brilliantly at the Pines, I feel that is quite as good as one can expect. I am much indebted to Mrs Shewan for taking a firm stand and insisting that you did not go to some rather sordid lodging house.

---

19 A more accurate figure is 3,414 women and children, civilian and services. http://gwulo.com/node/17063. 22 August 2015.
20 Peter's mother Agnes Dulley remained in her flat in Kensington, London for the rest of the war. It was said that her solution to air raids was a few stiff whiskies.

I enclose a copy of the three signals on evacuation,[21] which is all we know here to date:

1. This is standard and reassuring hooey.

2. This seems to indicate that we will have to pay 6s/6d for adults per day and 3s/6d for children; the American Red Cross, out of the goodness of their hearts, bearing the remainder.

3. This seems to envisage an eventual evacuation to Australia, which I sincerely hope will not be necessary. However, if it comes off, I feel it is most undesirable that you should be cut off from the official scheme and be left in the position of having to fend for yourself throughout. I am accordingly sending a chit to Petrie,[22] explaining the circumstances and saying you wish to hang onto the official scheme, but that it is most undesirable that you travel before the beginning of September at the earliest. By that time I hope that the major flap will be over, and if you cannot come back here, you can at least go down to Australia in a reasonably leisurely way.

I am still at 168 and will remain until something gets fixed one way or another. Bobby Geer is interested, but is not rushing as there is a big hoo-ha on in JM & Co. private office about rent reductions. Last Sunday he brought up a Govt. Servant named Davis who seemed quite keen on coming in with Geer, but there is a buzz that Govt. people may get their houses rent free, so he naturally cooled off and would prefer to keep on his old place, his wife having gone to Australia already.

Well, I don't take to being a grass widower any more than before, and the only thing is to throw oneself into one's nautical activities with a maximum of gusto. Steve and I are approximately ready for sea; we have done two trips already, one to a buoy in the harbour for twenty hours to collect coal and one to sea today for gun trials. Steve had his bridge windows and charthouse windows broken, whereas we had only four in the charthouse bust; that need never to have happened. I had all the windows lowered

---

21 This document is no longer with the letter.
22 Commander Petrie was Peter's commanding officer at the time.

in good time but some wretched dockyard matey felt he was getting a draught in the back of the neck, so put four up again and left them up while they were firing, so all four went.

It was my birthday today, but besides buying the troops a drink in *Cornflower*[23] I did not celebrate much. I don't seem to feel like celebrations these days. I have got used to celebrating with you and feel lonely without you. May this party be short; I don't like it.

I am sorry you feel low, lovey, but then to a fair extent we all do. The future is the big tip at the moment and we must concentrate on making it a good one. Do not worry unduly about things in Hong Kong. I feel sure the Japs, although they may make deep threats, will not do anything about attacking the British Empire unless things go very badly over the German invasion of England. If that happens we are all in the soup but I don't think it will. In fact I feel sure it won't. Hence we here are in for a spell of rumours and alarms but I doubt if anything more.

To Therese   14 July

As regards the Japanese, the Burma Road is only really a rallying cry to provide an excuse for why their army have not yet won in China. Whether it is closed or not will have little effect on supplies to China. I fancy we will stall and negotiate until the future is a bit clearer regarding the German invasion of England, and when that has been disposed of, with a consequent rallying of American and other support to our side, or at least a colossally increased confidence in our ability to win, then we will tell the Japs to go to hell and with the worst grace in the world they will do so. Frankly, I do not anticipate any trouble here, a bit of nuisance value interference with shipping possibly but no more.

As regards yourself, I have written to the Commodore[24] via Petrie (who incidentally has just collected an OBE) to say that I want you to hang onto the official scheme but that you will not be able to leave P.I. until mid September. If anyone wants to leave the official scheme they must say so before the 20 July. So it does not look as if there was a vast hurry to get people off to Australia. Shewan tells me he has booked passages for Mrs S and Jennifer, sailing for Australia early August. I feel that if you can hang around

---

23   An RNVR ship used as a Head Quarters.
24   The Commodore was Shields in the 1937 in HKRNVR photo on page 113.

in the P.I. until mid Sept, you would then be able to go to Australia well after the main crowd, possibly with an Amah, or alternatively sneak back quietly unnoticed. I am, however, very strongly against cutting away from the official scheme; we are living in difficult times and no one knows what will happen here. I think the prospect is small, but if anything did go wrong here, it would be much better for you to be a member of an organised party, than to be entirely loose on your own with a very small baby on your hands.

The good ship [*St. Aubin*] is now about ready for sea, and we start regular work late this week: I have had some trials and tribulations taking her in and out of the Dockyard several times this week, but beside bending a bit of odd iron on Steve's ship no great damage has been done.

I have lost all pep and initiative and seem to be rather like a soggy sponge. However, to the future boys and girls: this war will be won by the side that can stick it out longest, and by and large we have very little to complain of.

To Therese   19 July

My poor lovey, I am afraid you have been feeling very mouldy up in Baguio, and really don't wonder, no house of your own to mess around in, constant rain, a difficult period before the arrival of junior, on top of this enforced separation and the very worrying situation back in England.[25] I don't wonder you feel a bit low. So do I. Today I am taking a day off to complete the final stages of leaving 168, at least I got back from a night patrol, the third night running, at about 11.45 and I do not intend to do anything else until I start again tomorrow. Coming back to 168 since you left has not been easy, but packing up and going seems to be the final end to all our plans and dreams. On the sewing machine stand there are some oddments of your work, presumably for Junior, left as it was just before the evacuation order came along, and I have not the heart to move it or tell the Amah to do so. It is the last tangible personal link. Tonight I move to the E's, Geer is already at 168 but I have been on the high seas and in the HM Yard all the while.

I am afraid you bring the baby on the party, at any rate at present, but I hope it will be better when Junior arrives, as you will then be very busy. At the moment you have

---

25 The threatened German invasion.

too much time to think of the 'might have beens' and believe me it is fatal. It seems rather hard and unfeeling, but I try to keep off them, as they only make me want to cry and they do not help at all. It is naturally easier for me, as I have the new tug which is now in commission, but requiring a lot of work: however, when Junior arrives I hope it will be easier for you too.

I feel you were quite right in staying at the Pines. In times of stress hang onto what you have got and don't reach for the moon. I would not worry about Hong Kong and the Hong Kong situation: we seem to have given in on the Burma Road question but only diplomatically. In fact we have need to close it for three months when the rainy season normally does that for us, and not to allow transportation of material we have not got to send. A reasonable stall, which maybe gives the Japanese a bit of face, although it admittedly loses us a bit, but only to people who do not look beyond the surface. Admittedly, I would have liked to see the Foreign Office at home tell the Japanese to go to hell, as I feel it would surely have worked, but one must trust the people in charge of Foreign Policy to do what is right, having regard to the situation of the entire Empire. But if they were going to cave in, why evacuate you and all the rest?[26]

The latest news about your show is that service people in P.I. will travel to Australia sailing from Manila on the 28 or 31 July. The only exemptions are if you are medically unfit or if you wish to cut away from the official scheme, in which event you are thereafter responsible for your own arrangements and own expenses, without any assistance from the American Red Cross. People are being solidly urged by the authorities to move from the P.I. since they cannot expect to live on some charity forever and pesos will not be easy to come by.

In your case, mothers are different and I think I have established the idea that you stay in Baguio until mid September, when you would presumably be booked down to Australia on one of the normal passenger ship sailings, unless there is some most welcome turn in our affairs, which washes out the whole scheme. If there is any idea afoot of moving you too soon, just dig your toes in and refuse to budge. I am afraid, however, the idea of Australia has to be considered, if not finally accepted, and I have provisionally put you down for Sydney.

---

26 This is a puzzling statement but may mean that if Great Britain was to confront the Japanese on this issue, women and children should be evacuated first in view of the risks. However, if the Japanese demands were accepted there was no need for the evacuation.

Well the famous tug is now in operation and we have been out for the last three nights, but in by day, on a buoy in the harbour however, which does not make it at all easy when you have no proper boat routine.[27] Steve was to have started the party for a week, but after the first night they discovered the condenser was out of order. Its overhaul was to have been put out to contract with Taikoo,[28] but someone forgot to put in the list of work to be done, so it was just left. Net result an extra three days out of commission: can you beat it?

The new tug is undoubtedly a great deal more comfortable and pleasant to be in and live on than the old ones. Handling in the basin? Was a bit of a problem, partly because the engine room telegraphs were not adjusted properly when I rang half ahead, it only showed slow ahead in the engine room, also the rudder was not central. However, both those are corrected now and it is getting easier gradually. I have not hit anything yet, but I had an unfortunate accident on Tuesday when a berthing wire was wrongly placed so when the strain came on it flew up over the rails and hit one of the crew in the face. He was rather laid out and had to be carted off to hospital, shock mainly I think; most unfortunate but good experience for me, although a most undesirable way of getting it.

Well I have been up at 4.00 am for the last three mornings and feel sleepy, also very depressed about leaving 168 so I will close.

To Therese   23 July

I am afraid it was rather a sad, small voice from Baguio, but cheer up lovey, it cannot last forever. Nothing happened here and nothing looks like happening, so far as the local situation is concerned. I see nothing to stop you coming back except the rules. The prospective invasion of Britain is of course the big point on which it all hinges, but seeing nothing has yet happened in that direction, it begins to be slightly tinged with doubt whether anything will. I certainly do not see the Japs doing anything on their own; they will only act if the conquest of Britain looks a certainty and the prospect I utterly fail to envisage, so apparently does Hitler, otherwise he would have set about it already without all this delay. If nothing has happened by mid September, the approximate time you would be fit to travel, I think you can fairly safely assume

---

27 Regular boats to take the crew ashore and back.
28 A dockyard and engineering company.

that nothing will until next spring, by which time we should be far too powerful for there to be any prospect of success by invasion. In that event i.e. MID SEPT, and if everything else is quiet here too, I feel there should be a reasonable chance of your being able to infiltrate quietly and discreetly into Hong Kong.

Well, I wrote last as I was leaving 168 and it was a very sad moment, when I finally walked out of the drive in the evening. I will naturally be in and about there quite a bit, but it was the last real link with our most happy occupancy of the little house. On Monday we start our first four-day run, it being Tuesday today, so UE has not been unduly burdened with me.

The alligator pears[29] arrived and it was a most sweet thought on your part to send them: unfortunately the box in which they were packed was not quite strong enough, with the result they were rather broken about on arrival and had consequently got too ripe to eat. I was hoping to introduce UE to the joys of the avocado, but alas it was not to be.

We are nearly at the end of our fourth day out and I feel rather like one of the wild woolly fellows from the back blocks. Everything is giving out, except the iron determination, which gets the British Empire home. I am the only person with any cigarettes, matches are scarce, and we have just enough boiler water to get back to harbour if the Chief Engineer's calculations are correct. I never realised before that boilers used so much water; still live and learn; you cannot become a tug master in one day. The sailor that I inadvertently smote down with a wire rope has returned to the fold, not much the worse for wear; I don't know which hospital he went to, but he said they never gave him a bath and fed him badly, so possibly that speeded his recovery.

Well it is now 9.50 pm and I do a watch from 2.00–5.00 am,[30] so I must get a bit of shut eye. We have not yet decided whether to decorate the Wardroom with pictures of sailing ships or nude women, but I would like your opinion on the subject. Goodbye for the time being my love, and don't forget that I miss you badly and longing for you to be back in Hong Kong. Maybe by the time this arrives, the heir to the Dulley

---

29   He is referring to avocado pears and can only assume that they and maybe others called them this as the skin of some avocados could be described as dark and knobby like a crocodile's.
30   The traditional Royal Naval watch system was to divide the crew into Port and Starboard watches. Each watch would be of four hours duration apart from the two Dog Watches, which were two hours each. In this case, however, the watch is three hours. http://en.wikipedia.org/wiki/Watch_system. 31 August 2015.

millions will be in the world; if so I hope that Junior will be a credit to his or her parents and that you will not have had too bad a time.

P.S. Just in from Patrol and received Mrs Shewan's wire with the great news. Well done, lovey, I always wanted it to be a boy, but did not like to say so. I hope you are well and did not have too bad a time. Am wiring your mother and mine.

Notre Dame de Lourdes Hospital, Baguio, where HP was born

To Therese   27 July

First let me explain, if my letters seem a bit incoherent, that is because I scarcely ever seem to be ashore these days so that I only pick up your letters at irregular intervals. I finished our four-day patrol at 6.00 pm last night, had the evening and night ashore at No. 191 and was hoping for a little bit of relaxation over the weekend, but no it was not to be. The No. 1 Typhoon sign had to go up at 9.30 am, so we spent an hour or so getting some important jobs done and then they hived me off to take the Tug onto a buoy in the Harbour, where we are now and will stick there until it all blows over, by which time we will probably be due to start patrolling again. So, if I don't write very bright letters and don't get jobs like the Shewan's pram fixed up, it is because I never seem to be ashore, and when I am, I seem to be too confused to remember half of what I have to do.

However, I am so glad it is a boy. I hope you did not have too bad a time, my sweet, and that you are not feeling too exhausted. I managed this morning to get an announcement fixed up for the Sunday Herald and SCMP [South China Morning Post] Monday edition, the inestimable Joan[31] to the rescue, and I had to leave it to her to fix the announcement and send it to the papers.

With regard to evacuation to Australia, unless they change things in the meantime, I think you will have to go too, at some later date, much though I hate to have to say so. But I would not say it is definite yet, so don't give up hope. The unofficial members of the Council here are kicking up a hell of a hullabaloo in the Executive Council, asking what the evacuation is all about anyway and criticising its execution most heavily, so something may come of that.

The two points that arise in my mind are these: (1) If they have done this evacuation inadvisedly, it was a big job to do, so they are unlikely to admit their mistake and undo it, desirable though such a course might be; (2) We are passing through difficult times and I do not feel happy about the suggestion you cut adrift from the official scheme for naval wives. It is a very long chance against anything happening to me, but if it did you would be left on your own in a foreign land, on the opposite side of the world to your mother, having previously said, 'I am all right, I don't want any help.' I know it is dreary looking at the worst side of things, but when you make preparations such as a will, life insurance or an evacuation, you are preparing for the worst and you might just as well face up to it and admit it.

If you have to go to Australia, you should be able to travel as an ordinary passenger on one of the ships doing the run, and Townend in Sydney will find you accommodation, so it should not be too bad. The climate would be much preferable and the money would go further.

Well enough of all this morbid stuff about evacuation. I hope it all eases off quietly so that you will be able to come back in due course. I miss you badly, my love, and feel a very lonely little man without you. We have got so used to doing things together that I seem to have little incentive to do them alone.

---

31 Secretary/PA originally from Jardines Insurance Dept.

To Therese   3 August

I was terribly glad to hear that all was well after the great event, even if the production of infants is a difficult and trying affair. For several days I assumed all must be well, but I was a bit alarmed when I heard there was a wire for me; however, it turned out to be Harry Baines' very kind congratulations, which I forwarded to you with the local birth announcement. Big stuff, Mrs D, front page of the *Sunday Herald*. I assume from Harry B's wire that either your or my Mamma must have announced it in the *Times*, otherwise how would he have known.

Let me deal with your queries before I forget them. Birth certificate it does not matter two hoots how I am described and I think Hugh Peter is an excellent name for the heir to the Dulley millions; quite right having it registered with the British Consul, you cannot be too careful about the nationality question.

I am afraid my wire of congratulations was rather late in arriving and must explain that I arrived back from a four day patrol on the 26th, but was not able to go to the dockyard straight away; we made fast at Kellet Island at 1.30 pm and around 3.00 pm someone came along in a boat and gave me the cable with your news. Fortunately I had some cable forms handy and sent mine to you back on the same boat, but it then had to be censored and sent off, so I am surprised it even arrived at 7.00 pm. Since we got the tug going several weeks ago, we have been on the run fairly hard and do not get our first let up for another five days. By then the position will be this, out of twenty-three nights we have been thumping the seas for eighteen, tied up at a buoy for the typhoon for two and I have been off for three, the other two officers for two. During the day we have either been at sea, or trying to deal with repairs, stores or getting the ship going, with the result that one tends to settle into a state of apathetic languor, where the only thing, which will stir you is the sight of a bottle of Gin. Wrong by all means, but the natural reaction to trying to take more out of the system than it is intended to produce.

I have been hearing your praises sung in all quarters, always a consistent story. From Mrs Campbell, from Mrs Petrie [wife of Commander Petrie] both in a letter to him and in a very nice and kindly one she wrote to me, and from several other sources I cannot recollect at the moment. 'Mrs D is an example to us all, calm, collected, no complaints, no flap, just smiles, takes an optimistic view, knits for the future generation and shows us what we should be doing.' Hats off, my love, whatever your inner feelings may have been, you have performed that very difficult task of sublimating them, and have worked the thumbs up theory well beyond keeping your own thumbs up, but to that higher and more difficult altitude, where you are showing other people to keep theirs up, as a result. I have no wonder that you are a most restrained patient, I would have been surprised if you had not been, but I respect and love you and am proud of you for it nonetheless. Your trouble my sweet, as I have often said is that you understate yourself. If you want an opposite tack, with your talents, appearance and ability you would be a cinema star, a Florence Nightingale or a celebrated vamp.

Now as regards Australia. I enquired this week from Burgess in the Govt., who appears to be in charge of the evacuation racket, and the position on the 2 August was that they do not yet know, at this end, how many are left over in P.I. When they get the list of them in a few days time, they will instruct the HK Govt. Agent in Manila (the British Consul General) to fix the passages, as and when available, the word 'available' applying to both the passages and the passengers. The fares will be tourist, so if you have to go and do not like the accommodation, have no hesitation in paying the difference for something better. If they try to send you off before you feel fit to travel, dig your toes in and refuse to move, in that event I am perfectly willing to stand all expenses and not ask for help from anyone.

AE strongly advises you staying in hospital for three weeks, so I am wiring today to that effect, and I hope my wire will be sufficient to convince the hospital people. The Amah you had engaged came to 191 today and is now hard at it trying to make up her mind whether she wishes to travel. I am afraid that even the last few days, with these unrests of British in Japan, and Japanese in Britain, one has to admit that the situation has deteriorated. I don't mean by that there will be trouble here, but it will probably make the authorities adamant about people coming back and it starts to look as if you really will have to go to Australia. What I feel is that if we prepare for it, you would be able to do it in greater comfort and the preparations could always be cancelled, if they were not necessary. If we do not prepare, and you have to go, then you would have much less comfort. I am all for your idea of trying to get a ship via HK. It would be painful for us both,[32] but it would be worth it.

Well I must end now. I am very sleepy although it is only just before lunch, and I

---

32 Presumably he is envisaging that Therese and HP would not be able to land or if so, only for a matter of hours.

must close before I die of it. I miss you a lot, long to see Junior and will write you all about it while I am out on patrol.

To Therese   10 August

It is very difficult for me to feel like a father at this distance, but I fully understand all you write about wanting to share Hugh Peter between us, and I assure you I do too. I think about both of you a lot, and you need not worry yourself about getting out of touch. We have far too substantial and close a bond between us for mere separation to have any real effect upon it.

I think I told you in my last that I am all for taking a ship via Hong Kong, if you have to go to Australia. A second parting would be sad for both of us, but I long to see our small son: also it would make the question of your extra luggage a lot simpler, as you could pack it up here.

Hope your Camp John Hay arrangements have worked out alright, because being there with Mrs Brown would obviously be better than the Pines. The Amah seems to be a definite acquisition, even if a bit expensive compared to HK values, but then everything in Manila is, so there is no use in worrying on that score. The Amah you engaged through Mrs Butcher has decided she would not like to travel, so I will start afresh and make new arrangements.

UE is the Exemption King once again, and I gather things are easing up quite a bit, as in Mrs S's [Shewan] case, but there are not yet any signs of people being allowed to come back permanently. However, there is another month to go before the question of yourself would arise, so while there is life there is always hope.

The rain is proceeding according to schedule, although we have had a certain amount of fine sunny days. Rainfall is now 98 inches against an average of 57. The all-time record for a year of 119 was reached in 1889, so it looks to be pretty certain that we will break the record by a margin of about 20 inches. All very good for the Island's water supply. To cap it all, the Peak road has been washed out between Magazine Gap and the Hall's house, just where they were repairing it, so cars are at a discount and the peak Tram is doing a roaring trade. Both UE's and mine were at the bottom, which was lucky, but mine is now of very little use as it only came in for running up and down the Peak.

To Therese   15 August

I was glad to hear that Camp John Hay was a definite fixture, it must be a relief to you to be definitely fixed and I hope you are both comfortable there.

I enquired again from Burgess (Govt. here) to find if there were any cut and dried arrangements as regards yourself, and he knew of none. Apparently, and this is vague in the extreme, I let him know when you feel like moving and then a booking can be made. Alternatively the Consul General in Manila fixes it and tells you, Burgess did not seem to know. I have been to Cooks and found the two most likely sailings.

The Australia question still remains as before but there are slight signs of things easing off a bit, any way as regards people stopping over in the Colony for health reasons. Mrs Shewan and Mrs Armstrong are both doing so, they have passages booked, but their sailing dates are quite vague and so far as they are concerned will probably remain so. In your case, being an active service wife it would probably be more difficult to arrange an extended stopover; in addition, having given up the house produces complications, since we could not park on the E's indefinitely.

There is also the feeling at the back of my mind, that although I do not expect any

Therese (top right) at Camp John Hay

trouble here, if anything did go wrong, I would never be able to forgive myself for the rest of my life. All very difficult and I fancy the best thing is to discuss it between ourselves, when you arrive here. I am afraid it looks very much like Australia, but I would not call it final yet.

Today is the last day of our weeks standoff and I feel very much refreshed, having slept eight to nine hours every night. I played golf at Shek O with UE last Sunday afternoon.

Geer is still at 168. The coolie has apparently done another of his disappearing tricks, so I told Geer he had better fire him. I am sorry for his aged mother, but there are limits.

Well lovey, that is about all my news, and I must go down to the Naval Yard and argue about ballast.

Therese moves to Camp John Hay.

To Therese   18 August

Most galling that our wire to your mother said you were 'very sick', when I suggested 'very fit' especially to allay any worries on that score; if they cannot translate better, it as well not to wire at all. I forgot to say that a parcel has arrived from your mother with a woollen pram blanket, a woollen suit and a spoon, fork and napkin ring. We opened it so as to get things in the drying room.[33]

Please do not think your letters are too long and off the point; I look forward to them and thoroughly enjoy reading them. I am afraid mine lack the personal, chatty touch and are apt to be a bit businesslike, but then there seems to be lots of things to discuss and fix up, so that by the time I have dealt with them I have to go off playing at sailors again.

I enclose a copy of a letter, which Mrs F.C.H [Hall] received from Mrs Townend [see at the end of this letter], our Sydney Agent's wife: if you have to go there I am sure they will look after you well and will help you to find suitable living accommodation. FCH, incidentally, has made a corner in Australian bank notes, dear old boy, always preparing for the worst in an efficient businesslike way, and has offered to let me in on the ground floor. Extremely good of him and I accepted with alacrity.

---

33   The author of *Chips of China* (1930) states that because the Peak is shrouded in damp mist and cloud for many months of the year, Europeans had drying rooms in their houses. The room would be heated by a coal stove or an electric radiator. The contents would include clothes, linen, books, cameras etc. Woolf, p. 7.

Well, I am so glad to hear that you and HP are doing so well. I think of you a lot and miss you a great deal, but it will take more than separation like this to upset such an exceptional couple as ourselves.

It looks as if the German Blitzkrieg on England is a flop; they must have done a lot of damage but their losses are colossal and they cannot keep this up for long, so one would think.

The two letters enclosed with Peter's letter:

H Townend to F C Hall   12 August   Sydney   Re Mrs H W M Dulley
My congratulations to Dulley. I trust his wife and family are quite well.

Should Mrs Dulley decide to come here, I would like Dulley to let me know, when she leaves Manila and I will meet her on arrival. You mentioned she would probably be sending a Chinese baby Amah to Manila to travel down with her. If she decides on this I think he should bear in mind that Chinese are prohibited from entering Australia[34] and can only do so under certain Government regulations, what I cannot say offhand, but he could, or I would, if he preferred it, write to the Secretary of the Department of Interior at Canberra and ascertain the conditions and restrictions as prescribed by law.

My wife and I will be pleased to meet Mrs. Dulley and if she has no friends or relatives here we will do all we can to make her comfortable.

E. Townend to Mrs Hall   Aug 1940   Sydney
We are sorry to hear of the anxious time you are having over your way. In Mr Hall's letter he told my husband about Mrs Dulley's unfortunate position, and I thought I would like to write to you so that you could let her know that I should be delighted to do anything I could to help her. If she comes to Sydney, as soon as she is strong enough, we would meet her, and she could stay with us until she decided what she would like to do.

We are having a delightful winter, with plenty of sunshine – but rain is needed badly. They are talking of rationing the water. We may be short of bath water – I think I will try the ocean!

---

34 The White Australia Policy grew from the fears of Australians at the end of the Gold Rush days in the 19th century, that there would be 'swarms' of Asians, in particular Japanese and Chinese entering the country and undercutting the wages of Australians. http://en.wikipedia.orworkersg/wiki/White_Australia_policy. 13 November 2014.

Peter to Therese   24 August

Re travelling in the *Neptuna* early in October, has the advantage that you have to touch at HK on the way; I mention this because I hear that Army wives are not allowed to pass through HK on their way to Australia. I don't know whether this applies to the Navy and do not intend to ask; it is so much simpler not to know and to face people with a 'fait accompli'.

I was thrilled to see the small pictures of HP in the letter to your mother, but I must admit they were rather small to convey much to me; I feel I need to see him in the flesh to start saying I see likenesses. When your bigger ones arrive I will start to hold forth learnedly on family characteristics, but don't take it seriously if I put my foot in it. I was so glad to hear that you were putting on weight and that you are both fit and well. Somehow, I don't yet really feel like a father, and until I have seen you both I doubt I will, but if one becomes a father by correspondence I doubt if it is possible to have all the fatherly feelings.

Life goes on fairly quietly here and seems to be a succession of spells at sea and spells in harbour, which are supposed to be a stand-off but never quite seem to work out that way. I got a bit rattled and annoyed a day or so ago because we were hauled out of harbour to relieve a launch, which had run out of water.[35] Flap and bother, I recall the officers, recall the signalmen, crew, odds and bits and off we go. But all they wanted in the end was the water boat, so why send us out? Ah, there you have it, we are just volunteers and will stand for anything. The water boat people are professionals and have rules to say when they work and when they don't, mainly the latter apparently. I am afraid I get a bit sore periodically about being one of the dog's bodies who do all the jobs. However, things should be easing off shortly as all the tugs are now approximately in commission, so we should have a reasonable flotilla with which to carry on.

I went out to dinner with Gomp, Bobby Geer and Stafford on Saturday, first time I have been out since you left, and I will admit I had an idea of getting on a bit of a bender. We went soberly to the cinema after dinner, then Gomp trailed me off to a dance haunt at West Point, where he appears to have an understanding with one of the wenches. It is years since I have been at a Chinese dance place, and I recollect

---

35 Primarily for the ship's steam engine.

them as rather dull spots, so the general layout did not appeal to me a great deal, but I will admit I was curious to see Gomp's fancy. However, there was a notice on the door to say no one in uniform, irrespective of rank, would be admitted. So I trailed off to the hotel, left them to it, saw no one who interested me there, and had one drink and went soberly home with my bender not properly executed.

FCH still in a fairly deep state of gloom, anticipating a fairly early dissolution of most of the ordered and orderly functions in this world, as we at present know them.

To Therese 29 August

Many thanks for your two letters, which arrived together and were brought out to me by launch. Well, I am properly ticked off, a little harder than was really necessary, but I quite see that I have been at fault. My excuse is that 'I meant well.' You see lovey I am entirely in the dark at this end and can get no information from anyone I have so far tried. In addition, with this game of being a good five-eighth's of my time at sea, when I come in I am usually very tired and definitely not very intelligent. From what I would gather here, at some time unstated, someone in Manila[36] would tell you to move onto Australia, so I felt that all I could do was to organise it a bit, i.e. an Amah, better accommodation on the ship and a trip via HK, so as to make it better for both of us.

But don't for a moment think I was trying to send you to Australia. I dislike the idea just as much as you do. I was merely bowing as philosophically as possible to what I assumed to be inevitable. I did not realise that Camp John Hay held any prospect of being a permanency. I imagined it was only a temporary home until such time as you were shot on.

It is all so difficult to grasp from this end. Letters still take an absurdly long time and my life at the moment seems to be so bitty, there is never time to settle down and concentrate on anything. But please don't think I wished to shoo you off to Australia against your wishes and judgement, or that I do not realise what a rotten run you are having as an evacuated mother with a small baby. I do realise only too well and am extremely proud of you for the brave way you have stood up to it all, and your practical capability in organising all your own arrangements. I want you to do just what you think best for yourself and HP.

---

36 The British Consul?

As I said I did not realise there was any prospect of Camp JH being a permanency. At Ps 90 per month it is quite astonishing and if you like it and are among friends, I would be inclined to stay there until the cows come home, or until you are allowed to return to HK. I think it is extremely clever of you to have got yourself fixed up in a pleasant spot at so low a cost. When considering the question of staying on in P.I. I had visions that once the official assistance was removed, it would cost something in the nature of Ps 400 per month, or almost all of my salary, so that would only be a feasible proposition for a month or so, but not indefinitely.

I was thrilled to get the photos. He is a remarkably fine looking baby, but then what do you expect from parents like us? I think he looks like me, or rather like I used to at that age.

AE does a very handsome best to look after me, but it is not the motherly care of my little sweetie, and I miss the latter badly. I have to be quite honest, I have tried to work myself into a state of hard and brittle apathy; not that it has been a great success, but the other way merely leads to self pity and moping which does not really help one in the long run. I don't like the separation, lovey, and wish to goodness it would all end soon. I know that in many ways it is much worse for you than for me, being thrown out on the cold hard world, and I am so glad to hear that you have run into a crowd of kind pleasant people in Camp JH.

I have got myself mixed up, in a most conscientious way, in charging a steam launch and junk with going over a minefield. Now that our story is being dissected by the experts it looks a bit thin and apparently I am going to spend most of my stand-off time in Hole's Marine Court, with the prospect of being made to look rather an ass at the end. Oddly enough UE's Mr Brown is representing the defence and I feel he will probably make us look slightly silly in court. It looked all so easy at the start, the launch and Junk admitted their guilt, but now the signalman, who did the interpreting says, 'No, that is not what they said.' So our case and witnesses break down, when it is too late to stop the case. Such, is the result of trying to be conscientious over one's job.

To Therese   6 September

I hope you received mine of the 30th, in which I explained all my ideas of the evacuation. I very foolishly brought it on board with me and had to send it back to *Cornflower* via a Chinese signalman for posting.

Where we have gone wrong over the whole show is that you think we know what is happening up here and we think you must, because we certainly don't. In addition, I have been on the go pretty hard since you left and seem to have got into a routine of being perpetually short of sleep. As a result, when the opportunity to relax arrives periodically, I relax and do not spend sufficient time writing to you and thinking out your affairs.

Why I felt you should stick to the official scheme was roughly as follows. When you left I fancied the powers that be must have something up their sleeve and there was possibly a real threat to this Colony. If we had become cut off, and I had been unable to do anything for you as regards money etc., it would have been essential for you to be able to call on the Sponsors of the official scheme, to support you, transport you to Australia and find you lodgings there.

However, it has not worked out that way. I doubt if there was ever any real cause to put the evacuation into practice; the Army and Navy just did it as a drill movement and stampeded the civilians into following. As you rightly say, all you have so far got is a free fare on an uncomfortable ship, and all the arrangements in P.I. have been made by yourself. All you are now likely to get is another free fare to a place you don't want to go to, Australia to wit. So what the hell girl, what the hell? I entirely agree. I would not make any move off your own bat about cutting off from the scheme, but if they try to rush you into anything you don't want to do or consider unwise for yourself or HP, cut adrift by all means.

As I see it this evacuation is going to look sillier as the months go by. The tide of war may not have turned in our favour yet, but at least it has ceased to run against us. Hitler's idea of a short war shows no signs of materialising, the prospective invasion of Britain seems a flop, the French seem to have called the Japanese bluff in Indo China and the Americans appear to be saying a 'No' to any expansionist ideas on the part of the Japs out in this part of the world. As a result any prospect of immediate conquest and crumbling of the British Empire seems to have been removed and I do not see the vaguest prospect of trouble here. If we continue at peace here, with no prospects of trouble here, with no probability of change in that happy state, then it will be extremely difficult to maintain that the evacuation is necessary. It will not possibly be called off officially, because that would be a tacit admission of a previous faulty official judgement, but they will cease to harry people who trickle back. At present they are chasing up people who book through to another port and stop off at HK, but I think, and hope, that that will stop and that you should be able to return discreetly by Christmas, if not before. Hence stick around at Camp JH.

Now to answer your letter, I miss you badly, my sweet, and long to see you back here and to be introduced to HP. But if you don't mention this theme too often there is a method in the madness. If you think too seriously about this war, consider how our home has been broken up and how, what appeared to be a fairly rosy commercial future, is quietly dissolving while I hack away at an uncongenial occupation, then it is all too easy to sink into a welter of self-pity, positively bathe in it in fact. As a result, I find a modest amount of defensive armour against one's feelings is provided by an impersonal philosophical attitude, regarding the whole affair in a detached critical attitude. After all, while this war is on, one has got to keep going and do one's job as best one can until it is won, and bathing in self-pity does not fit in with that. I feel our parting deeply, but unfeeling though it may seem, I try to put it out of my mind as much as I can. Don't worry though, lovey, our marriage has three and a half years of very solid foundations, with HP now to cement them further, and it will take more than a war and an evacuation to affect them in the least.

No, I am afraid you cannot plead being domiciled in HK to avoid evacuation, you are only resident there, a very different thing legally. If we retired in HK and HP also settled there, then either he, or possibly only his children, would be domiciled in HK, until then they would be resident.

Well, not a great deal of news here. Life seems to consist of endless patrols then spells in harbour, which are always shorter than they should be, for some reason or another, one's time ashore being spent in arguments about your supposed misdeeds, writing reports, which presumably no one reads, and making arrangements about things which tend not to come to fruition. I will admit I am finding it a bit of a strain and one of these days I am going off on a colossal jag, before something snaps.

Last Saturday a most galling thing occurred. I was doing a day on board the tug, which was at the buoy in harbour and Dodwell's water boat came alongside to fill up our tanks. I explained that they must be careful with the FP tank[37] as it would overflow directly into the officers' cabins. Sure enough, some twenty minutes later, a tidal wave

---

37   Front Peak tank installed to provide extra water for the *St. Aubin* to carry out a long voyage.

swept through the wardroom and we were quietly inundated. I was extremely ill tempered with the water boat crew and made them mop up the mess, which took about half an hour. Hard words were used and I felt they would probably try to get back on me by pinching something, so I kept a careful eye on them, or thought I did. That evening, however, I could not find the lighter your mother gave me and I am afraid one of them must have sneaked it out. Most galling, and especially sorry as it was your mother's present to which I had become extremely attached, but what can I do.

To Therese   12 September   At Sea Hong Kong
Excuse the pencil but my pen is in dock, so it is pencil or nothing.[38] Your wire was forwarded to me in the ship, while at sea.[39] As it is very likely it got mutilated by being relayed, I will repeat it back to you so that you know what I am working on. 'Received notice from Consulate, passage booked *Taiping*. Refused. Asked option later sailing will need money from 21 September.' I have not done anything about trying to wire from *St. Aubin*, as I felt the process would be too complicated, but will send something of this sort when I get back 'Approve refusal of *Taiping* passage and apply Wise for money.' I feel that my reply is not urgently required, although you will naturally like to know as soon as possible that I am on your side over this show.

I am naturally a bit in the dark as yet, but I assume the Consul first sent you a chit to say you were booked in the *Taiping*, to which you replied nothing doing. So far so good. But does that in any way affect your living at Camp John Hay? I feel it should not as the Camp is an American Army place and in no way connected with the Consul. What I have been vaguely worried about, before we got ideas straightened out between us, was the prospect of refusing a free passage and then having prices put up against you in P.I. (by the removal of Concessions to Evacuees etc.) to the stage where it would be impossible to afford to live there. Since I wrote last they have enacted some Ordinance (Law) in HK, to prevent people coming back and to clear out those who already have. It all sounds very impressive, as most laws do, but I still feel that they will not be able to maintain the evacuation unless there is some sort of threat to the security of the Colony to back it up.

Somehow this routine in the new tugs gets me down, you never seem to get away from them, one gets a bit boxed up. I miss our evenings out together badly, more so

---

38 Presumably pencils were issued to the Navy as they would not smudge in wet conditions.
39 Transmitted by wireless.

as the rather scruffy atmosphere of a tug makes one want to put on one's best clothes, eat good food and see the gay lights, when one has an evening off.

To Therese   15 September 1940

I was so glad to hear that HP is gaining weight fast and that you feel better and less worried now.

As regards coming back to HK, I feel fearful of committing myself. I am still optimistic and feel they will not be able to maintain this evacuation indefinitely, but I doubt the wisdom of being premature in one's attempts to return. If they succeed lovely, but if they failed it would mean two moves, a trip to Australia, the loss of Camp JH and looking rather silly. Rest assured, I hold a watching brief for you, and will let you know as soon as I see any prospect of venturing with success.

UE is rather het up about the evacuation and I don't blame him. You recollect he was on an Exemption Committee with Tina Cock, Gillespie and a Govt. Servant called Sollice (?). A day or so ago a notice was published in the paper, appointing a new Committee, which is the first they had heard, or still have, that their Committee is now a dead number. There is a lot of mud being thrown about in the Colony over the evacuation and the sudden disappearance of a committee like that is bound to make people think that it is being hushed up. In point of fact the opposite was the case, they refused exemption to many people, including Mrs NL[40] and Lady Macgregor, only to be overruled from Govt. HQ. I gather that UE is going to ask for a public acknowledgement of the fact that the appointment of the new Committee in no way reflects on the old. I think he is quite right and that he has been treated disgracefully.

AE is a lot better and was to play nine holes of golf at DWB with UE today. I am afraid she is worried about Jack[41] and will continue to be so. He writes cheerful, interesting and intelligent letters, but I don't know exactly what he is doing in the flying line, and nor do I fancy do they.

We got in from our last about 5.00 pm on Friday (we now do mine sweeping exercises after our patrols, so we have to be back in the late afternoon instead of before lunch). Wads of papers, chat and complaints waiting for me in *Cornflower*, most of which I left behind.

---

40   Mrs N L Smith, wife of the Colonial Secretary, who resigned in late 1941.
41   Jack Davidson, her son, was a flying instructor in the RAF before moving to an operational squadron.

Who do you think popped up in the office when I was in there for a short while on Saturday morning, but Patrick Flannagan? They went on leave in April and a fortnight after they got to England he had a wire telling him to go back to the East. Fortunately there was not a ship for five weeks, which gave them seven at home, because when he got to Bombay and phoned head office in Calcutta, they did not even recollect that they had wired him, let alone where they wanted him. He is now in S'hai with Enid, who is expecting another baby in a month and they sent lots of kind messages.

To Therese   23 September
Over to the question of passage to Australia, it is very sweet of you to want to pay for it, but I feel you should not. Better keep the money, you never know when you may need it, or you could always spend it on something for HP. Buying steamer passages is a husband's job and such a dull thing for a woman to spend money on.

You ask me what are the prospects of your getting back and I will have to admit I am rather stumped for an answer. If I had known at the end of June how the whole show was going to pan out, I would have dug my toes in and said you could not travel, irrespective of what Andy said. But we were panicked into it and I thought that maybe there was some real threat to the Colony. As things stand now, I fancy the only way you can get back is by passing through the Colony and failing to go on. I don't like that very much, as you might be forced to do a double mover, Baguio/HK and HK/Australia, the latter without much notice and preparation. I also feel it advisable for this Japanese show in Indo China to blow over a bit, also to see how things develop after three months, during which we agreed to close the Burma Road, are finished. The American Presidential elections are a factor: it will be after then, if ever, that they will say that they intend to intervene actively on our side. If they do, there will be a very much more settled outlook here. I don't think there is the slightest use my taking it up officially; there are no grounds on which to base my request, except that I dislike you being away and that is scarcely enough.

There is a small consolation, that if you were here you would see very little of me. Life, re volunteering, does not seem to get any easier and I am stale and tired. I have expressed my views on paper to our worthy CO, but what will come of it I don't know.

I had a very sad piece of news in my mother's last letter. John Morgan is dead, killed in some fighting with tribes on the NW Frontier of India. One sometimes wonders, what is the good of all this fighting and killing. I am afraid Frances and Allan will take it pretty hard; I must try to write to them as soon as I can.

To Therese   25 September
One item of news that may cheer you up. A lot of the women who have come back from evacuation, have official notices to leave the Colony by 5 October. I felt that might come and it was apropos of that I did not want you to be premature in making an effort to return. I think the third week in October is a fairly critical period in the situation, since the agreement to close the Burma Road finishes on 18 October. So after that the future should look a bit clearer. The Indo China affair is quite beyond me: at one moment the French want to hand their Colonial Empire out to anyone who will take it and the next they talk about resisting all comers. What is one to think? Answer: wait and see. The USA seem to be gearing themselves up slowly and ponderously towards resisting Japanese aggression in the Pacific, a tendency which will probably gain momentum, so I still incline to the view that we will have no trouble here. All a bull point towards you coming back here.

To Therese   29 September
We had an inspection of the Force last Wednesday by HE.[42] The Governor, then a ceremony for handing over the new ship *Tai Hing*, in place of the old *Cornflower*, by Sir Robert Ho Tung to HE, representing the HK Govt. I had to Command the troops, who looked rather like the League of Nations on a Gala Day; it was very hot and we were standing in the afternoon sun. I, sweating by the bucketful, but all went off fairly well. We have been having a pretty hot spell to finish up the summer, the hottest so far I think, but there is a typhoon looming at the moment, which should clear the air and put us into autumn weather.

I have had two bits of good news since I wrote last. First your mother's lighter, which I had thought had been pinched by someone on a Dodwell water boat, has turned up in the pocket of a pair of overalls. Second, I hear that Jardines are to get a ten per cent high cost of living allowance, as from 1 September.

There is a reasonable hope that our nautical endeavours may shortly be curtailed,

---

42 His Exellency.

so that their scope is more within the capabilities of officers. I started to moan about it a short while ago and it has been forwarded to high places. So there is a fair prospect of things being rearranged so that we get more time off and occasional leave. I sincerely hope it does come off as we are all very stale and tired at the moment. And so are you too, I am afraid, my love. I realise only too well that you must be living in a constant strain and that it is impossible not to feel low at times. But you must not start thinking that there is nothing to live for. There is. There is our future together, Hugh P, any more HPs, which may come along, and lots of other things. After all, this show cannot last forever, however unpleasant it may be while it does. So look forward to the time it will all be over, to when we are together again and remember the Dulley motto is still 'thumbs up'.

To Therese   October

Re censorship: I had one of my letters opened, but I do not know whether the Honourable Edward[43] feels himself called upon to read them all through. Talking about Honourables, Gomp and I had a reunion tiffin party yesterday, with the Hon. Philip Samuel,[44] Viscount Samuel's son. He is out here with the China Light Power Co., Kadoorie's outfit, and arrived about last August (1939). We both remembered him at School[45] as 'Samuel P' and Jack [Peter's brother] had seen a bit of him at home apropos of the O/S League.[46]

You ask all about Japan and the Axis and I will admit the situation is growing a bit more complicated. Some people think it is very serious but I don't see it that way. I thought the Italy/Germany/Japan pact was a bit of window dressing to distract people's attention from things, the lack of success of the German air attack on Britain and the postponement or cancellation of the invasion, the slow progress of the Italian attack on Egypt, and the fact that the peoples of Germany and Italy have got to prepare themselves for a second winter of war. This last, I rate as being extremely important

---

43 Honourable Edward may have been Cmdr. Shields in a HKRNVR photo from 1937. There was an A L Shields on the Executive Council, and he would thus have the title of Honourable. If he used a different christian name, which was common, they could be the same person. If that was the case then he and Major Manners came through Japanese lines to persuade Major General Maltby to surrender during the Japanese invasion of Hong Kong in December 1941. Banham, p. 241.
44 In 1939 the Hon. Samuel became confidential office manager in Hong Kong and Shanghai for Sir Elly Kadoorie.
45 Westminster School, London.
46 Overseas League, a club in St. James, London.

from the viewpoint of morale. The only nations against whom the pact can be directed are America and Russia. If the USA joins in the European war then she is at war with Japan too. If Russia attacks Japan then she will be attacked by Germany. I think the chief idea is to deter America from becoming embroiled in the war, either in the Pacific or in Europe. I doubt whether it will achieve this effect. America is slow to wake up and realise her responsibilities, but she is now doing so at long last and slow though her progress may be it is progress and I don't think there will be any backward steps. With the calling up of her Naval Reservists, it looks as though she is definitely preparing to say 'No' to the Japs in the Pacific.

The Japanese position is obscure, as always and I fancy they are rapidly nearing the crossroads. Their basic trouble is that they are desperately keen to finish the China War, before they become exhausted. The Indo China business has the effect of cutting off one further route of communication between Chungking and the outside world, to wit the Haiphong/Yumman railway, but there is still the Burma Road. I gather, and sincerely hope, that we will reopen the road and tell the Japs to go to hell. They have to choose between giving in or fighting us and probably the USA as well. I think they will choose the former course, certainly if they decide on logical grounds.[47]

If they are going to close the Burma Road by force, they must start by landing at Rangoon, adding tremendously to their lines of communication and necessitating the capture of HK and Singapore and the command of the seas in the Far East. If the USA comes in with their navy this would be impossible, apart from the fact that with the trade of the British Empire and the USA cut off, Japan would dissolve economically within six months.

Over the next few weeks we must expect scares and tension. The Japs will storm, rage and threaten, but I feel sure their bubble will be pricked if the Americans show a firm front and back us up. It comes to this, if they plunge into a desperate war against Britain and the USA on top of their China affair, they will probably lose their Navy, occupied China and Manchuria. On the other hand, if they pipe down, they possibly will not be able to win the China War outright, but they will be able to hang onto, anyhow temporarily, large slices of occupied China, Manchuria and their Navy. The Navy is very important to their scheme, even if it is somewhat inactive; they have

---

47 Peter opens up the possibility that the Japanese might make plans that were not based on logic.

achieved most of their success over the last ten years by bluff, and without a Navy to protect their communications between Japan and the mainland, their bluff can be called far too easily.

The worthy tug is going into dock in a day or so and there is a slight hope that our fairly extensive list of troubles may be attended to. We are having about nineteen days without going to sea, seven of which are up today and I am fixing to go out to Fanling for a week next Friday. The big idea is to get right away from the sea, ships, the Dockyard and everything to do with them. I have fixed a Sunday golf game with Highet, of the Bank, and intend to have some lessons with the pro.

The E's had the news that Jack [Davidson] had been appointed about the end of August to an operational squadron. He is based at Newmarket; they use the heath for their aerodrome and they presumably bomb Germany at night. I am afraid AE was a bit upset, although she said nothing, but it had to come sooner or later. I hope he gets through this war alright, it will be such a tragedy if he does not, both for the E's sake and for the spoiling of such a great looking future.

To Therese   11 October   Fanling, Hong Kong

As you will see from the address here we are out at Fanling, having arrived in time for lunch today. Ample exercise, about thirty-six holes of golf per day, a modest amount of drink and about ten hours sleep per night is the routine and, as I hope to be out here for six days, I should return to HK a new man.

I do not see any real prospect of your being in any danger in Baguio. They must be at war with the USA before that can happen, which will certainly mean that they are at war with us too, and however mad they go I do not see them tackling both of us. I think we would naturally back the Americans up, but it is not yet so sure that they would back us up. Hence it seems to me more possible (not probable, mark you) that we should be at war with the Japs than the Americans and ourselves should be.

As regards coming via HK. I am a bit doubtful as to whether that is any longer possible. They are getting extremely strict of late and an appeal to do that was turned down a few days ago. People here are getting very pessimistic about this evacuation, Hall for one, although he is a natural pessimist, also Tommy Fairbairn. He told me a day or so ago that he had it from inside that women are not to be allowed to come back for a long while yet. All very discouraging, but I would not give up hope just yet.

I gather that the evacuation and the appointment of a Military Governor here shook the Japs badly, as it convinced them that we were going to defend the place. Putting up defence fortifications and telling them that we would defend it was apparently not enough, they just thought we were bluffing. So you can feel that you and HP are doing your part in the defence of the Empire, even if it does pain you being in Baguio all this while.

To Therese   20 October

On Friday night I spoilt most of the good done over the last week. Gomp is off to S'hai on Wednesday to take over as No. 1 from Mason, who is to have some months leave in Australia. Gomp had a cocktail party at 168.

The NL Smiths and Bish Lander came to dinner at 191, last night. Bish is just up from Manila, where he left his wife and child and is off to the Burma border of the Burma Road. APC [48] in HK sell all the petrol and oil to the Chinese Govt., which goes over the Burma Road, so they need a representative there to look after things for them. Apparently he is doing pretty well, as he was No. 2 in Manila and comes back here in about six months as No. 2 to Bonzo Beaconsfield.

Incidentally I hear that Landale[49] has joined the Navy at home; no details but I will let you know, if I get any. With J. J. [Paterson] back I suppose he feels there is no further call to hold the fort as the big businessman, so has done a very right and proper thing. Did I tell you I was thinking of selling *Monsoon*. I don't like doing it but feel the present is no time for sentiment: I have not the leisure to see she is properly kept up so it is better to get rid of her.

To Therese   27 October   Hong Kong

Not much news from here, life seems to meander on with the usual set of worries and mishaps. I feel fed up and lonely and long for days where there will be peace in the world once again, in place of this eternal killing, and we will be able to settle down again together and be quietly happy.

We took to the seas again last Monday after our docking, with only about half the

---

48 The Asiatic Petroleum Company, part of Shell. Allen, p. 312.
49 David Landale Jnr worked with J. J. Paterson as part of the senior management of Jardines in the 1930s. Keswick, p. 46.

work done, and when we got back I tried to get the Commodore to kick up a fuss about it, but he only informed me that it was my fault for not jockeying the Dockyard up to do their job properly. Not exactly what you would call backing your officers up, and not quite the line to get backing from them in return.[50] We were due in about 4.00 pm Thursday, but had a bit of an accident doing a practice mine sweep, by getting the sweep wire wound round the propeller, so we had to be towed back with considerable ignominy and arrived at 9.00 pm on a cold wet evening.

On Saturday evening they had a do at Kellett Island to open the new Yacht Club. Norton,[51] the new Governor, opened it, then cocktails, a buffet supper and dancing. I muscled in on John Potter's party, having met him at tiffin the day before and fixed it. There were wads of people there, about 500, lots of drink, and according to the Club stewards it was a pretty fair binge with which to start the new place. I left at 1.30 am as the dancing finished, but apparently people were still hard at it frying bacon and eggs at 4.00 am, when Vernal left, so it looks as if we really opened it properly.

---

50 This letter would have been censored and it is interesting that he felt he could say things like this about his commanding officer, without apparently any concern about any comeback.
51 Acting Governor.

CHAPTER 9

Planning the Return to Hong Kong
October to December 1940

Over the last few months Peter and Therese had been discussing the return to Hong Kong but now had come the time to act.

To Therese   31 October

Very many thanks for your two letters with all your ideas for passing through HK. I assume you would like me to get it all organised for you, but it is not so easy. If you could have told me how these dear souls fix their fortnight's stopover, I could then copy the same recipe; Mrs Hughes case is fairly easy, she has two passports, apparently, and uses her American when it suits.

    I have been routing round to the best of my ability and this is where I have so far got to. Naval volunteers are either Navy or civilians according to what suits and what gives us the dirty end of the deal. In case of evacuation we seem to be civilians; hence I checked up with Burgess and find that HK is not considered as being on the way to Australia and hence it is not a transit port. The only excuse acceptable to the Evacuations Exemptions Committee, who will have to deal with your case, is that one cannot get accommodation on a ship that goes direct from Manila to Australia. There is an opportunity now of making an application on that score, since the next two ships from Manila to Australia, the *Taiping* and *Tanda*, are fully booked. Further they call at Manila on the way down, so they would not give you leave to travel Manila/HK/Manila. The next ship after that is the *Neptuna*, leaving Manila on 18 December. It is not clear yet whether she calls at Manila on the way down, so I have booked you provisionally on her and will apply to the Exemptions Committee to give you leave to pass through the Colony on the grounds that is your only way to get to Australia. I might also suggest that you be allowed to come up by a previous ship, catching the *Neptuna* here, but I am doubtful of the wisdom of that. The *Neptuna* case, as it stands, seems fairly sound to me, provided they do not decide to send her to Manila on the way down, and I feel it would not be very safe to throw in something which might spoil it.

To Therese   1 November

Further to my last, I have made some real progress over your trip to Australia and your stopover in HK. Pat Sedgewick told me about one Luscombe[1] in the Passport Office, who seems to be the man to tackle. I saw him this morning and he appeared to be quite agreeable to your coming up here on the *Tjinegara* (JCJL) and catching the *Neptuna* here. It has to go to the Colonial Secretary for approval. The *Tijinegara* is scheduled to sail on 8 December from Manila but they are four days late on their schedule so she probably will not be off until 12th arriving here 14th, while the *Neptuna* sails from HK on 22 December. If the *Tijinegara* is too late you can always take the *Neptuna* and get your four-day stopover. On the other hand, if she sails as on the advertised programme you would arrive here on 10th and get twelve days. I hope it all goes through OK. (Blast this pen, it must be AE's and stops every other letter.)

To Therese   8 November

I enclose a cutting from the SCM Post [*South China Morning Post* – see Appendix V] which gives the official announcement, in case it was not reported fully in the Manila papers. The Colony is still a bit too flabbergasted to have digested the situation properly, so it is difficult to give you any news as to the implications of the new ruling. The storm has not yet had time to gather momentum and break, but when it does it will be a beauty. There is a husbands' meeting tonight at the Peninsula Hotel, organised before the recent announcement, and I feel it should be a fairly lively affair.

As things stand at the moment, those who are here can stay, while those who are away may not come back, in fact the people who evaded the evacuation have triumphed. I gather the inside reason for this lies in the fact that the Govt. had not the legal authority to force people to go. Six of the women, who were supposed to sail on Saturday for Australia, had filed writs under the HABEAS CORPUS ACT, against the policemen (representing the Govt.), who had served their final notice to quit and who presumably intended to implement them with force. The writs were due to be heard at the Central Magistracy on Thursday morning and, as the Govt. knew they had no legal case, they climbed down the day before and called the Saturday sailings off. There will, or certainly should be a glorious row about it, the outcome of which

---

[1] Luscombe was an assistant superintendent of police. He subsequently continued his duties at the height of the invasion. Banham, pp. 216 & 260.

is impossible to foresee, but is going to make it increasingly difficult for the Govt. to continue the evacuation scheme with its full rigour.

Your position, at the moment, remains the same as I told you in my last letter, with one important exception. In your case you did not receive the letter. I have not yet received any answer to my application, but I got the impression that it was likely to go through all right. If it does, I propose to let it stand and book the passages definitely, but here we come to the one exception mentioned above. It is just possible that you and HP might be upset by the sudden change of climate and so be unable to catch the *Neptuna*. In fact, if the Govt. were going to play fair over this evacuation and have the same rule for all, then I was also going to play fair over your transit trip in December. But if they deal in one way with those who keep to the rules and in another with those who don't, then I feel you are able to guess which category you will belong to. Keep it to yourself, however, and trust your little man to do all that is necessary up here. Also after this letter, if I refer to your passing though HK, don't be surprised. You will be passing through, but it may take you a mighty long time to pass.

I was so glad to hear of your success as a nurse and please put into your letters all about HP that you can. Of course it does not bore me, nor do your letters, I love getting them. I am afraid mine are rather dull. Men are not very inspired, they think their wives take for granted that they love them, so there is no need to keep repeating it. Women cannot hear it too often, just a difference in mental make up. Well, here you have it, I love you, my Darling, and miss you very badly. I just do, but am not good at putting it into words. Deeds are my strong suit, as I hope you will shortly be able to find out once again.

Haynes and Carter seem to be definitely interested in buying *Monsoon*, which is nice as I would like her to go to someone I like.

By and large conditions in the tugs and Naval Volunteers have improved, at least we are not doing some silly strings of nights straight off the reel, which we were doing in July and August. In addition we are settling down to them, and have got over a lot of the extra work incidental to a first commission. The same silly scraps with the Dockyard continue, rather like the poor, always with us.

UE has been appointed legal adviser to the Govt. over Income Tax. He hovered about taking it, as he cannot now advise Hastings'[2] clients about Tax; I wanted him to accept but did not like to say so. He gets $1,000 down and $100 per case and has already netted about $1,500, so he is feeling quite cheered about it.

Well my love, don't count too much on coming back, but I definitely think the situation looks brighter. All the best to you and remember I love you, even if I forget to say so.

To Therese   14 November

Very many thanks for your letters. I fancy the news of the change of evacuation plans had not come through, so all your queries are a bit out-of-date. As I see it, there is now no longer any question of you going to Australia, because it would only be further to come back from when the opportunity occurs as I feel it very likely will. The situation has not exactly clarified itself yet. There was a large sized husbands' protest meeting at the Peninsula a week ago, but that was merely an airing of grievances and a committee was formed to tabulate them. Jack Macgregor spoke and said he had been for an interview with the Governor that morning; the latter seems to be sympathetic and realises there is considerable injustice over the whole show. He said there was an outstanding political issue to be cleared up before the Govt. could consider revising the evacuation policy, and that is the only real pointer which has so far been given. He would not say what the political issue is, but I feel it must be connected with whether the Japs are going to have a stab at DEI. The impression given by the Governor's interview with Jack Macgregor was that if and when the political issue has been cleared up, then you may come back.

As far as you are concerned, I would draw on your stock of patience and stick around for the result of this transit permit for the *Neptuna* in December. I have not heard of anything further and in view of the changed circumstances, have not wished to appear to press things. However, it is now over two weeks since I applied to the policeman in question, so I will look him up tomorrow and see how things appear.

I don't feel your suggestion of seeing the Commodore would help and maybe you are very much better as a civilian than as services. If the Govt. call off the evacuation, the services can still say their wives may not return, under those or any other

---

2 Edgar Davidson was senior partner of Hastings & Co., solicitors.

circumstances. If you cheat the Govt. over the evacuation rules they can smack back at you by proper legal action, but services high ups have much more summary powers and can send wives away without any law to back it up, just by giving an order.

You ask whether I think that USA will come into the war and it is difficult to say. I should be inclined to suggest NO, not unless they think we will not win without their help. Last June [the evacuation of troops from Dunkirk] shook them badly but they felt they were then too late and anyway they would NOT make any appreciable difference. I think Roosevelt is well ahead of American opinion and would come in straight away, if he had a free hand. But he must educate public opinion as he goes; if he takes too forward a step, he would be ousted. I think he is working on quite reasonable grounds, as he is making a large army and educating public opinion at the same time, so that when the latter comes to the boil he will have the forces at his disposal with which to give effect to the decision of public opinion. In practice, I fancy it will be much the same as the last war; we will have to do the bulk of the fighting but the morale effect of the USA entering the war, as I think they will in a year or so's time, will be decisive as the Germans and Italians will know they cannot hope to win. Again, as the last war, the Americans will be able to say 'We won the War' and in a certain sense it will be true.

I agree, it is surprising and disgraceful that a Yacht Club show could be held without you, but there it is. There is the consolation that if the Yacht Club could not get on without our support, then it would be in liquidation [it did have financial difficulties because of the war] and there would be no Yacht Club left when life became peaceful and normal again. You ask why Beryl Fair, Joan Armstrong etc. are all exempt [from evacuation] but I cannot give the exact reason for each. They all have reasons, flimsy though they may be, and are all being made to take a fairly severe course in nursing and First Aid.

Continued   16 July

Life has had a setback and I feel a bit depressed, but not too much so, as it is not final and definite. I tried to corral the policeman yesterday but he was not in; today I succeeded in doing so, only to find that my application for your transit permit had been turned down by NL Smith. The policeman seemed to think it was a bit 'off', as others had been given similar permits, and it was agreed that I should get a letter from Gibb Livingstone, the *Neptuna* Agents in HK, saying that to the best of their knowledge at present the *Neptuna* is not going to call at Manila on the way down to Australia, and then tackle NL [Smith] with a view to having his decision reviewed again.

I went to a Mess night at *Tamar* yesterday evening, they are starting to have them every Friday with the idea of providing a common meeting place for all the very disjointed sections of the Navy in HK, such as the Shore Staff, the Destroyer Officers, the HKRNVR, the MTBs [Motor Torpedo Boats] and the Examination Services (mainly RNR). Quite a good evening. After it was over de Clair, Steve and I went to the Seaman's Home on de Clair's pretext of seeing how his sailors were enjoying themselves at a dance, and collected Miss Padmore and another nurse, whom we took to the Gripps. All very proper, as we had the Naval Padre with us too; one drink and a couple of dances and so home.

To Therese   23 November

It is very noble of you to write so often and I am afraid I come off poorly by comparison. I always seem to be rushed, tired or at sea and none of those states are conducive to letter writing.

Well this is a mouldy business spending another [wedding] anniversary apart and I feel sad and depressed, not a very usual state of affairs for me. It has all got me down a bit today, I hate our being apart. I am fed up with trying to be a sailor, all one hears of is killing, killing everywhere. When will it all end, what will be left and where will we both be?[3] An unprofitable line of thought, as all one can do is try to do one's own job as efficiently as possible and hope for the best, but it all does get on one's mind occasionally and I miss badly not being able to pour all my little worries out to you.

Re the transit permit: I was too late to see NL on Saturday 16th and had to take to the seas on Monday 18th not getting in again till the afternoon of Friday 22nd (yesterday). I went to beard them today with the Agent's letter, only to find Burgess away at Camp and NL off for a week's leave at Fanling. Altogether very difficult with these periodical five-day absences of mine, they make it all so slow. Incidently the *Neptuna* has been put back three weeks, but officially I don't know that yet. If the *Tjinegara/Neptuna* show is allowed, your stopover could then be not less than a month, even if we were stopped from making it permanent, which I don't think we would be. There is one

---

3   This was no doubt triggered by the Blitz on London and other cities, which continued throughout the winter.

thing of course to bear in mind re returning to HK, if anything were to go wrong here you would have to take your chances about getting out. Mind you, I don't think it will, as I feel the Japs are in a pretty bad way and not far from collapse. Also the sinking of the Italian battleships at Taranto will have freed three of ours, which are now potentially able to be sent to Singapore.[4] I think the risk of anything going wrong here is slight, but it is always there and must be considered.

Life in the Wavy Navy shows signs of easing up a bit in the future anyhow, as regards time on and time off, as we look like being in for longer than we are out, and the principle of a fortnight leave per year seems to have been accepted. I don't know if I am kidding myself but I am assuming this is as a result of my moan of a month or two ago. I have come to the conclusion that kicking up a fuss every now and then is a sound principle and I intend to continue it. I have a fairly fruity one on hand now, about accommodation for crew, and I will be amused to see what the reaction will be.

It is high time we were all together, necessary separation is one thing, but this, which I feel is so unnecessary, galls me beyond words. One is up against officialdom and a maze of regulations, and never having been accustomed to cope with either, I am not sufficiently well versed in the stratagems and cheating which are necessary if one is going to avoid being caught in a web of red tape.

To Therese   29 November

The news came through yesterday that your transit permit to pass through HK had been granted, but I did not do anything about it as I wished to see it definitely in writing that the *Tjinegara* was included as well as the *Neptuna*. I have not yet managed to do so and do not like to press the point, owing to the disparity in dates occasioned by the late sailing of the *Neptuna*.

Luscombe of the police tells me that he will be wiring to the British Consul in Manila to say you may leave for HK in transit to Australia and I hope he mentions the *Tjinegara* in his wire. I have booked your passage through Cooks, so you may apply to the JCJL in Manila for the ticket and, if there is any argument, say the British Consul has been advised from the Colonial Secretary's Office in HK. I hope it all goes

---

[4] In December 1941 the modern battleship HMS *Prince of Wales*, the battle cruiser HMS *Repulse* and four destroyers were sent to Singapore. The *Prince of Wales* and *Repulse* were lost to a heavy Japanese air attack on 10 December 1941. Beevor, pp. 254/6&7.

The Family   *Peter and HP*

HP and the Amah   *HP's first Christmas card – La Cigale 1*

smoothly your end and that you won't have any trouble. When you definitely get your ticket for the *Tjinegara*, and are all set to sail in her, send me a wire to say you are travelling in her.

If the *Tjinegara* section is not allowed, I doubt if there is much I can do this end. The transit rules definitely state not more than a week and people here (officials that is) are sticking to the rules like glue. It will then remain to wait for the *Neptuna*, which seems to be a rather movable feast, probably leaving Manila about the middle of January.

It is lovely to think of you back here in just over a fortnight and I feel there must be a catch to it. When I get your wire I will try to get 168 The Peak back and will also endeavour to find the Amah you had engaged. The question of the bond[5] is not yet definite, whether I have to put one up or not, but that can wait until later.

I am beginning to feel definitely optimistic about the war, mainly over this show in Albania. I fancy the Italians went in on their own without consulting Hitler and the Italian Army was against trying it in the winter, while the Fascist party said, 'Yes, go to it.'[6] Two rifts in the latter. There seems to be little question that the Italians are now on the run and once they start running they take a lot of stopping. If we can pound them good and hard with the RAF over the next few weeks, they may have a second Dunkerque on the shores of Albania, and they won't get out as well as we did. Stretching it a bit further, it might put them out of the war if we offered them an easy peace, which would solve the naval problem in the Mediterranean and hence the Jap question out here, as we would be able to put a battle fleet into the Pacific. This may seem optimistic but I don't think it is unduly so; Churchill believes in hitting hard when he hits, and I feel the present is a splendid opportunity.

I have sold *Monsoon* to Carter and Haynes for $2,100 and was sad to do it but it seemed the only thing.

Must end now, as I feel too excited to write sensibly.

To Therese   1 December
If it all breaks down we will have to wait for the *Neptuna* until the middle of January,

---

5   Maybe some form of guarantee that Therese would move on to Australia.
6   This is all correct, Mussolini did not consult Hitler, the army commanders were against the invasion. The Italians had eventually to retreat. Beevor, p. 148.

but I do hope you will catch the *Tjinegara* and be here for Christmas. It all seems too good to be true and I feel there must be a catch.

Therese's diary records that she left Baguio on 6 December and caught the 'Tjinegara' from Manila, arriving in Hong Kong 12 December. Peter took her out to a 'gala dinner' on the following Saturday, and thereafter there were many social engagements to make up for the preceding five months.

CHAPTER 10

A Sad Departure

March to April 1941

Peter and Therese had three happy months in Hong Kong, from 12 December 1940 to 5 March 1941, interspersed with Peter's naval patrols. They dined out, played golf, went walking and to the cinema. They cancelled the sailing to Australia on the 'Neptuna' on 13 January. This good fortune and gaiety could not last though; a policeman called at the house on 22 February to tell Therese that she must go to Australia. HP's christening was organised for 2 March.

She and HP sailed on 5 March 1941 on the 'Nellore'. Therese recalled in her diary that day she felt 'heartbroken and miserable' and Peter later said that they had made a bit of a 'scene' at the time of departure. They were prepared for the worst, as all the family photograph albums travelled with Therese. They did not resist the evacuation order, maybe unlike those who had resisted the original evacuation and remained in Hong Kong, the permit gave the authorities the necessary legal powers to enforce it. Peter states subsequently that he was very sad, but unlike previously he did not protest about the evacuation and say it was totally unnecessary. It was around this time that there were frequent provocations from the Japanese and the British Government was concerned that these did not escalate into war.[1] Maybe this and a change in Hong Kong thinking influenced him.

On her way the 'Nellore' called in at Manila, which must have been a sad reminder to Therese of the moment she left the Philippine Islands three months earlier full of hope and excitement for the future. A week after their departure they crossed the equator and Therese noted it was very hot. They finally arrived in Sydney on 22 March.

During their stay in Hong Kong, UE and AE had received bad news: at the beginning of January their only son Jack, who was in the RAF, had been killed in a flying accident in England.

Peter to Therese   6 March
I am writing this the day after you left so as to catch tomorrow's Rangoon airmail and make sure of having a letter to greet you on arrival in Sydney. Hence as you can imagine there will not be much news.

---
1 Welsh, p. 410.

HP's christening at the Peak Church. The Rev Brown, Peter, HP and Therese, Eva, Edgar and Fergie

It was miserable seeing you go off yesterday and I loathed it. Getting back to No. 191 in the evening with no sweetie and no little HP to greet me was also depressing in the extreme. Still, if it has to be, there is no use being too depressed and one must concentrate on the brighter side of things. The two and half months you were here were grand and as far as I was concerned, I think they were the happiest in our married life so far. We seemed to understand each other a great deal better and come closer to each other, not that we were exactly distant before. I suppose it is the result of having to struggle against something, to wit the evacuation, which makes one struggle as a team. It was a wonderful interlude in a pretty dead patch, and it was grand to see young HP for so long. I think he is a great little fellow and that he will develop into something quite remarkable.

After I had left the *Nellore*, I started to have horrible fears about your cabin and whether you were even going to be able to get the cot into it. I hope it has worked out alright or alternatively you were able to shift to another one. Possibly they had a folding cot on board, which you could put in the cabin.

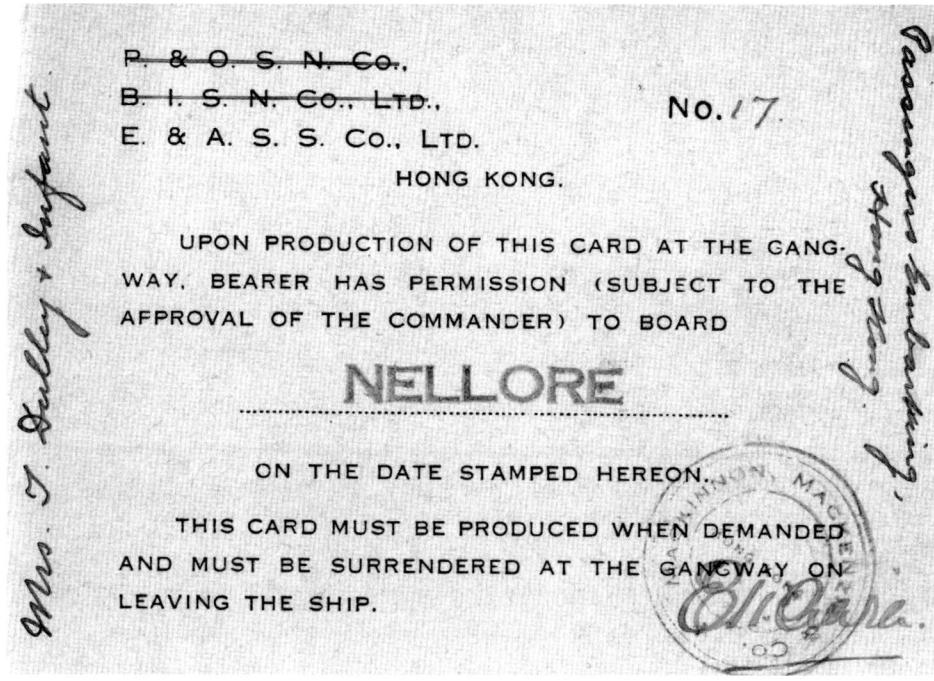

'Nellore' Boarding Pass

I saw Webb (Alex Ross)[2] in the street this afternoon and he told me I ought to get about $2,200 for the car (we paid $3,500 in 1938) so if I get an offer around that figure I will take it I think. Another link with the days of peace gone, and I am attached to our little EOF [their car: British registration letters] but there is no use suffering from undue sentiment in time of war.

I wired you today at Manila, so as to make sure of catching you and I hope you received it. I am going to dinner with Griff and Fergie tonight; if you recollect we were both invited to a party postponed from the last week of my leave. I had clean forgotten about it until I met Griff in the club at lunchtime, just after you had sailed.

AE is full of ideas to rig up 191 with all suitable ARP gear such as buckets of sand and stirrup pumps. UE is a bit sceptical, but willing to cooperate etc. if it shows the slightest sign of being useful.

I hope you will settle down soon into congenial surroundings with pleasant people, so that your exile may be made as affable as possible.

---

2   No explanation is given for using the two names.

Therese in EOF

To Therese   12 March

Very many thanks for your cable from Manila, from which I was very glad to hear that all was going well, even if rather hot. I feel deeply ashamed that I completely forgot to see the *Nellore* Purser before the ship sailed, to find out if you could have a double cabin to yourself. Shame on me, but what with the luggage not arriving, the shortness of time and the fact that neither of us felt just so hot, it was possibly understandable. However, I hope you coped with the situation in your efficient way and moved into a larger cabin fairly soon.

    Just as well I got off last week's letter to you in fair time as I was chased out on the briny wave at lunchtime Friday and I did not get back until Tuesday 4.00 pm (11 March). I got a letter off to your mother by the USA Clipper airmail today, telling her all about your leaving Hong Kong and about your prospects in Australia. Two days after you had left, we had a cable from her which read as follows: 'Tonbridge 6 March 12.02 – Dulley Davidson 191 The Peak Hong Kong – So disappointed very distressing for us all. Please convey loving sympathy [to] Therese Sander.' If this letter does not finish up too heavy I will put the actual cable in.

The following day, Friday, I got chased out to sea at 2.00 pm instead of 8.30 am Saturday, and felt very jaundiced about the whole situation. However, four days of the same old patrol routine brought me back to realities, and I am now almost settled into it again. So far as I can see from the present prospects, there is all the earmarks of a razz up on, so we are not likely to have much time in the future to sit down and harbour over our woes.

We got back about 3.30 pm Tuesday only to find the tugs and *Cornflower* were all out at the buoys in the harbour for an indefinite period. I will admit I was extremely annoyed about our being out at a buoy again, it put us back to where we were in July/August/September last year, but I was intensely tickled to find *Cornflower* was at one too. When the tugs were at buoys and *Cornflower* was alongside, the latter was extremely superior about the disadvantages of being at a buoy. Now, however, they will have a little practical experience of those disadvantages and I am interested to see that there is now an hourly boat routine from 6.00 am onwards, instead of four boats a day as there used to be when *Cornflower* was alongside and we were on the buoys.

Answer, for the time being slightly chaotic conditions, added to which I have got to do under strict instructions from Commodore, four Lewis Gun lectures, before the 20 March. I have not done one yet and there are only three more [training sessions] so I do not quite know how it is to be arranged, but I suppose 'God will provide.' This morning I was to do a Lewis Gun lecture in *Cornflower* (at a buoy in the harbour) at 10.00 am, probable duration one and a half hours, and an Anti-Submarine practice at 10.45 am in the Dockyard. So we plumped for the A/S practice and it went off rather successfully. On the first run, I having navigated the ship with considerable success, but in the last moment of crisis found that the glass over the indicator was all clouded up with damp and I could not see the tell-tale marks on the paper. We had time to wipe it over with a handkerchief, so I let the depth charges off fifty yards late. On the second run, I got one charge within ten yards of the submarine and on the third positively spattered it with depth charges. Most encouraging because the last time we did an anti-submarine practice, both Wilson and I were miles off it, and any submarine would have been perfectly safe in our immediate vicinity.

You will be pleased to hear that Amah has been taken on by Marjorie Fortescue from 1 June, so looks like having a reasonably settled job. I paid her up to the end of March so she will only have two months off the payroll and I will try to provide some additional help.

Continued   13 March

Mrs Hancock phoned up this evening and said she had seen you in Manila. 'Charming, resigned and happy.' I gathered that everything was going reasonably well on the ship and that you had managed to fit into your rather minute cabin, also that the stewardess was registering in an affable sort of way. I was very glad to get first news of you so early in the day and to hear that everything was going fairly well.

Antonia is on her way to Sydney, there have been difficulties, so I fancy she is [now] flying. Her address, so far is C/O Bank of New South Wales and I have given Potts yours, which he will send down to her, so I hope you see something of each other.

On the 16 March in the second half of the voyage the 'Nellore' picked up the Barrier Reef pilot near Thursday Island.

To Therese   19 March

I was so glad to hear that everything was going reasonably well and I hope the trip settled down after Manila, and was fairly pleasant from then on. My experience is that most trips on board ship look pretty mouldy at the start (unless you are frightfully young, inexperienced and enthusiastic) but gradually acquire a definitely human outlook as the trip proceeds and you get to know the more affable people on board.

Mrs Hancock was in this evening before dinner with her news of having seen you in Manila. I felt, but did not tell her, that you were giving a false impression; resigned possibly, but happy certainly not. However, I fancy she was trying to hand on a good and cheering report, so bless her for any slight in exactitude of description. She seems very worried about Marion, whom you will now have observed at close quarters [on ship as she was also being evacuated to Australia] so the following may amuse you: (1) Marion is full of life and intent on having a good time, as against settling down with one eye on marriage; (2) Marion will lack the steadying influence of a home in the years immediately after she leaves school; (3) Marion suffers from lack of any ability to distinguish between a gentleman and the other kind; (4) Marion is going to be away from them for at least three years, so they will lose her completely and be unable to help or influence her during her formative years. I sympathise with her over (2) but from what I have gathered of the wench, never having met her or set eyes on her, I should say that she will probably come out on the right side. She may be the world's friend with rather cheesy little ship's officers, just as she has been with second rate Americans up at Baguio, but doubt if she will come to any harm over it.

There is a new development[3] in the Naval Volunteer Reserve here, but I am not at liberty to talk about it at the moment. It may flare up in the newspapers, here and outside in a big way, in which case you will probably spot it. It concerns ships and is a turn very much in the right direction, but enough said beyond that until everything is decided. In any event we are due for a further period of change, but beneficial change so far as one can see.

I was up at 168 this afternoon and have sorted out the things to be packed up, also a few things to be brought around to No. 191. It was a sad business and I did not like doing it but there you are, it is no good being squeamish or sentimental. One may feel so but it is no good giving way to it. Life seems very dead and pointless here since you left and I feel very sad when I cannot manage to occupy my mind with other things, so I try the latter as far as possible. It is only for a definite number of months, probably for fewer than we expect, so it is up to us to remain cheerful as long as it lasts.

My latest occupation is navigation. I feel that it is high time I knew something about it if I am to look like a sailor and when I see some of the drunken old deadbeats that hold master's tickets and take ships around the world, I feel surely I can do just as well, if not better. By dint of a bit of 'organisation' I am now armed with a sextant (borrowed from *Cornflower*), a copy of *Norie's Nautical Tables*[4] (borrowed from the Marine Superintendent in JMs) and a *Nautical Almanac* for 1941 obtained on false pretences from the Chart Depot in the Dockyard. With these three weapons and an hour's 'Navigation for Children' from Stevenson I am equipped to find out, when sitting off Se Tanter,[5] whether I really am there by taking sun sights and applying formulae to the same. We get out tomorrow for three days and I feel rather like a prospective

---

3 This would appear to relate to Peter's journey to Aden and maybe AN Shields resigning his post as Commodore to the HKRNVR, and Petrie taking over with Vernall as his deputy and Peter as First Lieutenant.
4 These mathematical tables were first published in 1803. It has been a bestseller ever since, and despite developments in navigation, is an essential requirement for learning and practising astro-navigation http://www.sailingbooks.co.uk/norries-nautical-tables?search=nories.14 July 2015.
5 Clearly a place that Therese would have known on the Hong Kong coastline.

bride, all coy and fluttery. Maybe my next will register the depths of despair or not even mention it, but at the moment I feel just too bridal and virginal to be true. I have an interest and I am at the gates of the great unknown, so big things loom before me.

UE has written in a very shrewd letter to Govt. about the cost of your passage to Australia. There are apparently no legal grounds but from the way he has written the letter he has left them very little loophole to explain why they will not pay. In fact the idea is rather to shame them into paying. Did I tell you in my last their latest idea of a joke. You will probably recollect that quite a lot of people went, under their own steam to Victoria, British Columbia. Their husbands in HK have now had notice that after three months they will not be able to send them any more remittances in Canadian Dollars. Not a word about how their wives are to live or an offer of passage to Australia. Our wonderful Govt. again. When this war is over I feel I will probably start to lead a sort of Watt Tyler revolt amongst HK citizens.

I am still definitely optimistic about the outcome of the war, the only dark spot I see being our Merchant Supply losses. I have great hopes for the Balkan Campaign now we have definitely put troops in Greece. I feel the Germans are in Bulgaria to protect their flank, not to attack Greece and help the Waps,[6] who are just about sunk anyway. My bet is that we will move up the Eastern (Black Sea) Coast of Bulgaria and Romania, with a combined Naval, Military and Air Force manoeuvre, similar to that in Libya, which would put us preciously near the Romanian oilfields. Once we get those the Germans are sunk, but even if we don't get them we may be able to bomb either the fields or the transport of oil from them to such an extent that the fields are useless.

To Therese   22 March

I was glad to get your two cables, one from Townsville and the other from Townend in Sydney, saying you had arrived safely. I gather that airmail via Rangoon only take about ten days as I saw a letter of Townend's to Hall dated 14 March a day or so ago,[7] so I should be hearing from you quite soon.

We took out an American Newsreel cameraman, who took a shot of the ship, so don't be surprised if you suddenly see the famous tug on the silver screen.[8] I had my

---

6 War time slang for the Italians.
7 This shows that Peter still occasionally visited the Jardines' office.
8 The cinemas would show a weekly newsreel before the advent of television.

first experiments in navigation by the simple process of fixing our position exactly by compass, and then seeing how near I could get by sun sights through a sextant. It is nothing like so difficult as one would imagine, provided you are content to do it by rule of thumb and not worry about the 'whys and wherefores' of the formulae and are not distressed by such terms as log haversines.

On my first day's efforts I got the longitude correct to 600 yards on two separate occasions and I was so surprised I nearly fell overboard. Latitude was not so good and our nearest was about three miles out. However, it struck me as quite a fair start and I intend to build upon it.

On Monday I went to lunch with a French couple called Gardau, she being English however; you may recollect that I said years ago we should try to look them up. The connection is Aunt Helen and the place she goes to stay in France, Cancale by name. The Gardaus know Madame R, the widow who keeps the pension at Cancale; they are a pleasant couple of about our respective ages. He is in the Banque de l'Indo Chine and she was a Shanghai girl, which is presumably where she met him. They have a flat at the Peak Mansion (French flats near the Peak Train) and a small boy of three and a half.[9]

The E's seem to be a bit depressed and gloomy, partly at your departure and partly because the loneliness caused by Jack's death is starting to sink in seriously. It is inevitable that the first reaction is shock, tense and possibly rather theatrical, but when that wears off you have time to settle down and realise what you really have lost, and they have lost a lot. It is terribly sad for them but there is little one can do except be as bright and cheerful as possible. Lord knows, I don't feel very bright and cheerful although I can always put up a fairly good imitation of it. Your second departure has been a sadder one than your first, and I feel it down to the bottom of my tummy.

Harry Owen Hughes is in hospital with some undiagnosed complaint and suspected TB.[10] I hope for his sake it is not so as he will have to leave Hong Kong and how is he then to support a wife and four children. His father cannot keep on in Harry Wicking & Co. forever, and when he finishes what is Harry to live on if he cannot carry on the business? Not so good.

---

9 Like many of their compatriots across the world, as a result of being in Hong Kong they had avoided the invasion of France and the war for the time being.
10 TB was quite common among Europeans in the Far East at that time. Jack Dulley contracted it in India before the war.

I had a letter from Roger (Grieve) by a recent mail; he is still at Leith in the same ship. Dean Wilson has been appointed Bishop of Singapore an odd reward compared with Harry Baines who only got a slum parish in Birmingham or some such place. Northcote is back and Govt. House is on the edge of falling down.[11] All quiet here re the Japs and no further parries; Gardau told me he had it from a friend recently returned from Japan that the privation there is becoming very real and acute. I hope they will soon have had enough.

Au revoir, sweetie, and I long to see you again.

To Lizzie Blunt   27 March

Very many thanks for yours of the 23 October last, with all your good wishes [for the birth of HP], which I was most glad to get. It was good to hear that you were all well, since in these difficult times one never quite knows what has happened to everyone.

Since the war started my correspondence has got a bit out of control, so I have not the vaguest idea when I wrote to you last. I am in command of a sea going tug of some 470 tons, with three other British officers and a Chinese crew. We patrol the waters of Hong Kong with increasing vigilance and wait for the Japanese, who don't come and to my way of thinking won't either. I have learnt a certain amount about how to be a sailor, mainly by bitter experience, but of course it is very boring work patrolling forever, with very little incident. However, if we did not do it, the Navy would have to, so one can feel that one is relieving RN officers for duties for which they are better fitted.

Everything is perfectly quiet and normal here. HK is a pretty lethargic place and we do not work ourselves up into a panic about the prospect of an invasion. If it comes, it comes, and we will do our best to repel it, but until then we just go on with our normal lives and try to get the local volunteer units as large and efficient as possible.

The evacuation of course is a definite pill. Someone, as yet unknown, but said to be from the home government, panicked them into it, and a fine panic it was. There was little or no previous organisation and no legal powers taken to enforce it, with the result that those who refused to go, or who came back quickly, are still in the Colony and sitting pretty, while those who went like lambs at the start and stayed away, cannot get back until it is called off, presumably at the end of the war.

---

11 Sir Geoffrey Northcote was governor for a relatively short time during which he suffered from ill health. Welsh, p. 403.

Therese went out with the first lot and HP was born in Baguio, a hill station in the Philippines. Therese stayed on at Baguio for a while, after the main body of evacuees had gone onto Australia, and in December I managed to arrange for her to pass through Hong Kong on her way to Australia. I hoped that once she was in the Colony, the Govt. with their usual inefficiency would lose sight of her, but not so. She was forced to move on just over three weeks ago.

As you probably know my mother is back in London again, which I do not much like, but you cannot manage people's affairs for them. I have not heard from Jack for a while but I gather there is some prospect of his getting into the clerical side of the RAF. Evelyn is safely down near Shrewsbury with the transplanted convent [from Bayswater, London. She was Mother Superior to a Catholic teaching order and like many schools in London they moved out of London to avoid the Blitz].

As regards the war I am a convinced optimist. I don't think the Japs will do anything out here, as they have already had about a skinful with the Chinese war, and taking on a new one is no solution to their present troubles.

When I read of the air raids at home, I fear you must all be having a pretty bad time, and it makes me feel a bit of a cad to be out here where all is quiet and peaceful, not even any black-outs. However, I hope and think it will be over soon and we can then get back to being civilised human beings once again.

To Therese   10 April

Very many thanks for your most noble fifteen-page letter written from the ship. I was sorry you had it so distressingly hot on board the *Nellore*, but that is now a thing of the past and you will be into autumn [in Sydney] by the time you get this.

It was most noble of you to cope with washing nappies in all that heat on board, and I admire you for it. Don't wear yourself out doing too much, lovey, our funds are not colossal but they should be enough to keep you in reasonable comfort. As regard the guesthouse, I feel that should be OK. As a bachelor I used to work on the idea that one's board and lodging should be only one third of the total income, in order to allow a reasonable amount of money to spend on amusements and small luxuries.

I am almost never in the Club or the Hotel in the evening. I much prefer to go back to 191 and have a quiet evening with the E's. Somehow I seem to have lost the taste for bachelor drinking parties. I suppose you have domesticated me.

AE had it from Bill Williams that he hopes the evacuation might be called off next September, if nothing goes wrong here or at home. I trust that is not her imagination or exaggeration: I fancy what he meant that by next September we should know whether there really is any Japanese threat to this place, and if there is obviously not, then the evacuation is rather futile. I saw Ralph today; he seems to be rather chafing over the whole show, which is not surprising, and has some rather wild schemes for getting Mrs Ralph back. Mrs Bonsfield is back, incidentally on health grounds, but goes on to Canada in a few weeks' time.

I felt possibly that Townend might be able to fix for an Amah to enter Australia much more easily, so I have approached him about it in my letter. I have a vague idea that the whole show may be off as they will not allow any more Amahs[12] to be sent. However, if you feel you would like one, wire me and I will start things at this end.

---

12 Owing to the White Australia Policy; see footnote 34 in Chapter 8.

CHAPTER 11

Preparing for the Voyage
April to May 1941

At the beginning of April Therese went house hunting in Sydney at Double Bay and it was possibly there that she booked a room at Miss Garra's at fourteen shillings per week and moved in on 18 April. Maybe to celebrate she bought a bottle of wine and sherry for five shillings and nine pence. Therese went out sometimes for lunch and tea, but there is no mention of anything for her birthday on 23 May.

Letter of 10 April to Therese   continued from Chapter 10

It is about ten days since I wrote to you, as I had to post my last before going on patrol. When we got back we had a hell of a scramble to get the ship ready for the Dock on Monday, having only heard about it on Friday afternoon when we came in. No change in fact, everything done with a grand last minute scramble. Everything is now dirt and chaos with Chinese everywhere, as it will continue to be for some stated period, about three weeks probably. However, it gets us another of those Deepwater Bay shows,[1] which is developing next week. I feel being out there again so soon would remind me rather too keenly of your last week here.[2]

The Dockyard are working for most of Easter, so I suppose I will be hanging about the place, wondering if there is something I should be doing but am not.

I still miss you badly and feel there is a blank spot in my life, which will not be filled until you return. Somehow your two and half months here seem to have rubbed things in a bit. I think it was the happiest so far in our married life.

PS: AE told me she intentionally tried to remain cheerful last January so as not to be a gloom spot for your stay in HK, which possibly explains a lot in her attitude to Jack's death, which we both found difficult to understand.

---

1 HKRNVR training.
2 From when the policeman had called at their house they had met for lunch each day at Deep Water Bay and even managed to go for a walk one afternoon.

The Peak, above and HMS 'Tamar' in the RN Dockyard, right

To Therese   15 April

I am starting my letter a bit early this week, as I am tied up in the Dockyard with *Cornflower* and the rest of the bunch are round at Deepwater Bay for a few days, so I have to send my letter out there to be censored.

We came out of dry dock last Friday (Good Friday) there seems to have been a bit of a frisk up in the Dockyard routine recently. We have been alongside the wall since then, with hordes of Chinese workmen doing not very much; however there seems to have been a tendency, so far, to do slightly more work than a year ago, which was my main experience of Naval Yards, so things seem to be improving slightly.

I spent a major portion of the weekend messing around the Dockyard and I got very bored in the process; we have another tug also docking, alongside us. But our

officers are getting shipped off one by one, so we are down to myself and one other, while the other tug has a cadet and a spare Sub Lieut. for the time being.

Val Killery is definitely going to Singapore, on some rather ill-defined job which is probably connected with Ministry of Economic Warfare.[3] He is presumably flying out there and has possibly arrived, Peggy[4] is not going with him.

---

3 The origins of Ministry of Economic Warfare can be traced back to cabinet approval for the Special Operations Executive (SOE), which was officially formed by the Minister of Economic Warfare, Hugh Dalton, in July 1940, to operate in occupied Europe. The same year they were preparing plans for operations in South East Asia. They organised resistance organisations and guerrilla armies in those parts of China occupied by the Japanese. They also launched 'Operation Remorse' (1944–45), aimed at protecting the economic and political status of Hong Kong. In China, Force 136 engaged in covert trading of goods and currencies and raised £77m to assist Allied prisoners of war and to enable the smooth return to pre-war conditions locally.
   http://en.wikipedia.org/wiki/Special_Operations_Executive#Later_analysis_and_commentaries. 13 November 2014.
4 His wife and Therese's cousin.

Well this is my last sheet in the block so I must finish. I heard from my mother that Jack [Dulley] is now in the land side of the Air Force, so I have written to congratulate him. All the best, my sweet, and I have seldom felt so low as last Saturday with you, HP and the E's all away, and myself alone.

To Therese   24 April

I was glad to hear you had achieved something reasonable in the way of new quarters and I hope they may prove pleasant and a permanency, as you naturally don't want to be moving all the while. I quite understand what you mean about leaving the homely, friendly atmosphere of the Townends and having to strike out on your own. It is a shame you should ever have to do it. I hope you will find some companionable people at the Guest House and manage to get hold of a reasonable girl to help you with HP. I feel that would be more satisfactory than an Amah; the latter is rather a responsibility and would work out pretty expensive if you were only in Sydney for a short stay. I agree you do not want to get permanently stuck in a house and turn into a drudge. I want my attractive wife returned to me in due course, not a household drudge.

I went to see the film *All This and Heaven Too* (Bette Davis and Charles Boyer) with AE the other afternoon. The production and acting was excellent but of course it is somewhat gloomy. We went to the 7.15 show, as I had been out at Fanling with Griff in the afternoon and so on to the Gloucester's for dinner afterwards. I think AE enjoyed her little toot and I will try to repeat it. UE did not come, as it is a bit off his beat.

The worthy tug still sits alongside the Dockyard wall, receiving the loving but somewhat ponderously slow ministrations of those famous repairers of ships, HM Dockyard. We should take to the seas in a few days' time, but it is anybody's guess whether we will. If we do it will be a grand scramble at the last moment, which is all rather galling after vast hordes of coolies have been sitting doing practically nothing for weeks on end. The war news does not look too hot at the moment and I gather from today's papers that there is a section of the population in Australia, which is pretty sore about Australian forces bearing the brunt of the show in Greece.[5] I sympathise with them up to a point, but you must leave it to the Higher Command to hand out the dirt impartially between forces from various parts of the Empire.

---

5   The expeditionary force consisting of Australian and New Zealand troops had to be evacuated from Greece with the loss of 2,000 killed and 14,000 taken prisoner. Beevor, p. 163.

I fancy we will be lucky to hang on at all, even in Southern Greece, but at least we seem to have inflicted very heavy losses on the Germans in an area where they presumably expected to get their result by treachery as against fighting. If they get the whole Balkans, I suppose they will try a drive through Turkey at the Persian oilfields and another drive eastwards from Tripoli to the Suez Canal. I feel, given the forces, we should be able to scotch the latter with considerable loss to the Germans, while the former depends very much on whether the Turks fight or let the Germans through. However, even if the Turks don't fight (which I think they will if attacked) it is a very long trip over difficult country and they will be acquiring extremely long lines of communication, which do not lend themselves to Blitz warfare at which they appear to be artists.[6] I feel that their moves in the Mediterranean Zone are really blinds before the invasion of Britain either this spring or this summer, and that they will have to go for a decision this year or see their military machine go off half cock much as it did in the last war, with the prospect of disintegration on the home front, which means a complete eventual breakdown. If they try an invasion I have no doubt as to the outcome and we should then be able to see the end of the war in sight by the autumn, even if it has not ended. I received a letter from you just before I left the Dockyard this evening, but I was superintending a move of two tugs along the wall, mainly done by wires and hope, and as it was raining I put it in my oilskin pocket. When I got back on board to change before returning to 191, I then left the letter in the aforesaid oilskin and am unable to answer it at the moment.

Continued   25 April

Yes, I am getting all keen about navigation but have not done any since we have been in Dock. Falconers were looking out for a sextant for me and have a quite nice one for $65, but I do not think that will be necessary as I hope to get one from Naval Stores. At the moment I have *Cornflower*'s and I will not put down any money unless I have to. After the war they will be going at four a penny and I will think of buying one then.

To Therese   3 May

Re the tea question, I fancied I had explained in part that the favourite Australian meal

---

6 In June, Turkey entered a friendship agreement with Germany and later declared neutrality in the German-Russian war. https://en.wikipedia.org/wiki/1941-in-Turkey. 14 September 2016.

is 'a dish of tea and a lay off'.[7]

Our three weeks docking was due to finish on Saturday, 26 April. On Wednesday 23rd the after peak tank[8] was leaking into the stokers mess; it was repaired and when we filled it again on Thursday it still leaked. Repaired again but on Saturday it still leaked. In the meanwhile we had got steam up, but when Lloyd's Survey tested the safety valves at 11.45 am Saturday (Zero hour for completion 12.00) one of them leaked and the forward boiler had to be blown down.[9]

I then considered we could not finish on time, so packed up at 1.00 pm Saturday and got off on a bit of a tootle with Wilson, his wife and Vernall.[10] We had dinner at the Wilsons' flat, went to the VAD's show, *Pure and Simple*, at the China Fleet Club (produced by Fortescue) and repaired to the hotel, where Vernall and I drank far too much whisky. Sunday was not a good day, but I found the engineering end of the Dockyard had slipped a quick one across me by repairing the safety valve so soon as the boiler was blown down (someone must have burnt his fingers getting it off) and then harrying the crew to get the steam up again at 6.30 pm Saturday. So the engineering wallahs could say they had finished it on time (i.e. on the Saturday).

We were due to go out on Monday but we just sat on the wall until they repaired the after peak tank, which they finished at noon, I then fixed for 150 tons of coal; we started coaling[11] at Kowloon at 4.00 pm Monday, finished at 3.00 am Tuesday and sailed at 8.00 am.

On Tuesday afternoon we were hauled back to the harbour for orders, arriving 7.00 pm, were served out three lengths of towing wire (one so rusted it could not be used) 'Scout's'[12] chart folio, three days food and a navigator and told to find a lighter that had broken adrift from a tow off Amoy,[13] *Thanet*[14] (Mowlem's ship) was also on the party and got away an hour or two ahead of us. We sailed at 11.00 pm, cleared from Waglan at

---

7   Australian slang for a rest.
8   The after peak tank was used for storing fresh water for the crew and boilers for a long voyage.
9   To reduce the steam pressure in the boiler.
10 Peter's Acting Commanding Officer.
11 This was often carried out by large numbers of coolies carrying sacks of coal on their shoulders.
12 An 'S' Class Destroyer.
13 Amoy was on the mainland opposite Taiwan. It had been a Treaty Port until the Japanese invaded it in 1938. http://gwulo.com/A-brief-history-of-international-Amoy. 18 November 2014.
14 An S Class Destroyer. She left Hong Kong on 8 December, just before the invasion, but was later sunk by the Japanese Navy off Endau in 1942. Banham, p. 31.

midnight and at 12.30 the navigator started to spew. He was the skipper of the ill-fated *Sirdhana*,[15] which blew up on the minefield at Singapore, and who is now a Lieut. in *Cornflower*. By 1.00 am the navigator was out cold and did not revive until 8.00 pm next night; I have never seen anything to touch it, every time he stood up he was sick. Well, there we were, on our first trip to sea, with a passed out navigator, so I had to assume those functions.

Our troubles, however, had not properly started; we were bucking into a NE monsoon swell, water everywhere and soon the flanges of the anchor hawser pipes (which had just been repaired during our docking) started to leak, with the result that the floor of the cabins and wardroom were awash and had to be bailed out constantly. I turned in about 1.30 am (Wednesday morning), was sick once, went to bed again and then the mushroom cowl to the ventilator over my bunk was not properly screwed down, so a large green sea came straight down the ventilator and onto the bed. I then proceeded to be sick again, three quarters of an hour's sleep and it was time for me to do the 4.00–8.00 watch. When daylight came we were well out to sea, no sign of land and the navigator still passed out. At 8.00 am I slowly and laboriously worked out our dead reckoning position,[16] got a sun sight, worked it out and it was only about three miles off our dead reckoning position. Bending over the chart table was not my strong suit and I was sick again. This process took about one and a half hours as I found the old brain was not concentrating very well. Breakfast was conspicuous by the poor muster; most of the crew were being sick. I then snoozed for an hour or so and repeated my navigation efforts at noon. I got what later proved to be a very fair position at noon, and we then decided to cut in towards the next promontory and make for landfall. This panned out almost perfectly, as we picked up a lighthouse by Swatow first shot and we could not have been more than a mile out; we then carried

---

15 A colleague of Oliver Lindsay (see Bibliography) may have experienced the minefield episode. On reaching Calcutta he was put on board the *Sedana* [The ship was named *Sirdhana* in Peter' letters and a wreck website confirms this was the ship] a small cargo ship carrying passengers. On leaving Singapore on 13 November 1939 he heard an explosion the port side, followed by screaming. The *Sedana* had entered a British minefield, watched by a gun battery on shore, which was not authorised to warn the ship. The minefield had apparently been marked in the wrong place on the *Sedana*'s charts. Rescuers were reluctant to enter the minefield. Twenty passengers were killed. Lindsay, p. 30.
16 Dead reckoning is the process of calculating the ships current position by using a previously determined position, or fix, and advancing that position based upon known or estimated speeds, time and course. https://en.wikipedia.org/wiki/Dead_reckoning. 26 July 2015.

on up the coast to meet HMS *Thanet*, who had already collected the lighter[17] and met them about sixty miles SW of Amoy at 11.30 pm Wednesday; when we turned to come in company with them all was lovely in the garden. The swell had already run off a lot and was behind us so we had scarcely any motion; it was a lovely night and Thursday was a beautiful day, real picnic stuff. We got to the Ninepins at 4.00 pm and took the lighter over from Thanet at 7.00 pm off Stanley. Mowlem made very heavy weather of getting in the towing wires and cables. I wanted to suggest we did it on our winch, but I felt RN would not appreciate suggestions from RNVR so I let well alone. They had most of the *Thanet*'s crew on the lighter heaving it in by hand, and they were so fed up when they finished that they proceeded to sink a junk on their way home.

We got in about 9.00 pm Thursday, and Friday was a grand flap making arrangements about going back to dock to get various leaks fixed up. So I am afraid I did not manage to get a letter off to you. Today (Saturday) we are back in the naval camber and maybe the Dockyard, if they feel very kindly disposed, will start work on Monday.

Continued   4 May

Thinking over the trip to Amoy, in slightly further retrospect, I am very glad that I had done something about this navigation question in advance, as otherwise the only sensible thing for me to do would have been to turn back and I don't like letting the side down that way. I assure you I am going to have some pretty keen classes in navigation and pilotage for the other officers over the next month or so, as I don't like to be left holding the baby with no one else knowing his backside from his elbow, as was the case.

I would not sweat yourself about the war news too much. As I see it, the Germans have done three very successful campaigns (and hats off to them) Poland, Flanders and Greece. Their technique in all this was as old as the hills, bringing overwhelming force to bear at a given point. In each case they massed colossal forces on the border, struck without warning and very hard and had short lines of communication until the battle was won. In Poland and Greece they had the opposition heavily outnumbered, while in France the French packed up. But can they go on doing this? In Libya, which I think will be their first major reverse, they are trying to attack the Suez from Tripoli with no sea communications along the coast and presumably only a sketchy one from

---

17   A lighter is a cargo-carrying barge.

Sicily to Tripoli. When the Balkans Force is reformed in Egypt, and possibly a lot of our troops are withdrawn from Abyssinia too, I fancy we will evacuate Tobruk and wait for them at Mersa Matruh near Alamein,[18] this giving them an extra 150 miles of desert to cross from Sidi Barrani. It will thus be a bit like a league football match: we on the home ground and they away. I will be very surprised if they get anywhere and if they don't, a mechanised army spread out from Tripoli [some 900 miles west] to Mersa Matruh will look like two cents. If their supplies of petrol, oil or water break down they will either die in the desert or get stuck at oases with their food giving up fast. As regards Turkey, I do not like to prophecy. I fancy the Turks will fight, which will make any attack on the Persian oilfields a long and dangerous venture with the knowledge that the oilfields will probably be blown up if and when they get there. If the Turks don't fight, not so good, but they will have terribly long lines of communication before they meet whatever force can be whistled up into Mesopotamia.[19] Not at all the show they brought off so successfully in Poland, Flanders and Greece.

Chan came to me in great trouble a day or so ago, to say he had been fired as from 7 May. I don't know why, but will see Geer.

To Therese   8 May

St. Aubin is now repaired and we are back at the patrolling job once again. Wilson has dropped out of our crew and the Naval Volunteers, as he has picked up a job as acting Company Secretary to Whampoa Dock, Teddy Cock's outfit. I am very glad for his sake as there was no future for him in Lowe Binghams; being an unqualified man in a firm of chartered accountants is a bit of a dead end and you have to get out into commercial employment. I suppose the fact that the dock are building lots of standard ships provided suitable grounds for leaving the Naval Volunteers. I am sorry he has gone, as he was a most pleasant and useful member, but glad for his sake as it should be a first class opening. In his place we have Hindmarsh, just returned from Australia, where he has been visiting his virgin bride. He was the man who was married on the morning of the evacuation and spent his wedding night on board *Indira*[20] at a

---

18 On the coast further East.
19 Situated where the modern borders of Syria, Iraq and Iran meet and encompassing large parts of the first two countries.
20 The *Indira* was an APV: Hindmarsh was subsequently made captain of this ship.

typhoon buoy. Case has left us and in his place we have one Glover, a Shanghai policeman. Parkinson[21] and I are the two surviving members, so we are a bit of a scratch crew at the moment.

Apropos of your going away (from HK), maybe it is just as well, if there is to be trouble here, which I still doubt. They have brought out a billeting scheme, supposed to be very secret, and Mt Killett seems to be a Chinese reservation. In an emergency both 191 and 168 will be crammed full of Chinese, so you and HP would have looked a bit lost. AE would presumably move to Matilda [Hospital, The Peak], I to my ship, but what happens to UE I don't quite know, nor does he and I imagine it is naturally not too funny to be lumped around like a sack of potatoes.

I think I told you I had a letter from Jack [Dulley] who is now down in Bournemouth training on the non-flying side of the RAFVR; he presumably finishes up as a Station Adjutant attached to the RAF. Betty has a job typing with the BBC in London and they have placed Jacqueline in a home near Reading. He sent me a photo of JM who has developed into a very sweet little girl.

I have not got much further with Chan's troubles; he was to have seen me yesterday morning but I had to be away unexpectedly by 7.00 am so have fixed it up for Sunday next. I saw Geer for a moment, but he did not open up on the subject at all. Of course I can't do anything about it. If Geer does not want to keep him, I cannot make him do so, all I can do is to keep in touch with Chan, try to find him a job and see he gets a regular bit of money to carry on with.

Thanet and ourselves got a quiet pat on the back from the Commodore over our venture up to Amoy. I was amused to hear they had quite a dirty trip too, started gaily at twenty-five knots but soon came down to fifteen. There is apparently no prospect of salvage or prize money as the lighter was already an Admiralty commitment.

The weather has suddenly turned from cold to hot and thick clothes have been cast in quick time. We had quite a bit of rain shortly after you left so that most of the reservoirs were full by the end of April, a rather unusual sight. It has, however, steadied up recently and the weather is now lovely.

To Therese   16 May
I don't think you will go to the dogs on a glass of sherry and a glass of Chablis

---
21 Parkinson did not go to Aden.

per day. My impression of the Australian wines was that they were very fair, except for a certain heaviness about them, which I fancy comes from the iron in the soil. However, I commend your taking to the wine of the country, also wine is much better for the young than spirits!!

Of the other sinners [who had not been evacuated], Mrs Proulx was the only one I knew by sight; Proulx is one of our mine watchers and he tells me that he sent her off to Macao. She comes over every now and then but is not allowed to land, so he sees her on board the river steamer. Not a very satisfactory arrangement as Macao must be a deadly hole in which to live and would probably provide no more safety in the event of the Japs running riot here.[22]

If the Japs don't do anything this summer, then I don't think they will at all. Fortescue had got an idea of wives back in September. I am playing golf with him on Sunday so I will ask him about it.

I fancy Hitler's bid to Japan is about this. I will take Suez, you take Singapore, then the two bottlenecks, which stop the union of the Axis Fleets, are opened. The Jap fleet can go to the Mediterranean and help the Germans there. All very nice except for: (1) I don't think the Germans will get Suez; (2) I am sure the Japs won't get Singapore; (3) the Japs want to be helped themselves, not to help Hitler out of his troubles of having taken on a first class naval power without a fleet of his own.[23]

I am not the least pessimistic about the news. Hitler has finished Easy Conquests on the home pitch. He is presumably in fairly urgent need of oil supplies, so his choices of what to do seem to be: (a) a double drive at the Mosul oilfields via Turkey, also via Libya and Suez; (b) a crack at the Russian oilfields North East of the Black Sea. If (a) and (b) do not look like being successful by, say, the end of June, he will likely have a desperate shot at the invasion of Britain to try to finish the war this summer.[24]

As regards his prospects of success in these ventures it is difficult to speak. In Libya, with very week sea communications to Tripoli and none along the sea

---

22 Mrs Proulx subsequently returned to Hong Kong with her two sons and was in the Repulse Bay Hotel, when it was under siege near the end of invasion. Banham, p. 328.
23 The Japanese did take Singapore but Hitler did not take Suez.
24 Britain's stiff resistance to the German air raids, both in the air and among the civilian population resulted in Hitler postponing the invasion in October 1940. The proposed invasion was named Operation Sealion and was postponed until the following spring i.e. April 1941 but was never resurrected. However, it suited Hitler that the threat remained in British minds. Beevor, p. 139.

coast to Alexandria, I think we will starve them of supplies, knock them about fairly badly in the big bases like Bengazi, wipe up their spearhead near Salum and Sidi Barrani and leave the rest to rot in the desert.

If they make no progress in Libya, I think the Turks will fight, in which event it would be a colossal undertaking for the Germans to get to the Mosul oilfields, only to find they are blown up when they get there.

The idea of attacking Russia is not so hot, as it then involves Germany in a war on two fronts, which is entirely against Hitler's creed. It thus comes back to the old story of being forced to invade Britain with the odds loaded terribly against Germany. Hitler is a gambler and may easily try, and I fancy it was the prospect of this that made Hess go off his rocker and fly to Scotland. He did not want to be party to this tremendous slaughter of German youth, which their overbearing military ambitions must sometime produce. Take it from me lovely, the Germans have had their successes, but this year is going to see the start, if not the finish, of their failures. The Hess news is only just out a day or so ago, but local opinion seems to think the Japs won't take it too well. If a Jap General gets a bit stewed up he commits suicide, he does not fly over to the other side. In Germany too, I fancy, it should have a deplorable effect, as it will instil that horrible seed of doubt which is so bad for morale. I hope our propaganda people use it cleverly even if they have to stretch the truth a bit.

To Therese   21 May

We got kept out an extra day at the end of last week, due to someone's steering gear breaking down for the forty-seventh time. Or, more correctly, we were sent out again just after we had got back, so Hindmarsh and I were the only two officers available and we had to borrow two others.

I eventually finished up on Saturday afternoon, very tired, but managed to slip in ten hours' sleep, which corrected things a bit. On Sunday I had a grand day out at Fanling with Fortescue and in the afternoon we picked up a couple of gunners for a four ball. The Fortescues came to dinner at 191 in the evening: He is now working with Sedgwick on this Economic Warfare stunt. I think F is reasonably bright and clever, well above the average in fact.

I have been giving Hindmarsh lessons in the little bit of navigation I have so far learnt and I find him a most apt pupil. Trying to teach it to someone else is quite a fair idea, as you then find out whether you know it yourself. I think I told you that Hindmarsh was the man with the virgin bride in the July evacuation; he is now just back from sixteen weeks' leave in Sydney where he has presumably corrected that oversight. He is a very pleasant fellow and I wish he were going to stay with me in *St. Aubin*, but he is senior to several other officers who have already got a command, so I fancy he will be put in command of another tug when we have a big shuffle up which is just around the corner. Our new Sub, one Glover by name, is an ex-Shanghai policeman who went down to Singapore to join the Army, found it was a frost when he got there and joined the HKRNVR on his way back to S'hai. He started his life as a trooper in the Life Guards, the very ornamental laddies who are on duty at the Archway leading from Whitehall to Horse Guards Parade. Solid as the day, about thirty-five, and the right sort of person to have on your side if there is any scrapping to be done. We have introduced him to the joys of sea sickness and he seems to have gone into rather a run of it, but with the calmer weather coming he should recover. Our other officer thinks more of girls and jitterbug dancing than of becoming a naval officer, so is not very dependable. He was educated locally and they never seem to get their bottoms kicked, with consequent poor results in the products they turn out.

AE has been a bit seedy, the result apparently of eating iced fruit salad for dinner, she seems to get upset very easily. UE is in his usual good health and was out shooting with the Husilliers[25] at the Kowloon Range on Sunday, where he got the very respectable score of seventeen out of twenty at 300 yards.

They have had a lot of bother over the photos of Jack[26] in uniform: apparently no photos can be sent from the UK as there is a scare on about them being used for code ciphers. I hope various ones of you and the christening arrived safely. I sent some to Aunt Helen today and took the precaution of having them censored on the back, but not having heard about this difficulty I naturally did not think of it for the earlier ones.

I came down the Peak yesterday with Bonzo Bonsefield. He tells me Pooh is in Victoria BC [Canada] and he was flying off today on six weeks' leave. Very nice but not much after four and a half years.[27]

---

25 A group of elderly volunteers, named after their founder Hughes [some books refer to them as Hugheseliers], who during the Invasion tenaciously defended the North Point Power Station. Lindsay, p. 106.
26 Their late son.
27 The pre-war norm in Jardines was six months' leave to go back home every four years.

To Therese   27 May

No, you were not letting the cat out of the bag re Townend's moan, I had seen all the correspondence up here. If the gun goes off here and HK falls, it automatically becomes enemy territory and the assets of all companies with their head offices in HK (such as the HK Bank and our insurance companies, JM, automatically become frozen). Townend will then have to cease business until such time as the assets in Australia become unfrozen, a period of say three months or however much longer the Australian Govt. like to take over the unfreezing process. He wants to form a separate company in Australia, with our Australian Assets (about A£100,000[28]) as a backing, so that he can carry on whatever happens. But he has forgotten that he could not carry on the Australian business without doing a lot of reinsuring in London, which he does through our London Agents and that their assets would be frozen as well, so they could not either do business for him or pay for his reinsurances. To carry out his scheme with any real effect we would also have to form a separate company in London on the same lines, with our London Assets as backing to the company and that would cost us about £6,000/£8,000 in Income Tax, with endless complications on top of that. Admittedly it is hard on Townend if his Australian business and livelihood packs up on him through no fault of his own, but we do not feel inclined to go into all these complicated manoeuvres, with the added knowledge that we will have to enter up to £6,000/£8,000 in Income Tax p.a. just to keep Townend's business alive. 'C'est la guerre' and everyone must take his chance. The Union weren't willing and moved to Sydney in order to avoid just these same troubles, but we are sitting pat and chancing our hand.[29]

I was out for three days at the end of last week and felt rather broken down when I started. I had had, apparently, a chill on the bladder and Dr. Griffith gave me something to clear it up, which on Wednesday gave me a very decided belly ache. That night I went on a small farewell party at the Parisian Grill for Mayo, who has been teaching us the anti-submarine stuff. He is off shortly and has been so helpful and pleasant that we wanted to give him a big send off. As usual I found gin was the universal healer, but really having something to heal for a change I possibly looked at the gin bottle a shade too hard. Anyway it was a good party, I refused to be lured into the HK Hotel and felt

---

28 Australian £s.
29 'We' means Jardines.

not so hot the next day, but not half as cold as those who had gone to the hotel.

We had an uneventful three-day trip, a bit of navigation practice but cloud and rain at the end, so we were not able to carry out all the experiments in navigation we had planned. When we got back we found all future arrangements were rather chaotic as some of the changes I had previously mentioned are coming to a head. We and our twin [tug] are off shortly to a place you know; you landed there in 1938 [Aden], but did not call there on your way out in 1935. That should give it to you, so write all future letters to the Ship Fleet Mail Office at the aforesaid port. I am rather cheered. I am bored stiff creeping around the shores of HK, and if I am supposed to be a sailor I might as well get out there and be one. Our trip will take around six weeks to two months depending on how long we stop over at ports, and these will be almost entirely ones I have not visited.

To Agnes Dulley   31 May

I go in my own command of the sub-division of two. It is really rather comic when you come to think of it. Before the war my sole nautical experience was to tool around the shores of HK in a 4-ton yacht and now, after eighteen months, I find myself taking two 500-ton tugs on a 6,500 [sea] miles voyage in wartime conditions. However, 'c'est la guerre', and one must do one's best. I think we will get there, but possibly the method of so doing will not be in the best traditions of the RN. Actually the affair is quite out of order which makes me rather keen on doing it. To start with, the RNVR officers are not usually in charge of ships of this size. RNR (Merchant Service) usually command with RNVR under them. However, for lack of RNR officers here, they have had to put our RNVR officers in command and we have now done it for nine months with perfectly reasonable results. Next, RNVR navigators are completely taboo, but again we are breaking the rules, although here not so much so.

Our navigator is the ex-BI Skipper, who came up to Amoy with me a month or so ago and was so sick that I had to do the navigation for him, so I appear rather definitely to be the spare navigator and possibly the only one if it gets rough. The Commanding Officer of the other tug is one Watson, a junior from the HK Bank out on his first trip East, who knew even less about it than I before the war. He, incidentally, got married two days ago just to add to the joy of it and I held a sword outside the cathedral after the ceremony.

Lt. Watson HKRNVR and Isa Lammert's wedding, 29 May 1941. Peter is marked by a cross for Therese's benefit (the photo was taken by the SCMP)

The letters that follow are continuations of the letters of 27 May to Therese and 31 May to Agnes Dulley. They have been split up in order to place events in sequence

To Therese   27 May continued

Our officers are the navigator, Glover, the ex-Guardsman, and I am trying to wangle an extra officer as I will probably have to do the navigation myself, judging from the results of our Amoy trip. For some completely unexplained reason we drop our Sub Lieutenants at Singapore and pick up two Straits RNVR Subs;[30] as they will probably try and palm off a couple of their worst duds, I will try to slip them and sail on with our own.

Everything completely vague as yet, but when we get there I may stay on or come back to HK, in which event I would be back here in about four months. I naturally feel a bit sad, in some ways in leaving HK, my stamping ground of so many years, but now

---

30 Sub Lieutenants.

you are away it is a dull lonely place, in spite of the E's kindness and I am only too glad to be going and feeling at long last I am really starting to help in the war.

To Agnes Dulley   Continued   31 May

Well, there we are, off quite soon. The Dockyard are working on us like beavers, or as near like beavers as they could ever become. We still have not half the information or instructions, but I suppose the 'Lord will provide' although his provision will produce an almighty scramble at the last moment.

To Therese   Continued   27 May

The Dockyard are in a grand flap and are hard at it talking rot about stability, coal consumption, water consumption: in fact chaos reigns supreme as usual. Today we had a conference of all Dockyard departments, Vernall and myself and it was agreed that working overtime, providing everything went well and there were no hitches, then we might start on Friday, 6 June at the earliest. Against that apparently the whole matter has to go back to the Admiralty for confirmation so we may never start, but I think we will go all right.

I have done nothing about cabling you and will not do so until things are more definite. I have enquired about the censorship regulations and gather that it is fair to tell you we are going to Aden. Possibly that is not correct and we have only been told Aden to fox us. Any of your letters which arrive after I have left will be forwarded onto the FMO there.

By and large I feel a bit like Columbus starting out to find America and I feel the trip should be the most wonderful experience and training. It is against all RN rules that two ships should go off with only RNVR officers on board, which is one reason why I want to make it, just to show that the somewhat despised RNVR can do their stuff. The main difficulty of course is the route; you remember the *Chitral*[31] in 1938 and the filthy trip we had from Penang; well the *Chitral* is 16,000 tons and we are only 500 so the usual Penang, Colombo, Bombay trip is no good in the SW monsoon. As a result we will have

---

31 A P&O Steam Navigation Co. ship. Could carry 203 First Class and 103 Second Class passengers. In 1939 she was requisitioned by the Admiralty for service as an armed merchant cruiser and converted by her builders. Her after funnel was removed and seven 6-inch and two 3-inch guns were fitted.
http://www.clydesite.co.uk/clydebuilt/viewship.asp?id=3579. 11 February 2016.

to go by devious ways, keeping to calm water which will suit me, but complicating the coal situation owing to the distance between ports. However, I put in a bit of work with the navigator this evening and I reckon we have got it all reasonably fixed up.

To Agnes Dulley   Continued   31 May

I hope they let us tool along the equator as we want to do. It should be a grand trip, fine weather and the SE trades pushing you along. I cannot mention the name of the tug, according to the censorship rules, as I have stated the port to which we are going, but possibly you will remember it or can get it from my Christmas card to various members of the family.

When we get to Aden all is vague. Officially we are only taking the ships there and we then return here, but I don't intend to do so. I am fed up with beach crawling round HK and will look around for something in the Near East. They are fairly sure to be short of officers with reasonable experience and by then I should be one. Actually, I have a sneaking affection for the old hooker and would like to carry on with her at Aden. Some sixth sense tells me that any given centre is always short of officers with dependable experience, so I should not have much difficulty in getting fixed up in Aden when we arrive. I have also got to try to get our navigator parked when we arrive, because the only reason why he is being sent with me, is not for his capacities as a navigator (or any lack of confidence in mine), but just because they want to get rid of him here and this is a grand opportunity. That does not worry me a great deal since when the trip is over I shall not need him any more (I doubt actually if we will be on speaking terms) and I don't give two hoots if he drifts back to HK or not. The simplest thing, of course, is to leave him behind at some out of the way port en route, but I don't know enough about King's regulations and Admiralty instructions to realise what the complications are (and answers to the inevitable questions) if you arrive one officer short. Possibly they won't know how many we are supposed to have, but I fancy somehow they will, so intense complications would surely arise unless some pretty keen bit of Active Service came along to obscure the slight contretemps.

The news today is that our trip is held up until further orders; other sources maintain we are sailing the day after tomorrow (quite impossible, but they don't know that) so you can imagine the glorious state of uncertainty in which we live. However, it is all a new experience preparing for a very long voyage, so I am learning all the while.

Actually, I will be very disappointed if it does not come off. If one is dressed up as a sailor, one might as well try to be one and a trip like this is just what we want to teach us things and to give us confidence.

Peter sailed from Hong Kong on 5 June. After that, although he kept sending letters to Therese when he could and no doubt she wrote regularly, he did not receive any of hers until he arrived in Aden and the rest when he returned to Hong Kong, so she was given a very delayed response to her letters.

CHAPTER 12

The Voyage to Aden

June to July 1941

During and after his trip to Aden Peter wrote to Therese, his mother, sister, brother and Eva Davidson. Naturally there was a considerable amount of repetition between the letters. They have therefore been distilled down into one narrative, unless otherwise stated, in order to paint a full and colourful picture of his journey. The voyage to Aden started on 5 June and is shown on the Map of Journey to Aden and Back (pp. 18–19).

We sailed from Hong Kong in considerable disorder the day after I had lunch with Uncle Edgar and Aunt Eva at the Club. Our departure was twenty minutes late, the mess man had not appeared and then we had just got off the wall, to the cheers of the assembled multitude, when he came up on the bridge to say the cabin boy was not on board as he thought we were sailing two hours later. I felt I could not start to worry about cabin boys, so I just carried on, but the shore experts came the coco. When he turned up in the Dockyard and found he had missed the ship, he made such a holler that someone borrowed the Commodore's barge, stopped us by signal[1] and he was put on board some fifteen miles out south of Lamma.

The trip down to Singapore took seven days, five of which were fine and calm, while for two days off the Indo China coast it was rough and unpleasant. When these tugs get into a bit of rough stuff they are most uncomfortable. They have a quick motion which is far too much for most stomachs. There is water everywhere so you have to be completely battened down, with the result that the air just gets ranker and ranker. Most of the officers (myself included) and crew were sick and I once again had the pleasure of introducing a new candidate to seasickness, to wit Gemmell, our CERA,[2] who had been in the Navy for ten years without succumbing. The worthy tug gets very dirty over a prolonged trip, ash from the boiler room everywhere, and one has to go easy on the fresh water so one cannot do much about cleaning up. We also had trouble with food, as our mess man did not get enough ice for the ice box (he said the dockyard police would not let him bring it in) and a lot of fresh meat went bad before we had time to eat it.

---

1 Presumably sent by wireless.
2 Chief Engine Room Artificer.

Here we are at our first port of call [Singapore] with everyone trying to shoot us out before we have really arrived. However, I soon scotched that with a pretty handy list of defects, with the result that we stayed three and a half days. It looks as if our stay here will be just about as much of a scramble as our last week in Hong Kong. That was horrible; the same old story, no one seemed to know what was to be done or how to do it; chaos all the way. The main idea was to get us out of Hong Kong so that the people there did not have to bear any blame for our starting late. I find one needs all one's wits about you on this party, to remember the various things to be done and to absorb the information which staff officers shoot out in a very airy way and then expect you to remember and act on in a week's time.

We arrived just after tiffin and are out at the Naval Base at Seletar, on the north of the Island, some fifteen miles from Singapore, so are rather marooned. I had vaguely hoped to contact the Le Flemings [old friends of Peter's] and had written to them in advance; also Jim Henry, but I doubt if we will have the opportunity to get over to Singapore the way things are working out.

I have been doing a bit of work on the navigation line on the way down and results have been quite reasonable, rather more accurate than the navigator I fancy. He is a bit of a trial; he complains continually, rubs the crew up the wrong way, and his navigational efforts seem to be most slapdash and inaccurate. I had to show him how to adjust the error on his sextant!! It makes it all rather difficult for me, when he has a master's ticket and has been a Merchant Service Captain for a long while past, as I feel naturally rather diffident at suggesting he is wrong, even if I really think he is.

Mrs C's five shillings given to me at Christmas 1934 is a great standby;[3] I can do the sun sights with fair accuracy during the day, but have not yet got on to star sights, chiefly because I don't know which of the wretched things are which.

To Therese   12 June   Singapore

Our route on from here has not yet been fixed but we are to call on the high ups tomorrow morning to be told what to do. In theory we return to Hong Kong after arrival in Aden, and if we do it occurs to me that there will be very little prospect of a direct ship, so we might very easily go via an empty troop transport to Australia[4]

---

3   Used to purchase a secondhand sextant.
4   This may have been an optimistic idea, as the majority of the Australian Army was in North Africa by early 1941. Beevor, p. 175.

and so up by ship [to Hong Kong]. It would be a grand idea if we do, and I could on arrival in Sydney, find that my distressing but all to prevalent complaint needed attention, which it will certainly need to have some time, so why not in Sydney. If we went that way and I could fix a bit of stopover leave, it would be grand.[5]

I have heard no war news for a week, but gather today on arrival that we have gone into Syria without serious opposition.[6] Thank goodness we are taking the initiative for once in a while. It makes life look much better. I don't fancy the French have any fight in them and if we alienate Free French sympathies it won't amount to a row of pins anyway, so we might as well charge in and get there before the Germans.

Well it is getting late. I would have started earlier but my cabin was 102°F at teatime, so I had a bath at the officer's club instead. We are at present in a creek, which looks rather like Lessy's abandoned attempt at the Panama Canal.[7]

To Therese   20 June 1941   Singapore

Here we are, still in Singapore, after two unsuccessful attempts to get away. I wrote to you last, about a week ago just after our arrival. On the original scheme we were to be here for three and a half days to pick up coal, water, stores, fresh food and get some minor repairs done. The night before I was hauled out of bed and told to get up steam chop chop. I thought it was just a bit of the usual official cussedness, but we got going just after 03.00 and found in the meanwhile that there had been quite a serious collision between two ships and we were to standby to tow. We got back from that party about 05.30 next morning, and topped up with coal and water and were off again around 15.00 the same afternoon.

About sixty miles out of Singapore, around midnight, a ship was crossing us from port to starboard. The officer on the bridge, Goodwin, switched on the navigation lights. The ship altered to starboard and passed to port of us, and then ran into our twin[8] some six cables[9] astern, who had not turned on her navigation lights. She was hit a pretty handy whack on the port bow and the Engineer Petty Officer was very lucky not

---

5 Therese and HP had been evacuated to Sydney in March 1941.
6 Syria was a French colony under the control of Vichy France, who were allied to Germany.
7 Peter had passed through the completed Canal on his trip to Chile in the late 1920s.
8 The lack of any mention of the other tug while on the voyage was no doubt because of censorship.
9 A cable is a nautical unit of measurement equal to one tenth of a nautical mile which equates to 185.2 metres; six cables would be over 1,000 metres.

to be killed, as his cabin was completely stove in and the other ship's bow cut his bunk clean in half while he was sleeping in it. With traditional naval sangfroid, he grabbed his lifejacket, climbed out of the hole in the ship's side and eventually came to wandering about the foc'sle.

Fortunately she was only holed above the waterline and did not fill in consequence, so we turned back and steamed for the Naval Base again. Our twin will take some weeks to repair and it is quite in the air whether we wait here or go on alone. All rather annoying as it should not really have happened, as they ought to have turned on their navigation lights and not assumed the other ship had seen them. I was hoping we would get through the trip without any such contretemps, as the answer immediately arises: 'If you send ships out with RNVR officers that is what you expect.' They have also a Court of Enquiry hanging over them and will require some changes in officer personnel before proceeding, as the man on watch when the accident occurred will probably be sent back to Hong Kong and they will require a navigator, as we have the only official navigator of the party. Official navigator is about the right term, as being the official one is about as near as he gets to navigation. Regularly in the morning when I take over from him at eight o'clock he tells me he does not know where we are and leaves me to find out.

I had a bit of a chill the day before we first arrived here. I tried to get it out of the system with a hot whisky and lemon, but it seemed to hang around for a bit, so I felt rather mouldy for the first five days after we arrived. It all seems to have cleared up now thank goodness, as it is a rotten job being in command of this circus and not feeling up to the mark. Being detached from our base we are now quite independent units and have to do a lot more thinking for ourselves than we did in Hong Kong. It is the old story, you are the captain and it is up to you. Nobody suggests things and if you don't think of them for yourself you find yourself away off at sea without something essential.

As we are out at the Naval Base, I have only been in for one rather rushed and short visit for about a couple of hours to get some money and do some shopping. I phoned the Le Flemings at KL and found they were away from home.[10] However, I am off for the evening tonight with Goodwin and Glover, as it does not do any good to hang around these small tugs too much. They are hot and the temperature in my cabin is 90 degrees at the moment, with afternoon sun on it, it is 102 degrees.

---

10 In less than five months Malaya was invaded by the Japanese and surrendered on 15 February 1942.

Goodwin is the new officer we picked up here; he is a tough New Zealander of about forty. He has considerable yachting experience,[11] keen, a hard worker and seems to know his job fairly well. He is also very abstemious, serious, conscientious and reliable, definitely a useful addition to the party. Our other two officers are Glover and the navigator. Glover the junior officer, has had a bit of a chequered career, ran away from school at fifteen to join the Army and became a trooper in the Blues,[12] then in business for a bit and so into the Shanghai police, where he has been for about fifteen years. He has been in the HKRNVR for about nine months. He does not know much about it all but is a hard working and talks the Shanghai dialect, which is an advantage as all the crew are Shanghai Chinese. I think they have the savvy to realise you can't put anything across a man with S'hai police experience. Our last man is Gemmell a CERA, or a sort of Engine Chief Petty Officer from a gunboat in Hong Kong, who lives with us and ranks to all intent and purposes as an officer, as there is nowhere else for him to go. He is a nice fellow of an excellent type and was a bit unlucky a while ago in not getting a commissioned rank. I think he has received some shocks since he joined us. We don't run things on hard and fast Navy lines, my motto is that it is the result that counts and by and large we get it.

Well, there you have our officer compliment and I feel we might easily have fared a great deal worse. The navigator's old womanly fussing and continual complaints is the only fly in the ointment, which has so far developed, but I feel we are a sufficiently forbearing lot to cope with that. We have put him in charge of the food so that he cannot complain about that any more.

To Eva Davidson   21 June   Singapore

The Naval Base positively bustles with Admirals, Commodores etc. and I never talk to anyone unless he has a brass hat. If you are not a Commander you are no one here, so I make a rule not to deal with underlings. All the staff people have been very nice to us and I feel there is a lot in the quotation about 'A prophet is not without honour etc.' In HK we were just the despised Naval Volunteers, but here I am the senior officer of two detached ships and I say I want so and so doing. We have collected almost all the stores we were refused in HK. I have swapped my Navy sextant, a rebuilt model, for a

---

11 The idea was to recruit yachtsmen to the RNVR.
12 The Royal Horse Guards, which were known as the Blues. Now merged to become 'The Blues and Royals'.

new one of the very latest pattern; we have had lots of bits of odd work done to the ship without demur or argument. If I want something I just make a signal to that effect and it is done, if it is at all possible. It is certainly a blessing in many ways being on one's own, but it has the effect, of course, that you have to be rather on your toes, otherwise you leave a port without some of the vital abracadabra which is necessary in wartime; also there is a tendency for separate sections of the staff to give you conflicting instructions.

I put forward my ideas about the route, which were quite kindly received and cabled on to C in C East Indies, but could not be adopted due to lack of coal at one of the proposed stopping places. I understand, incidentally, that there are no raiders left in the Indian Ocean, the Navy having had the forethought to sink them before we arrived in this part of the world.[13]

The repairs to our twin will take about three weeks and it has now been decided that we go on alone. I am glad because the prospect of sitting on the wall at the Naval Base for three weeks with nothing much to do was beginning to appal us somewhat. The last few days of comparative peace and quiet have given us an opportunity to get the odds and ends squared up, the ship painted and cleaned up, and generally get ourselves somewhat under control.

Letters to Therese and Agnes   Singapore and Padang

The latest news is that we will sail almost at once. I cannot tell you our future route, as these things are supposed to be kept frightfully hush hush, but we go to one port you know. Don't worry about me, as I am probably even safer scouring about the ocean in my present conveyance than I was sitting on the beaches of Hong Kong.[14] We have perfect weather since Singapore, except for a few rain squalls.

Incidentally I censor my own letters now, as you will see from the envelope and I am extremely vague about the rules. I have to be rather discreet in mentioning future ports etc.[15]

---

13 This was not entirely the case. HMAS *Sydney* was sunk off the coast of Australia by a German raider 'Kormoran' flying a Dutch flag in November 1941. It was suspected the German raider was not alone as there may also have been a Japanese submarine there. Beevor, p. 265.
14 Meaning patrolling around the islands.
15 It would follow that he censored the crew's letters, but this would have only been the small number of English speaking members. The Chinese may not have written any and if they had he would not have been able to read them.

An example of the censor's stamp and signature

To Therese   28 June   Padang

I last wrote from Singapore, just before we finally left, we have now moved onto this land of the Lotus Eaters, which is on the West coast of Sumatra, about half way up. Our twin was left behind so we are now on our own, which is a bit of a relief as we do not have to bother whether she is still following at night. I have one regret which is a personal one; here, at Padang, we are in a foreign port and according to the King's regulations and Admiralty Instructions the senior ship (that is us) must fly a Senior Officer's Pennant, so as to let the local dignitaries know on whom to call. We had procured two pennants in Singapore, but being here on our own we naturally don't fly it. I fancy it is quite likely the first occasion an RNVR officer has ever flown a Senior Officer's Pennant and I am sufficiently conceited to like to be mixed up in little events like that.

Over the last five days since Singapore, it was very pleasant: calm seas, bright sun, just a few rain squalls and a long, easy, rolling swell at the end. We have been coasting and have had some excellent practice in pilotage. We came successfully through the fairly narrow straits, the Rhio[16] and the Bangka Straits,[17] a pastime for which merchant ships usually have to pay their captains a fee of £5 if they don't take a pilot.[18] I have also learnt how to work lighthouses when coasting along the shore. Altogether a most instructive and pleasant trip. It also gave us practice in pilotage i.e. finding where you are when in sight of land. In Hong Kong it is all too easy, I know what all the islands look like in almost any conditions, so all I have to do is to take bearings and put our position in on the chart. Usually I know what that is too, at any rate to within a mile or so. In this game, I do not know the lie of the land, so I have to establish the identity of the landmarks one by one and then get a position. Goodwin, our new officer, is excellent at it and very reliable. Glover finds it all rather beyond him, but is trying to learn, while our navigator makes a lot of fuss and noise and often puts our position in wrong.

We arrived here [Padang] yesterday morning and the place …

Although Peter had 'censored' his own letter, ten lines were subsequently censored [or cut out so both sides were lost] by the Dutch Authorities.

I played golf in the afternoon on the six-hole course at the race course. Very rustic, both race course and the golf. The grandstand of the former is a wooden affair mainly populated by chickens and goats, while the fairways of the latter seem to be kept mown (or not) by the attentions of the local cattle. The Javanese population bathe in the river which runs beside it and all is peace. Levinson, the Consul, appears to have taken up golf at around fifty, but in spite of some twenty years assiduous practise he has failed to master the fundamentals. I referred casually to the British community to which he replied, 'I am the British community.' Great fun to be a Consul with only yourself to look after.

The only thing that is not peaceful in Padang is the harbour …

The Censor has cut out more of the letter; this may have been because Peter made some oblique reference to the harbour defences, and their concern that there would be a Japanese invasion.

---

16 Between the islands just south of Singapore.
17 Off SE Sumatra.
18 The Navy eventually paid him £2.6s.10d (pre-decimalisation).

As a result we were too late for the evening festivities, which consisted of going to a bazaar in aid of the Spitfire Fund. All the Dutch are very pro British, have photos of their Majesties and Churchill all over the place. We come in for some of the reflected glory and have been showered with entertainment, also presented with lots of pictorial papers (British Consul) one bottle of gin, two boxes of cigars, 1000 Craven A[19] and two large parcels of novels (Rotary Club). I have not even any proper stationery on which to write a letter of thanks. Yesterday evening when we got ashore we had Chinese chow and beer at the house of a young Dutch couple called Veth. They came down to the ship this morning and drank some gin, so I got to know them a bit.

Letters to Therese, Agnes and Evelyn   Padang
The following morning was great fun. As we were flying the White Ensign, on the Consul's advice and under his direction and management, I called on the Assistant Resident (the Resident is away in Batava), the Major in charge of the local garrison and the Burgomeister. The calls were delivered at 7.30, 7.45 and 8.00 am (please note am). They all trooped back on board the tug at 9.30 am to return the call, dressed up like a Ruritanian Musical Comedy. Imagine the four of them and four of us in a wardroom. The Major insisted on wearing a sword, in spite of the Consul tipping them off that swords were taboo as we had not got one. A coal burning tug is no place to do social honours; the fan in the wardroom had just broken, the ship was still covered with coal dust from the previous day's coaling and we sat in the wardroom, sweating profusely, making strained conversation and drinking whisky and soda at 9.30 am, a habit in which I do not usually indulge.[20]

The whole effect was rather comic opera, but it does not do as they say to take it very seriously. It all seemed to go off all right, but we did burst ourselves laughing when we were able to relax.

To Therese   Continued   28 June
I have your three portrait studies in my cabin, the one of you and Pip sitting by a stream, also several of HP. Seeing these people [the Dutch] united and happy here

---
19 A popular brand of cigarette at the time.
20 His sister, Evelyn, was a Mother Superior in a convent. Peter acted the naughty younger brother but the last sentence was probably written for her benefit, although she was very broad minded.

HMPS 'Perla' showing the smoke a coal-fired tug could produce

makes one rather envious,[21] but they must have their troubles as lots of their relatives are in occupied territory.

To Agnes Dulley   11 July   Padang/Seychelles

I wrote to you last just before we got to Padang and here we are a fortnight further on with our trip. The British Consul at Padang was an ex-BI Skipper, who was looking after our various affairs, told me he had come to Padang thirty-one years ago on a holiday and had just stayed. One could quite understand it. Luxuriant tropical vegetation with lots of bright flowers; out of the hurly-burly of the world, delightfully rural and sleepy. Nothing is done fast, why should it be, is the idea.

On the Saturday night we went to a dance at the club in honour of Prince Bernhard's birthday; they were also having a sale of work etc. in aid of the Spitfire Fund, which rather surprised me as Nevison, the Vice Consul, comprises the entire British community. The Dutch appear to be very pro-ally; you see photos of Churchill in their papers, they talk of what WE including their silver[22] are doing, but one cannot

---
21 Sumatra was invaded by the Japanese on 14 February 1942 in order to secure the oilfields and the Dutch Shell refineries. Beevor, p. 265.
22 Presumably this means their donations to the war effort.

help wondering what their real feelings are.[23]

There is a delightful swimming pool near the town, where we had a bathe. An artificial pool at the bottom of a gully, with a freshwater stream running through it and all the surroundings, trees, etc. as they originally were. A Dutch couple called and took us to it. She was very nice and quite attractive with a brother commanding a Dutch submarine, now operating with the British Navy, but I had my doubts that he [the husband] was so pro-British as he made himself out to be. In different circumstances I would quite see him being a fifth columnist. The dance at the Club was a bit odd to our ideas, about what you would have expected in the Portuguese Club in Hong Kong, like the VRC [the Victoria Recreation Club], black, white and khaki all (the races) mixed together on an equal footing.

We are now on our eleventh day out of Padang and nearly at the end of the longest leg of the trip. We were a great sight when we started with 40 tons of coal in bags, a live pig and several chickens on deck, and under the White Ensign. My Lords of the Admiralty would have had six fits, but they weren't there.

The idea of coming by this rather roundabout route was to miss the heavy weather which always accompanies the SW monsoon. It was my idea and I managed to 'sell it' to the staff at Singapore and Colombo. They were a bit dubious as to whether we would have the endurance in coal and water to make the passage of 2,800 miles. I maintained we could,[24] but I did not tell them about the 40 tons of coal on deck, as the Chief Constructor would probably have had a fit and talked ominously about stability. From what I gathered from the weather maps it looked like a calm passage at the start, so I was quite willing to take responsibility and have a crack at it.

We have had bright fair weather the whole way, but a long ocean swell on the beam, so that we have been rolling quite a bit and all felt pretty livery at first until we got used to it. This is a lonely stretch of ocean, as you will see from the map, and we

---

23   Peter's suspicions possibly stem from WWI, when the Netherlands were neutral. Goods imported by the Netherlands proved vital to Germany, but were stopped by a Royal Navy blockade in 1916. Up to 1940, the Netherlands was a neutral country, generally on good terms with Germany until the invasion. In May 1940 Queen Wilhelmina escaped from Germany to London; the Dutch government followed. The government-in-exile faced a dilemma, the Vichy French government was collaborating with Germany. The Dutch government was still in control of the Dutch East Indies with all its oil. Wilhelmina realised that if the Dutch collaborated with Germany, the Dutch East Indies would be surrendered to Japan, so the government stayed in exile. http://en.wikipedia.org/wiki/The_Netherlands#World_Wars_and_beyond_.281890.E2.80.93present.2912. March 2015.
24   The consequences of failure in the vast Indian Ocean would have been serious, as although they had a wireless, a ship would have to be found to take them to the nearest port.

have not seen a ship since we left Padang or land since we left the outlying islands. We make our landfall, or hope to, on a small flat island with a lighthouse on it, some fifty miles from Mahé, the principal island in the Seychelles group. I will get a hell of a thrill if we hit it dead bull's eye and hope that tomorrow, our last day, is nice and clear so that we can take plenty of sights.

Well, I hope that all goes well with you; I have had very little news since this trip started and naturally no letters. I sent you some tinned butter from Hong Kong just before I left, but judging by some we have just started on, it will probably be rancid. I did not realise that tinned butter was not a success.

To Therese   16 July   Seychelles

It is now over a fortnight since I wrote to you last, but this, let me hasten to mention is because there has been no opportunity to post anything. Lord knows when you will get this letter, there is a ship due here in a few days, which will reach Singapore in twelve days after she sails from here, but the Post Office say they can make no airmail arrangements. However, Goodwin and I are going to try to hit a bargain with the Postmaster, whereby he encloses our letters, together with a Singapore dollar note, in a cover to the Postmaster at Singapore, asking him to stamp them suitably and send them on airmail.

We sailed from Padang on the 30 June, to this spot (Seychelles). You recollect what a filthy trip home we had in 1938 from Penang to Aden; well we would have got that anywhere North of Latitude 2 degrees N. Hence keep South was our motto. We had a shock on the first day out when we found that we were burning 18 tons per day of the South African coal we had loaded at Padang, as against our estimates of 15 tons per day for Indian coal on the way down from Hong Kong to Singapore; an extra 20 per cent in fact, which was just about our margin of reserve coal.

I felt very depressed for a day or two, as I had sponsored the Seychelles route and taken responsibility for it, so I actually did not want it to go wrong. We had also allowed for adverse current of one knot throughout the whole trip, and as we did not meet this we finished up at the Seychelles, to my great relief, with 48 tons of coal out of 280, 15 tons of water out of 66, and thirteen days out of Padang as against an estimated fourteen and a half.

As a result of the ocean swell all the way, we never had the fiddles off the table. The food situation got a bit out of control, as we could only carry fresh food for six days and we finished on a diet of corned beef, dry corned beef hash for breakfast, cold corned beef for tiffin and what do you think for dinner? Why, cold corned beef again.

The navigation got quite slick on the trip and the navigator and I were getting the noon position to within a mile or two of each other by independent sun sights and workings. As long as you keep off fancy stuff and leave hidden reefs by at least fifty miles, the ordinary straight-forward navigation by sun sights is not at all difficult. When I knew nothing about it, I used to be impressed, but now having been initiated into the sacred brotherhood of navigators, the mystery of it all looks a bit thin. We had to make our land fall after twelve days in the open ocean, on a small flat island, which only rises some six feet out of the sea and is then covered with palm trees. We both did star sights at dawn that morning, but somehow they went wrong and our positions landed up miles apart. However, with the true British spirit of compromise, we split the difference, changed course accordingly, raised our island dead ahead at 9.15 am, half an hour after we expected to see it, not too bad I thought.

We anchored here at 4.00 pm the same day and will be here for nearly a week as we are cleaning the boilers. This is a first class poverty stricken place: fish, copra[25] and cinnamon seem to be the main industries. There is no bank, no cinema, no telephone system and they have run short of butter, cheese, ham, bacon, beer, gin and most other things you want, chiefly due to HM ships stocking up from the island's slender resources. Fortunately there is a Fleet oiler in port at present and we have replenished our larder from them; we hope to do the same with the drink situation, but we don't want to panic them over it.

The place was originally French but was taken from them by us after the Napoleonic Wars and is now a British Crown Colony. Eric Grimble's cousin, Sir Arthur Grimble[26] is the Governor and I called at Govt. Ho. and had a chat with him the other day. He told me all about his four daughters at home, how the eldest had just got married to a Canadian RNVR officer after refusing him about eight times, how the youngest was on the stage etc. etc. and did not seem at all interested in our affairs. I fancy he was rather glad to talk to a fairly kindred soul, as most of the people here seem to be half-castes or beach combers or both.

---

25 The dried kernel of a coconut.
26 Sir Arthur Grimble was a British colonial governor and ethnographer; resident commissioner of the Gilbert and Ellice Islands from 1914 and Governor of the Seychelles and Windward Islands (etc.); after retirement his most celebrated book *A Pattern of Islands* was published in 1952. http://www.britishmuseum.org/research/search_the_collection_database/term_details.aspx?bioId=39389. 5 May 2015.

He lent us his car for a drive round the island yesterday afternoon. It is very pretty, there is coral and palm trees, cool, no malaria – quite the South Sea Island. We are in the depths of winter at present and the climate is certainly very pleasant. You wear whites, but don't sweat and I have been using a blanket at night. When we returned from our drive we had tea off very Victorian silver plate in an ultra-Victorian and rather ramshackle government house. Such is the Seychelles.

There is a club, of which we are all visiting members, a broken down ramshackle sort of spot, with the League of Nations for its membership. The chief building materials here seem to be corrugated iron, rotted match-boarding and old petrol cans. I forgot to mention the Island's icemaking plant is out of commission so we will have to do most of our next leg on tinned food.

I sent you a wire from here to say we had arrived OK. The Services have now a system of numbered telegrams such as 'All well'; 'In hospital not expected to recover'; 'Arrived safely send money.' There is a beauty No. 47 'You are ever closer to my thoughts darling' and I think I must send you one of those. If you get it without previous warning you will presumably think I was tight.

Still no news about our eventual destination, or whether we stay with the ship. My bet is that they will use her to help salvage Italian ships sunk in the Red Sea, mainly at Massawa. Whether we stay with her is open to bet too, but I would far sooner do salvage work in the near east, than return to the deadly round of patrolling Hong Kong.

I think the war situation is distinctly encouraging, as the RAF seem to be giving them [the Germans] a first class hammering, while the Russian campaign shows little signs of being a smash victory. I still hold the theory that they will try to invade Britain in August: but if they don't it would appear that their ideas of trying to force a victory have rather disappeared.

To Therese   31 July   Aden
[With some pieces from the letter to Agnes Dulley of 7 August.]
The last day we were in the Seychelles two HM ships came in[27] and I wanted to get some

---

27 The names of the two ships were not disclosed because of censorship. The ships must have been HMS *Hermes*, an aircraft carrier and HMS *Enterprise*, a light cruiser. Both ships patrolled the Indian Ocean together between Colombo and the Seychelles from June 1941. Peter also met Lt.Cdr. Bristowe who was on *Hermes* in 1940. Ironically, at the outbreak of war in the Far East *Hermes* was in Simonstown naval base in South Africa for a long-overdue refit. McCart, p. 46.

HMS 'Hermes' (Australian War Memorial)

dope from the Signal Officer of one of them. Imagine my surprise when I found it was none other than David Block; we had been at prep school together at Gadebridge Park.[28] We had quite a good evening ashore, along with the first Lieut. from his ship, lots of bad whisky in the Seychelles Club and then dinner at the Hotel (rather one horse) but we resisted going to the dance at the club, where the Ships band was playing.

Next day I had to go on board both ships on business; they were fair sized and with lots of officers and sentries, telescopes etc. at the head of the gangway, and imagine my consternation when I was piped on board. It had not occurred to me that being in command of my somewhat dubious tub entitled me to a pipe, but of course I am. Also I had not been piped on board before, so did not know if there was any special drill.

I gave my friend half a box of Padang cigars, had some very soothing gin in the wardroom and scrounged 20 lbs of fresh beef from their paymaster, so we parted friends.

We had a most amusing incident just before we left that afternoon: one of our quartermasters, who had been carefully hiding out of sight for the last day or so, came up onto the bridge with an enormous swelling on his face, abscesses in the gums by the look of it. I was not going to take him on a seven-day trip in that condition, so we handed him over to the HM ship, where they proceeded to take out seven teeth and sent him back in their boat trussed up like a chicken in a Navy stretcher and still under anaesthetic. He got a hell of a jar when he woke up a few hours later; we were

---

28 A preparatory school near Hemel Hempstead, Hertfordshire.

Peter in tropical uniform

well out to sea by then, but he was as right as rain in two days and very glad that we had taken a firm hand. The boat he came back in was the one that depth charged the *Richlieu*'s propeller at Oran last year, and I met Bristowe the sportsman who did it.[29]

If he had not been spotted before we sailed, we would probably have had to operate on him with pliers and cold chisels to get the teeth out and let the poison out as well; not an enticing thought. That is the sort of thing I have been coping with for seven weeks and I will admit the responsibility of it has tired me a bit.

Seychelles to here [Aden] took seven days, and we had much better weather than we expected for the first four, no SW monsoon at all. The last two days up to Cape Guardafui we had a heavy following sea and plenty of wind but the old tub does not mind it behind her. Unfortunately, on the last night and morning the current carried us away out from the coast of Africa and we would have needed to steer with the sea beam on (quite unsafe) to make landfall at Ras Asir, a bit south of Guardafui. Round those parts you have the strongest ocean current in the world, running up to one hundred miles per day, so accurate navigation is not too easy.

Fortunately the sun was out, so we got a fairly accurate position at noon and in the afternoon the swell went down a bit, so I said to hell with the Pope and put her slap across it, heading nearly west. She nearly rolled her guts out, but we picked up Guardafui at 5.00 pm, before the light failed and we were all pretty relieved when we ran into the calm water in the Gulf of Aden. The trip up the Gulf of Aden started

---

29 Lt.Cdr. R H Bristowe on 8 July 1940 took *Hermes*' crash-boat, loaded with depth charges, and attacked the Vichy France battleship *Richelieu* moored in Dakar Harbour. Unfortunately, owing to the shallow water in the harbour the depth charges did not go off, but six Swordfish subsequently managed to damage one of the *Richelieu*'s propellers, thus temporarily disabling her. Bristowe's crew were all awarded medals and he was given a DSO. McCart, p. 41.

calm and pleasant, but a head sea soon got up and I regret to say that I lost my early morning orange on the very last day of the trip.

Aden

CHAPTER 13

Life in Aden

July to August 1941

Peter's arrival in Aden was to be an anti-climax after his long and successful voyage from Hong Kong. Added to this, Aden was very hot and lacking in the facilities he had become accustomed to in Hong Kong. Once he had handed over 'St. Aubin' he had very little to do until he was able to start his journey back to Hong Kong.

To Therese   31 July

It was grand to hear from you again and know you are both well. The last I had from you in HK must have been about 20 May.

You don't say anything about my wire from S'Pore which must have been sent off about 14 June, so I presume someone must have been sitting on it for a week or two, in this affable way they have, with a possible view to assist the censorship.

Our arrival here was rather an anti-climax. I expected someone to say 'well done thou good and faithful weekend sailor' but not a bit of it.[1] We had done the job we set out to do; done it right on schedule and without any hitch or accident. I know it sounds like neck shooting on my part, but I feel pretty sure there is not an officer in the Navy or Merchant Service who has been in command on a 6,500 miles sea passage after less than two years afloat. Those sort of games seem to be reserved for the somewhat despised RNVR.

When we got here we imagined it was merely a matter of handing over to the new crew, but things did not quite work out like that. Goodwin and Glover were pinched for some job ashore and the navigator and I were left to do a programme, which looked like twenty-four hours a day of tug work. I assure you I felt pretty sore, to be handed a pup like that within twenty-four hours of arriving from a fairly strenuous ocean passage. We started on our first afternoon of towing, and we were very light in the water so that the ship was nearly unmanageable in a high wind. They lent us a tug master to show us what to do, and he stood on the bridge watching in a very

---

1 His RNVR contemporaries did however recognise his achievement, which is recorded in *The RNVR: A Record of Achievement.* J L Kerr and W Granville, p. 257.

supercilious manner, as I had about four shots at picking up a barge. I was very fed up with the whole show by then and when the tug master asked if he could have a shot at it, I said yes. He started slamming around in great style, full ahead and full astern, that's the way we professionals do it, but finished up with the tow rope wrapped around the propeller on his first shot; it is now three days later and the diver has only just finished unwrapping it.

I gathered that there was a bit of a prospect of our sitting about the harbour towing mud barges and the prospect did not appeal to me, so I saw the Senior Naval Officer next day, apologised for the accident and told him that harbour towing is well above my mark, which is true by and large as it is a specialist job. I also trod on someone's corns by criticising the proposal to put in an Indian Serang (boatswain) to run the tug for harbour towing: (a) because the Chinese crew would not work under an Indian and (b) because his service certificate showed that he had always been in big ships, hence he could not have any knowledge of handling small ones. After that I laid off as I was quite unpopular enough already. I fancy there had been a lot of kniff-knaffing as to what they are going to do with the tug when she arrived, and I have now exploded their scheme for running her, so there is a lot of vagueness in the air. Gemmell, our PO engineer, left on Tuesday, so there is only the navigator and myself left, and we are waiting to hear what they are going to do with us. I used to think that they were a bit dippy in HK, but here they seem to be absolutely crackers. It is a godforsaken dump and I want to get the hell out of it and back to HK as soon as I can.

Well, lovey, that is about the drift of it all. We have got here, the trip was an excellent experience and I now feel a bit more justified in being dressed up as a sailor. But having arrived, no one seems to love us and I want to get out. This trip has made me realise how much we are in velvet in HK: cinemas, golf courses, pleasant people, no shortage of anything, two restaurants where you can get a really good meal.

I saw the M.O. over the prospect of returning via Australia, so as to have my ancient and honourable ailment operated upon in a good climate;[2] I did not hold out high hopes but they seem to be used enough to do anything. Nothing doing, he said they would have to be trailing on the ground before they could recommend that. Nothing like a try, however.

---

2   The likely cause of the ailment would be an abdominal hernia, which can result in scrotal swelling.

I think the war news is most decidedly encouraging; I only seem to get it in little scraps, these days, but it looks good. It seems the Germans are having whacking great casualties in Russia without really getting anywhere. If that venture fails and they have an unsuccessful invasion of Britain on a big scale, with corresponding appalling losses, I think they will crack. In fact I still stand on my old idea that we will see the foundations of victory laid by late September.[3] The Japs seem to have been made to eat a pretty terrible pill recently[4] and I do not think we will have much sauce from them. In fact, I see precious little reason why we should not be together again before Christmas, so drop all this chat about grey hair and dying. This life in an entirely male atmosphere does not suit me too much.

To Agnes Dulley   7 August

I have come to journey's end, and am, at present staying in that most fashionable and up-to-date hostelry, the Crescent Hotel, Aden. Possibly you remember it from when you passed through in 1930.[5] It is a dirty, ramshackle dump and you cannot even get a cool bath as the water tank is out on the roof and the water comes out almost boiling from the sun's heat. Aden in August is not exactly a haven of rest and my ambition is to get out and away before I get snipped for a job in the Naval Intelligence Staff, which is vaguely hanging around in the offing.

When we got here we imagined it was merely a matter of handing over to the new crew, but things did not quite work out like that. I got mixed up on the wrong end of departmental petty bickering and, being new to the port and its ways, I was always wrong whatever I did. However, after a rather painful and almost completely wasted week, I managed to hand over the worthy tug, and am now a gentleman at large, trying to get out of the place before anyone spots that I have not got a job.

I am very glad we did the trip. My previous efforts in HK to forward the cause of democracy had left me with rather a feeling of futility, but having done this trip and got away with it, I feel I have justified myself to small degree, at any rate in my own eyes, which is what counts as far as one's own self-respect goes. That may all sound a bit abstruse, and I find it difficult to explain, but I hope it conveys.

---

3 In fact the foundations were laid over a year later with victory at El Alamein.
4 From 1940 the USA had been placing embargoes on Japan, and in July 1941 all Japanese assets in America were frozen. Keay, p. 168.
5 Possibly visiting Peter in Hong Kong.

All the best for the time being and I hope you are not too lonely in London now that Frances and Daphne are gone.

To Therese   10 August

Incidentally, your remarks about recruiting in Australia were not all approved by the censor and some were cut out.[6] As regards the question of your return to HK, book straight off as soon as the ban has been raised and pay the fare yourself if necessary. I don't think we have much hope of getting the Govt. to pay the fare, and if we tried to do so it would probably have the effect of your being put back to the last in the batch. I should not fly if I were you, as you would have to leave most of your luggage and the Lord knows when you would see it again. The only thing that might cancel the above is if I can get short leave to Australia when the war is over. If I can, I would be well advised to take it while Wilmer is still there. JM & Co. should pay all fares and we could then travel back together when all the rush is over. I will only be too glad to get out of this hole by any route and any ship.

The Shuffle up in the RNVR, about which I could not write in HK, was that the Commodore went on leave to Australia, Vernal took over command and I went ashore as First Lieut. I did not like the idea but could have worked with Vernal perfectly OK, however, when the Commodore came back from Australia, Vernal then had to go on leave which left me working with the Commodore. He has not given up his shore job and tried to learn his RNVR one properly. He had not gone when I left HK early in June, but this trip should have scotched the idea of my being First Lieut. as they will have had to make other arrangements before I get back.

I have had several letters from my mother forwarded here. Some of her news was not so good; Frances and Daphne Morgan were killed in an air raid on London, while Jack,[7] who had just been gazetted in the RAFVR has had a recurrence of his old trouble and will have to go to a sanatorium for six months. Poor Alan Morgan, all his family wiped out in a year and he left to go it alone. Alan is now serving as an officer Commanding Troops in Transport and apparently I overlapped with him here but never ran into him.

---

6 In June the Australian Government was making plans to enlist more men into the armed services. *The Times*, 19 June 1941.
7 Peter's brother.

For five days after arrival they did not know what they wanted to do with us, and I seemed to be the scapegoat of the party, chiefly I fancy because I told them that some of the arrangements they had already made re the crew were quite unworkable. They later proved to be, but they did not like my saying so. I spent the next three days handing over the tug, the usual muddle and chaos, not knowing what to do and how to do it. Eventually that was finished and I came ashore to await passage to HK, also act as nurse maid to the Chinese crew who are going back as well.

As you can imagine Aden in August is not exactly paradise, the temperature is a steady 90–92°F day and night, and the wind blows the dust everywhere. There is absolutely nothing to do bar read detective novels, drink and, of course, think of you. I went to the cinema the other evening with a tough-egg RNR Lieut. from Yorkshire. What do you think we wore for the local mess kit? Black shoes and socks, white drill trousers open neck shirt with shoulder straps and a black cummerbund; we should have had a couple of banjos and blackened our faces, because we certainly looked the part. That is the Red Sea Rig apparently; I must try it on the HK Hotel some evening. I hope to get a ship in a few days and will certainly be glad to be out of this benighted hole.

There is one thing that may cheer you up, namely that except for my natural tendency towards the bottle, I have been leading a most austere life since I left HK. Except for Mrs Fairbairn in Singapore, some Dutch women in Padang and a ginger-haired half caste at the Seychelles, with whom Glover and Gemmell were trying to get fresh, I have not spoken to a single woman at all. Is that chastity or isn't it?

Why the Germans started their Russian Campaign, God knows. Possibly they decided the invasion of Britain was not a go, so they must have oil and wheat to last out in the hope that their blockade of Britain would be successful. But all they seem to have done in the first eight weeks is to pick up whacking casualties and, if we can stage an autumn offensive, they will then be fighting on two or three fronts, the one thing Hitler has always tried to avoid. That is where your foundation of victory is coming.

Well I think that about finishes me off. Correspondence in this oven of a place is not too easy. Keep cheerful, my love, because I feel sure we will be together again before you expect.

LIFE IN ADEN

To Therese   15 August

It is very sweet of you to be concerned over my safety and general welfare, but you really must not upset yourself. Aden is not in the 'War Area' and scarcely ever has been. When the Italians were going strong in Abyssinia they apparently used to do rather half-hearted air raids here, but they did not have much success and have made absolutely no signs of any damage to the town. That, of course, is all over now and Aden is out of bombing range for the Germans, whose most advanced base is presumably Crete. Suez and the Canal area seem to be catching it a bit, but we are 1,300 miles on from there, which means 2,600 on the return trip, nearly the width of the Atlantic.

Our twin is due in next week. Its officers were Watson, Poole and Milne and also Pollock as far as Singapore. Watson was married for a few days before we sailed, so his sweetie bought the baby a bit. I will be very interested to hear what happened to them if I am still here. I have had no news since we left Singapore, so I do not know whether they changed the officers apropos of their unfortunate smash up.

The censor seems to be getting quite interested in your letters as there was again a piece cut out. You had been talking about the Mansfields – next piece cut out – then reference to someone speaking French and German and a good salary. Presumably some job that Mrs M is onto.[8] As you see from the address, I am still here awaiting passage and getting very fed up in the process. The difficulty seems to be the Chinese crew, who have been put ashore here and due to be repatriated to HK. Almost any ship could take me, but it is not too easy to find one to take me and thirty-six Celestials.[9] Goodwin and Glover were given jobs as watch keeping officers in a ship, which was a bit short, and got off over a fortnight ago on their way back. The navigator has a temporary job in the Examination Service, filling in until a relief arrives, so I am the sole survivor of the wreck.

I have been ashore for twelve days now and apart from a few odd jobs there has been nothing to do at all, absolutely nothing, and I have reached about the height of boredom. Living in a third rate hotel with one's suitcases all packed so as to be able to make a quick getaway, is not exactly conducive to settling down to anything seriously, so I drift rather aimlessly between odd drinks at the bar (usually

---

8 It was alleged in an earlier letter that Mrs Munro had a supposedly secret job in intelligence.
9 In this case another word for Chinese.

lukewarm), detective stories and half-hearted attempts at writing letters. The one thing that scares me is that I may get caught for some job here if I don't get going and out of the place. People seem to settle down to this spot and like it alright, but the prospect of getting stuck here fills me with the deepest horror.

I am now sharing a bedroom with a Ltr. Cdr. RN called Turnbull. He and another two and a half striper called Low are awaiting passage to Durban on sick leave. I am trying to fix that I go into the first available ship and that the navigator brings the crew back when he gets out of the Examination Service. That sounds grand to me, but the personnel officer, a Ltr. Cdr. RNR is probably afraid that the navigator may get stuck in the Examination Service, so that he, the personnel officer, will get left with a Chinese crew on his hands.

There is one bright spark on a sombre horizon; everything and everyone in Aden is a bit dippy so you may expect the pay situation to be out of control as well. Apparently I draw, at my rate for the first month, a Subsistence Allowance of about RS 300 per month, out of which I pay some RS 3.50 per day for my food at the Hotel (the room is free), leaving me a net profit of RS 6.50 per day. This apparently is a local allowance for officers passing through and is not taken off my pay when I get back to HK, so there seems to be profit in staying here, boring though it may be.

Keep cheerful my sweet, it can't last a great while longer. The Germans have had colossal losses in Russia, about a quarter of what they were in the last war, but all done in eight short weeks, so we are that much farther on. There seems to be some truth in the rumour about Goering and General Milch being in a concentration camp, as the Italian paper at Massawa had it five weeks ago. If it is true the break up from the top started by the Hess' flight, is continuing, so it all looks good from our point of view. If we do a successful autumn offensive in Libya and the Russians hold out, we ought to be able to crack them this autumn and the end will be in sight, it will be a matter of months not years.

I long for the day when we are both together again, settled down at No.168 with little HP playing around the place. A settled life, knowing where we will be tomorrow and knowing that we need not be parted unless we choose it ourselves. It looks pretty good to me.

To Jack Dulley   17 August

Do you recollect the Crescent Hotel, the big one on the Plaza?[10] That is my present abode and has been for a fortnight. I spend my time between the Crescent Hotel and the Union Club and have become an adept at wasting time. It is the only way to keep out of the bar and if one settles down then it means that one would be inebriated for the bulk of the time.

---

10 When Jack worked for a bank in India he would have stopped in Aden going out or on return.

CHAPTER 14

The Return Journey
August to September 1941

Peter eventually left Aden about 22 August. He was at last on his return journey to Hong Kong, which was to prove very different to his outward bound journey. He travelled by a variety of means of transport during which he experienced some of the basic aspects of travelling in the East at that time. This, however, gave him time for letter writing. On the international scene, Churchill, after visiting President Roosevelt in the USA, made a speech to the [British] nation on 24 August, which included reference to the Far East and chided Japan for its aggression in China and Indo-China and the threat it posed to other countries in the region. He asks Japan to negotiate with the USA.[1]

To Therese   24 August   At sea Aden/Colombo

As you see I am now on my way back to HK and the deadly boredom of waiting at Aden is now finished, thank goodness. I had two and a half weeks at the Crescent Hotel and a further week previously when I was getting rid of the tug, and you may imagine three and a half weeks in Aden is just about enough for anyone.

The Chinese crew from the tug went off in a Danish Merchant Ship, while the two wireless ratings and myself got a lift in a cruiser,[2] 'taking passage' as it is technically termed. I have fallen on my feet pretty well, as I have been given the captain's spare cabin and am very comfortably ensconced. Your photos in the leather case and the one of HP in his pram taken at Sydney, both sit on the chest of drawers so there is a homely atmosphere about things, but somehow I feel badly out of my element. I do not know the big ship routine, customs, habits or anything about it all; people are always blowing bugles, pipes and what-have-you and giving orders over the loud speaker system.

---
1   Wheeler, p. 324.
2   The cruiser was probably HMS *Cornwall*, a Kent-Class, County type heavy cruiser, deployed as a Flagship of 5th Cruiser Squadron, China Station in September 1939, commanded by Admiral Sir Percy Noble. This would explain why Peter and the officers had mutual friends. She visited Aden in July 1941 and was deployed to the Indian Ocean from August to November. Sunk by the Japanese in April 1942 with heavy casualties. http://www.naval-history.net/xGM-Chrono-06CA-HMS_Cornwall.htm. 3 September 2015.

Steam ships in Colombo Harbour

The officers are a pleasant bunch and some have been in China and Hong Kong, so we have plenty of mutual acquaintances, also she is a 'happy ship', which is a great help. But somehow the transfer from a small ship to a big ship routine gives me an inferiority complex and I feel rather lonely and forlorn. Childish, of course, and maybe it will pass off in a few days.

As I am merely 'taking passage' as far as Colombo, I have not been given a job of work to do, but have been filling in a bit of time with the navigator, in practising star sights, a side of navigation on which I am extremely deficient. In the few days that I have been doing them, I have learnt quite a bit about quick methods for working them out, and how to lay out the work. I hoped to pick up all that sort of thing from the *St. Aubin*'s navigator. Incidentally I left him stuck in the Examination Service at Aden and just before I left I heard that he might be sent to Massawa,[3] so I think I did fairly well as I had a private and unofficial arrangement with Vernal before I left HK, that I would try to lose him on the trip.[4]

---

3   On the Red Sea, now called Mitsiwa in Eritrea.
4   For which the navigator was probably very grateful, as events turned out.

Did I tell you in an earlier letter I was chalked off good and hot by the Naval Officer in Command at Aden for not having collected a new crew for the tug, when I never knew I was supposed to be doing so. I was a bit sore at the time, as I felt it was one over the odds, but did not blow up as the NOIC (Naval Officer in Command) seemed to be a very tired man and working under considerable strain. That worthy gent a Captain RN, went off his rocker a week later and will have to be invalided home, a fate which apparently happens to many who stay at Aden for over a year; you may understand that I was glad to get away.

As I said I go to Colombo in my present ship, and then apply for some further mode of conveyance. If I have to wait about in Colombo for a bit, it will be a vastly preferable spot to Aden in which to do it. I hope Nicholson is still there and if so, I will be quite shameless about battening down on him. Otherwise, if I have any length of stay, I think I will try and get up to Neuralia if it is not too expensive. I am a bit fed up with the hot weather and this ship in the Gulf of Aden with all the portholes closed at night has been a beauty.[5] Oh for the days of peace and those weekends with the two of us in the yacht. Don't they look good now and at the time we did not realise how good they were.

To Agnes Dulley   29 August   Aden/Colombo
The trip [to Colombo] has been quite interesting, even if I have not learnt much. In Hong Kong before the war we never had any opportunity to do any training in HM ships and since the war started we have been running our own tugs and so forth, with Chinese crews and on lines which have little connection with that bible of the Navy, King's Regulations and Admiralty Instructions. As a result I have very little idea how things are done in the Navy proper and have been pretty well adrift in this ship.

There is always someone blowing a bugle and I never have the slightest idea what it is all about, so I maintain a masterly inactivity and do nothing about it. I have filled in a bit of time with the navigator. In an HM ship the navigator navigates and does nothing else, so the whole show is done with no inconsiderable precision.

When I get to Colombo I then start once again with trying to get some ship to take me on a further leg of the journey; travelling by sea in wartime is very complicated. You cannot breeze into Thos. Cook and say I want a ticket to Hong Kong. You have to go to a Sea Transport Officer, usually a retired Merchant Skipper with an RNR

---
5 The portholes would have been closed to maintain a blackout at night.

The Grand Oriental Hotel, Colombo

Commission, who knows very little about the prospects of travelling and whose one ambition is to get you on to another port and so off his books. Still, at least I am going to a fixed destination which cannot move. Joining a ship is far more difficult, as it has usually just left before you arrive.

Well, I am afraid this is a very dull letter, but I have no news which would pass the censor.

To Therese   2 September   Colombo
I arrived here on 30th and am now settled down at the Grand Oriental Hotel (the hotel opposite the pier where you land), waiting once again to start on the next leg of the trip. It appears that I go to Madras[6] by train and get a ship from there, but there is nothing in view for another fortnight, so I am trying to fix to go to Neuralia[7] for a bit of cold weather and some golf. I wired you on arrival here to say I had got here and that

---

6 On the coast of India, north of Ceylon.
7 Neuralia was a hill station.

I was progressing slowly, and I hope you received it alright. Letters seem so slow and uncertain, and I have not the vaguest idea where you have got to with my news, so it seems best to wire you from each port so that you will have some idea where I am.

Nicholson is still here and I ran into him within an hour of arrival, with the result that I have been most handsomely entertained and have been having a pretty beery time. He is still a bachelor, lives in the same bungalow, where we had lunch in November 1938, which he shares with two other men. Colombo is a bit too hot for me though, the standard of drinking is well above my modest tastes, so I am fixing up to go to Neuralia. We ran into a friend of Nic's at the Colombo Club last night and he is going to get me fixed up at the Hill Club, right on the golf course, so I will get a bit of exercise, which I have been badly needing for a while past, also some cold mountain air and, I hope, a spot of quiet, healthy life.

To Therese   3 September

I heard yesterday afternoon from the Naval Office that I am going to Madras by train on Saturday 6th, so I have had to scratch the Neuralia idea. It would have meant going up on the train on Wednesday night and coming down by the Friday night train, so I did not think it worthwhile, especially as the train fare is about RS 30. A pity I could not have had all my Aden time in Colombo, as I could have used it to far greater advantage.

I don't do so well here on the 'Sustainable Allowance'. Here everything seems far more expensive. You pay one rupee for a microscopic drink and everything else seems to be a match.

I will be glad to get back to HK, but it will be quite a while before I get there. I do a night in the train to the NW corner of Ceylon, an hour or so in the ferry and then twenty-four hours in the train to Madras. I don't know what sort of ship I will pick up at Madras, probably a British/India ship to Penang and wait then for a Jardine ship to HK, so I should eventually arrive about the end of September. Did I tell you that we past our twin tug at sea when we were about thirty miles out of Aden. I knew she was due that day, but had not had any news from them since we left Singapore about the middle of June, so I do not know what happened at the Court of Enquiry i.e. whether some of the officers were replaced or not.

The war news, so far as Russia is concerned, seems to be eminently satisfactory: they seem to be holding out OK and doing that very necessary job, slaughtering Germans by the thousand. If we can give them a bit of a knocking about in Libya, then life should not look too good when they start the third winter of the war.

To Agnes Dulley   5 September   Colombo
Well, I must get off to the Naval Officer, fix up about tomorrow's journey, and get this censored. It is an awful curse not being allowed to pop your letters in the nearest pillar box.

To Agnes Dulley   15 September   Singapore
I left Colombo by train on Saturday night with the two wireless ratings from the tug and a Commissioned Warrant Officer from the RAF, who is on his way to Singapore. We go to the NW coast of Ceylon and by ferry for about fifteen miles over to India. I had never before realised that the sea crossing to India is so short. We caught the train on the Indian side at about 11.00 am and then a rather dull train journey to Madras which we reached at about 7.00 am the next day.

What surprised me about Colombo and Madras was that it seemed so cool compared with my ideas of a HK summer, where the temperature is not high, but it is intensely damp.

I don't quite know what I will do when I get back; there is a vague project of another trip to Aden, but the tug in question may have already gone. I fancy we should have some newer and far more elegant patrol craft by the time I get back, so if it is to be patrolling in HK waters, I hope my days of dirty coal-burning tugs are over.

To Therese   16 September   At sea – Madras – Penang
Here we are, well on the way back to HK; we reach Penang tomorrow, the ship takes me on to Singapore and from there I should be able to get up to HK quite quickly and easily.

Nic continued to entertain me in a very lavish style in Colombo. I staged a return party in the form of a dinner dance at the Galle Face, for which Nic produced a couple of definitely attractive popsies.[8] We had quite a good evening but I did not enjoy it as much as when we were there together in 1938.

The Paymaster's office seemed to be a very trusting lot, whenever I wanted to pay the crew, I called on a completely unknown Base Accountant Officer, said I wanted a

---
8   Slang for young attractive girls.

thousand rupees or so and was handed it over the counter without a murmur.

Madras seemed a sleepy spot and at the Navy office people either weren't there or did not know. The Merchant ship, which was to take us to Singapore was already in port, so we went straight on board. We had two days and a night in Madras, and on the second afternoon I had a very pleasant bathe at the Gymkhana Club. I also ran into one – MacCarthy, who used to be in the Group's [Jardines] mess in Shanghai, where I stayed when I was up there in 1936. Madras cannot forget that it was bombarded by the *Emden* in the last war.[9] Although that is now twenty-seven years ago and the city is about as far removed from hostilities, actual or possible, as it is possible, they religiously have a blackout every night. They improve on that, however, the lighthouse which is the first sign of the town which you would pick up at a distance, and which is also in the middle of the town, is left on. Surely an odd mix of war mindedness and vexatious regulations.

The first four days were taken up loading cargo at Indian coast ports, so progress has not been phenomenal. The trip has been pretty dull, as there are no amusing passengers; I share a cabin with an RAF lad. The Skipper, on the other hand, is unlimited, but his conversation is entirely about himself and his great deeds. We are going through them for the second time and some for the third, so I am at considerable pains to avoid getting stuck with him and having to listen to the recital of his greatness. Why can't people realise how boring such recitations are and what a giveaway.

I have filled a bit of the time by organising a passengers' gun crew for the four-inch gun on the stern and we have the drill fairly pat. After we had been practising for about two days, the Skipper, true to form, told a lady passenger how he always liked to organise a gun crew, as it gave us something to do and kept our minds off things.

Well, my sweet, I will soon be in HK, and I hope to have lots of your letters waiting for me, your last received at Aden, was of 21 June [nearly three months ago] so it seems a terribly long while since I heard from you. I think of you a lot, my love, also young HP and I miss you more all the time. But it won't be long now before we see each other again. I feel that a war of motion, like this one, produces results far more quickly than a war of attrition like the last, and I feel we will soon be smacking the Germans in the West, while the Russians do their stuff in the East.

---

9   The SMS *Emden*, a light cruiser in the Imperial German Navy in WWI, was a raider and in 1914 she attacked the city of Madras at night and opened fire on the many large fuel oil tanks of the Burmah Oil Company. The raid did little damage but was a severe blow to British and local morale.
    http://en.wikipedia.org/wiki/Bombardment_of_Madras. 14 September 2015.

To Therese   20 September   Singapore
[On British India Steam Navigation Co. Ltd. paper]
We arrived at Penang a few days ago. Had a twenty-four hour stopover, but I did not go up to the Crag Hotel, as I would have liked to have done, as I felt it would be too full of memories of our last visit there. I tried to get onto the Flemings at Kuala Lumpur, with the idea of looking them up, but found they were still on leave.

In the evening I went to the cinema and wondered into the E & O [European & Orient?] after for a drink; then I ran into Robertson of the HK Bank. You probably will not remember him. Apart from getting rather bald he has not changed a bit, and was hard at it, 'a deux' sucking someone else's wife. She seemed to be enjoying the process in no mean way. I then had lunch with him at the E & O next day and we had a chat about the days when we were young and foolish in Singapore. I also saw Prentis, which was rather a surprise. He has just been transferred to Penang and he tells me that his dear Esme is shortly flying up to join him. Lucky man.

To Therese   26 September   At sea Singapore/Hong Kong
We are nearing HK and smelling the stable door at last. I feel very much like the prodigal son returning. Land has just hove into sight so I must go up and have a look at it.

We arrived at Singapore on 20th and I transferred straight over to a somewhat decrepit Jardine cargo ship which has recently taken out a passenger licence in view of the shortage of accommodation for passengers these days. We sailed at 3.30 pm so I did not have much time to spare there.

I am the only passenger on the ship bar my two wireless ratings from the tug, who are travelling second class, so I am rather thrown on the company of the Skipper. Quite a pleasant bloke in a very limited way, but it is terribly difficult to hold any sort of conversation with him for two reasons: (1) because he never listens to what you say and (2) because he immediately interrupts you if you start to say something. I am beginning to wonder if the Merchant Service Skippers suffer from some sort of complex, whereby they feel the world at large is thirsting to hear their rather ill-informed views on all and sundry questions, which tend to crop up in general conversation.[10] I have been playing around with doing a bit of navigation on the way

---

10   No doubt they lived a lonely life, set apart from the rest of the crew and therefore took every opportunity to talk to passengers.

from Singapore, partly to keep my hand in and partly to while away the time. I find, as usual, there is a certain amount of surprise that an RNVR officer should know anything about navigation so I have replied, rather unkindly, by asking people with Masters Tickets questions on the theory of navigation, which they presumably knew when they passed their Masters but have certainly forgotten since.

This navigation business amuses me quite a lot. To understand the theory completely is quite a difficult job, but to be able to do it by rule of thumb, with a modest knowledge of the theory, is not difficult for anyone of reasonable intelligence, and I pride myself that I have that. But I sit back and say I am not a sailor, but just an accountant, so when Merchant Services people find I can slap out navigation just as well as well as they can, they get rather perplexed and annoyed, while I am pleasantly amused. Catty possibly but rather human.

When it comes down to 'Honest to God' and bedrock sentiment, I am not very good at expressing myself, as you presumably know only too well by now. But believe me, I miss you very badly my love. I loathe being on my own, I feel lost and incomplete. We have nearly four years of married life, living together, and in that time we have become so much of a team, being together, arguing together and doing things together, that I for one, do not want to do them any other way and I feel lost when you are not there. I know I am not good at expressing all this but I assure you that it comes right from the thing I use for a heart and I feel it is far more genuine and deep seated than I can ever express in words. Believe it or not, it is there just the same.

To Agnes Dulley   26 September   Singapore/Hong Kong

I put in a bit of time with the ship's navigator on the cruiser. I found out from him that I am due for some pilotage money over our trip in the tug and, which is far more important, got hold of the right form on which to apply for it. In the Navy it does not matter how much you want something, or how good your claim to have it, if you don't apply on the right form you don't get it.

We arrive at HK tonight, but will get there too late to be received until tomorrow morning.

I don't know what sort of a job I will get when I return to work; whether it will be in command of a Patrol Launch or an executive job ashore. The former I rather hope. However, I will know in a day or so.

CHAPTER 15

The Last Few Months
September to November 1941

Peter finally returned to Hong Kong after four month's absence. Although he was away a comparatively short time, much has happened since he left. He would have been briefed by his friends at the Hong Kong Club and Therese's uncle, Edgar Davidson, now on the Executive Council. The latter would have retained the confidentiality of the Council, but seeing his depression, Peter would no doubt have read between the lines. Peter also admitted to a bout of depression and there was the debacle over their wedding anniversary date.

As Andrew Roberts in 'Letters from the Front'[1] points out, soldiers writing from the Front get to the point quickly and tend to tell the truth, apart from their chances of being killed. Although they will have considered it themselves, they want to protect those closest to them. This was likewise reflected throughout Peter's World War 2 letters. Latterly the emphasis he places on the future and the happiness it could bring is to compensate for his thoughts about a likely Japanese invasion. He wants to think of something positive and above all have hope, that very basic human need. Both Edgar and Eva Davidson and Peter were socialising more, no doubt to build up a feeling of comradeship and to temporarily forget the ever-present threat.

In Japan, Prince Konoye resigned in mid-October. The Minister for War, General Hideki Tojo was asked to form a cabinet. He stated that he wanted to see a new order in East Asia.[2]

To Therese   26 September   Continued on 28th
We arrived in HK yesterday morning and I have been hard at [it] since, saying 'What ho' to people. I am back at 191, which is very nice for me, and the E's seem quite pleased to see me. It is extremely comforting to be back in an ordered household, amongst our own people as you might say. UE is now the Hon. Mr D[3] in place of Stanley Dodwell, who is presumably in Australia, he seems to be pretty busy, what with the Executive Council, and some new war work in place of the Huseliers.

---
1 Roberts, p. 10.
2 Wheeler, p. 325.
3 Edgar Davidson was appointed to the Executive Council. All members had the title Hon. http://www.legco.gov.hk/1941/h411113.pdf. 1 August 2015.

On return I have received many of your letters. There seems to be so much to answer and so much to tell you about now I am back, that I doubt I will manage it all in one letter. I was terribly sorry to hear you had been feeling so low, but don't let things get you down. The war news is not bad, it is definitely good, far better than is evident on the surface. The Germans have lost probably about three quarters of a million killed in their Russian Campaign and will inevitably lose a lot more. That means we are saved the bother and loss to ourselves of killing about one million Germans; and in the last war they packed up when they had had two million killed, so a very big dent has been made by the Russian Campaign in the slaughter necessary to stop them.

As regards the Japs, my feelings are still precisely the same. I will give ten to one against them taking the plunge in the Far East. The Russians using Vladivostock as an air base, really could knock hell out of their industrial cities and probably the Japs know it. To my mind the position is much the same as it was when you were here, except that the Japs have now three potential enemies (Russia, Britain and USA) instead of two (Britain and USA). The Japs are still stuck solidly over the China Campaign so will the acquisition of a new opponent assist them? On the other hand if they stick in the Axis they have got to put up some show which I feel will consist in going through the motions of starting a war, in fact everything short of a war. As a result the situation here will probably continue to have a threatening appearance, regular crises, diplomatic moves and counter moves but no actual fight. Unfortunately from our point of view I see little prospect of our being able to bring sufficient force to bear out here to blow the gaff on the Japanese bluff. So it will continue until we have cleared up the Germans in the West but will decrease as their threats and big talk regularly fails to be translated into words and as the German military strength grows weaker ours grows stronger.

The only final settlement out here is to bring the British and American fleets out to the Pacific and tell the Japs to get the hell out of China, Indo China, Manchuria and Korea. If they don't, their fleet will be sunk and their Merchant fleet captured, so that their army will be left stranded on the mainland unsupported and will slowly be annihilated by the Chinese guerrillas. On the other hand, if they do get out [of China], the military party will be discredited and broken, their dreams of a new order in Asia, for which they have sacrificed so much, will disappear like mist before the morning sun and the country will be thrown into a state of chaos and revolution. But we cannot take a strong line out here until we have finished off the Germans in the West. Till that day comes, which I confidently anticipate next summer,[4] we have got to soft pedal out here and I am afraid that means for us a series of abortive crises which will stop the repeal of the evacuation idea. But don't worry my love, I am not sitting on the top end of the inferno.[5] The Australians appear to be windy,[6] but no one is here and Hong Kong's crisis appears to exist in the press of the outside world as against in and around Hong Kong.

Well, I seem to have been off on a very long digression, so what about answering your letter. I was very relieved to get away from Aden, as I think I have said before. If I had stayed I would only have got a shore job, and all the naval people ashore seem to be suffering under some rather ill-defined strain, boredom, frustration, drink or some such thing and lots of people have become unbalanced and had to be sent home.

I was glad to hear your lunch party at the Australia Hotel went off well; certainly if you entertain, do it well and don't minge.[7] I will be amused to hear if you eventually met Kitty Metcalf; she and I caused some scandal by sitting at a table for two crossing the Atlantic in 1934. People were curious as to what the relationship was and became scandalised when we failed to react to pumping. I fancy Mrs Owen is definitely socially minded in Sydney, but I thought that through her you might meet a strata of society which you probably would not meet otherwise.

From the chat I have heard since I have been back, HK seems to have got right out of control during my absence. Scandals everywhere: Inquiries into Govt. Depts., people in the PWD shooting themselves apropos of questions asked about the cost of ARP tunnels, divorces pending by the score, Charles Boxer living in sin with an erstwhile friend of Ursula's, who is about to produce an illegitimate child at the WM Hospital,[8] Suzette married to some questionable gent in Singapore after the [her] parents had tried to stop the wedding, and so on ad lib. Everyone is agog with scandal, licking their chops and waiting to hear the next and even more shocking disclosure.

---

4 There was victory against the Germans in North Africa in autumn 1942. However, the USA, by placing an oil embargo on the Japanese, were placing serious pressure on them in 1941. Beevor, p. 248.
5 In two and half months Hong Kong was invaded.
6 Australia was requesting that the two remaining brigades in North Africa should be returned to bolster the defence of Australia. Perry, p. 17.
7 Be mingy.
8 The War Memorial Hospital.

To Therese   3 October

Many thanks for your cable, which arrived today. It was very sweet of you to think of wiring me apropos of my return to HK welcoming me back and I was very touched.

I thought the snap of HP in the wicker chair outside was grand. He looks so robust and cheerful and a great credit to your care in looking after him. I hope you manage to get someone to help you with him as it is no good at all to be tied to him and the house all the while. I hope your prospective domicile with Mary Williams comes off and that it is a success. Living in a flat with someone you know is vastly preferable to a guest house and if you are in the Rose Bay area I feel you should be more in touch with people of your own ilk.

HP in the wicker chair

Incidentally your last letter had about one third of a page cut out of it [censored]. It was between some remarks about Mrs Gordon Spencer and the Leadbetter's [Peter's relatives] connection, and my trip on the RN ship from Aden. Unfortunately the stuff on the back of the page was lost too, that was all sentimental remarks about one of our last weekends in Port Shelter. Most annoying.

I was glad to hear about Robert's[9] shift up in pay, I feel he certainly deserved it. It was fortunate that he was able to get well installed in his job before the start of the war, and I should think he would do well at it.[10]

I am sorry that you have been feeling so mouldy and depressed down in Australia, but cheer up sweetie. No one, naturally, can say when the war will be over, but the Russians are undoubtedly making a nasty hole in the German war machine. When the crack comes in Germany, I fancy it will come from the top; if the Ribbentrop, Goebbels etc., see that Germany is not going to win, they will get out and try to live on their ill-gotten gains abroad.

Petrie is still down in Australia, so Vernal is in command of the RNVR and I am to go to *Cornflower* as First Lieutenant. I don't much appreciate the idea but at least it will be a change of occupation and doing those patrols round the beaches would be a bit tame after one's deep sea ideas collected on the trip to Aden. I will not have to live on board *Cornflower* and I hope we can get things organised so that it is not a seven day a week job.

I spent last week clearing up the odd jobs from the tug and paying off the crew, who had got back here two days before me. Also trying to collect money for various expenses incurred while away. I find I am due some money for pilotage at Singapore, so have filled it all up on the requisition form and await results. If anything is forthcoming, I intend to split it with Goodwin, the New Zealand officer who has just been transferred to MTBs [Motor Torpedo Boats].

While on the question of money, if anything goes wrong up here, apply to Townend, who will pay you £30 per month, whether you need it or not, so as to make sure of getting it. The position is a bit obscure but works roughly as follows: if HK is taken by the Japs, the Canton Insurance Office funds in Australia will be frozen temporarily and will be under the Control of the Custodian of Enemy Property in Australia. To

---

9 Robert was Therese's brother-in-law.
10 Robert Stewart worked in research on gun sites i.e. the aiming mechanisms. Peter does not say what his job was because it was secret and a concern re censorship.

The old HMS 'Cornflower', built in 1916, which was adapted for the HKRNVR

obviate the difficulty we have put some money in the name of Townend's firm, Geo King & Co., which will not be frozen. This can be drawn on by JM & Co. people, but will only last for about six months, by which time the Canton Insurance office funds should be unfrozen. You can then continue to draw Canton Insurance office funds from Townend in what quantity you require.

I am not panicking over the matter, as I still think the prospect of anything happening here is fairly small, but I thought I would tip you off as to what to do. I will send some more money in due course, so that you will always have £500 in hand against emergencies. Incidentally, to help working my accounts at the end of the year can you let me know how much you have left as on 31 December.

To Therese   12 October

It is so nice to be hearing from you every week again and letters of only a fortnight or so ago: it makes us seem far nearer together and that is a start on the way to being together again.

I am afraid I cannot apply Jardines' rules[11] for my leave to the RNVR arrangements.

---

11 At Jardines there was six months leave every four years, which enabled staff to go back to Great Britain and would have meant that he would have been due for this in 1942. Therese was hoping he would be able to go to Australia, but the RNVR were much less generous.

I hear Antonia Potts' transit permit was refused, they seem to be rather down on them these days and I fancy we had the cream of that. Mrs Ernie Mitchell passed through here the other day, on her way to Macao or some improbable spot and they had a policeman on board to see she did not land.

I was so glad to hear you had got a reliable soul to look after HP for you when you want to have a bit of time off, and I hope you will make plenty of use of her as it is no use getting stewed up and lonely for lack of never going out and seeing people. I was thrilled to see the studio photos when they arrived, the two small ones were very sweet but he seems to be changing so much that quite soon I will not know the young man.

I was interested in what you said about Hughes and HH. When I heard the story from AE on my return, I felt possibly your letter to me with the bit cut out, had been the start of the trouble, but it is absurd to say you are at fault. If she has a job, the continuance of which depends on people not knowing what it is, then she should not tell people what she is doing. If she does tell anyone, it should be under the darkest pledge of secrecy, yet apparently all the HK folk in Sydney know all about her job.

I have settled down to working in *Cornflower* but have not officially been appointed to any job. Vernall has been promoted to Commander in place of Petrie, and is in Command of the Force[12] and I am to come in as First Lieutenant (Second in Command).

There is some odd bobbery[13] about Petrie's leave as he will apparently not get back here on time and there is a rumour sculling around that he is not coming back at all, although I do not see any justification for it. If he does not it is rather hard on Vernall as he is overdue for leave and is waiting until Petrie comes back before he takes it.

The E's have been quite gay recently and out to dinner quite a bit.[14] One evening last week, when they were out, I had Goodwin into dinner and to the cinema after; he was the New Zealander we picked up at S'pore.

Chan, you will be pleased to hear, has got a job with Col. & Mrs White at the Austin barracks. Long may he hold the job because I did not feel I could go on paying him $25 pm for ever, but I did not want him to starve.

---

12 The HKRNVR was known initially as the HK Naval Volunteer Force, and there are photos of them at the King's Birthday Parade June 1934. They became the HKRNVR in 1935.
13 A noisy row. Chambers, p. 115.
14 Perhaps Eva Davidson felt that Edgar needed cheering up and he on his part had become resigned to the invasion.

PS: Do you remember the man who travelled in the 'Chitral' in 1938 [on the way back to Hong Kong] with the 'Spanish looking' wife? He was Capt. Hobbs who shot himself over this ARP enquiry,[15] so perhaps we are better off with an Austin 10.[16]

To Therese   19 October

My heart goes out to you lovey over your life in Sydney and I wish I was able either to do or suggest something that would make it brighter and more cheerful. I am not trying to lecture you, but I feel you are overworking yourself over HP and leading too lonely and shut up type of existence. I would feel far happier if you could get a flat in the Rose Bay area[17] and a bit more domestic help with HP, so that you would not have to work yourself so hard and would be able to get out a bit more and relax amongst people you know and like.[18]

I have at last got on with the job and done something about the present situation, which I fear has got badly out of control apropos of my being away for so long. I have never sent your birthday present [23 May], our wedding anniversary will be here shortly after you get this and Christmas will not be far off, so I made one fell swoop of the lot. I have collected, with AE's assistance, and will shortly despatch the following – a white lace cocktail blouse and a white victory brooch, a dark blue bag and a dozen assorted handkerchiefs from the 3'Lai Handkerchief Store. They may not sound inspired presents and I am afraid they are not, but in these hard days I felt utility was the mark. Poor presents though they are, the thoughts which go with them will have to make up for the lack of originality in selection.

The chief item of local chat is the arrival of the Boxer-Hahn baby, a girl of 5 lbs. Did I tell you that Miss H has put out feelers to AE and Mrs Hall to the effect that 'They were two women in the Colony, whose esteem she would like to retain.' Can you beat it? AE has met her twice at lunch and is expected to repress her religious scruples and the ingrained social values of a lifetime[19] in order to assist some almost unknown

---

15 A programme to build air-raid shelters fell into disrepute owing to the fixing of contracts. Snow states that Wing Commander A. H. S. Steele-Perkins was the ARP Director. Snow, p. 42.
16 Their small car.
17 This was an attractive suburb, which she did move to and the flat had views over Sydney Harbour.
18 She followed this advice, judging by professional photographs of Therese walking down the streets in Sydney and the friends she made.
19 Having been brought up in a well-to-do Victorian family and being a regular churchgoer.

women laugh off the arrival of an illegitimate child, whose father is the husband of one of her friends.[20] Some people have odd ideas and I tell you that Vera Armstrong held a 'Shower Party' several weeks ago, to which people brought gifts for the baby.

You remember sending me a letter from the Evacuation Officer in Australia shortly before I went to Aden. Well I have attended to it at last and have arranged for the Treasury here to remit you £5 per month starting 30 November. This is only a nominal remittance, to get your name on the list and if anything were to happen here, you just apply to have it increased to whatever you want, or whatever they reckon my pay will stand. Don't for a moment imagine from this that I consider we are about to be invaded, I don't. But if you are to be kept in Australia apropos of the prospects of an invasion here, it seems so untidy not to make a job of it and settle up the financial side of things. You will now have Geo King good for £30 per month and this Govt. remittance which you should be able to increase from £5 to about £40/50, so you should be insured against most of the shocks of this world.

I gather the Pacific is at present suffering from a crisis due to the resignation of the Japanese Cabinet. I met FCH[21] [F. C. Hall] at the Club yesterday and was choked off for being flippantly optimistic when I said I would give five to one against war with Japan over the present crisis. FCH has settled down to the 'Doom is near' attitude, has ordered in a couple of cases of whisky to help with the siege, and now that is all clear cut and near at hand seems quite cheerful over the whole show. I feel that the Japs have shot their bolt and ineffectually, from the military point of view, they are degenerating into a nuisance value stage.

I think I told you that Antonia Potts has been refused her transit permit for HK; they seem pretty scared of anyone landing in HK these days as they know quite well that they will cheat for a certainty.[22] Not much news so far as I am concerned. I spend my days hanging around *Cornflower* with no definite job, as I have not yet been appointed First Lieutenant. There is a rumour around the Dockyard that I am to take command of [HMS] *Redstart*,[23] but don't mention it to anyone in Sydney, as I

---

20 His wife, Ursula, was evacuated to Australia in 1940.
21 Peter's boss Hall from 1936.
22 Which the Dulleys had done.
23 She was one of two of the first secret Indicator Loop Mine Layers. The post of captain was taken by Lt.Cdr. H. C. S. Collingwood-Selby RN before the invasion. She was scuttled on 19 December. Collingwood-Selby, pp. 192 & 196.

don't want it shooting back at me. I would vastly prefer that to First Lieut. *Cornflower*. I would have a ship of my own, an approximately independent command, and an interesting job with about three months of each year down in S'Pre, just to give one a change. Of course it is only a rumour, but somehow these Dockyard rumours often have a smack of truth about them.

You may be interested to know that Bish [Lander] dislikes being a grass widower just about as much as I do. I find he dislikes it more and more as the months go by instead of getting reconciled to it. The fact is lovely, that I miss you very badly and feel very lonely without you. Believe it or not, I think of you a lot, much more than I used to do when you were first away down at Baguio. However, the day will come when all this mess is over and we will then get down to it and make up for all we have missed.

To Therese   25 October

Poor Sweetie, I gather from your letters, although you don't say so in so many words, that you are pretty fed up with life and I don't blame you, you have every reason to be so. I have been feeling rather low and dispirited over the last week or so and you are at the bottom of it, as I take a perennially optimistic point of view about the progress of the war and every other aspect of life. It is the knowledge that you are sad, lonely and unhappy in Australia which upsets me, added to that I hate being a grass widower. We have got too much into the habit of doing things together and enjoying things together, so naturally I feel lonely and lost when you are not here. If I go to a party, I feel it difficult to enter into the spirit of things but I manage to keep my end up by having a liberal libation of spirits and talking a lot of hooey in a loud voice. Much though it pains me to say it, that can only be done on spirits. I have an ever present sinking feeling in my tum, which reminds me, if I needed it, that you are not here, so I am only half present. To put it all rather baldly, we have been very happily married for nearly five years now and have become part of each other's lives. I suppose I could seek consolation by frequenting houses of ill fame or acquiring a mistress, but as regards the latter, I am far too late in the market and anyway, as regards both, it does not seem to present any solution.

No, my sweet, there is no solution to our present dilemma, except biting on the bullet and cherishing what we have had in our married life so that we can take it up once again when we are allowed to be together. Keep it and take it up unimpaired;

many won't, from what I can gather but let us be two that will. And don't run away with any ideas that it may be many years before we see each other again. I am all depressed about you being away and lonely but not about the war. Cast your mind back to 1918, when you were about five years old. The Germans seemed to be winning all along the line since 1916, their offensive in March/April 1918 nearly broke the British armies and let them through to the Channel Ports. When that failed, they returned to the Hindenburgh [sic] Line in June 1918 and everyone said it would go on for another ten years. But in July the Hindenburgh Line was broken and from there until November 1918 it was a rapidly increasing rout. I was talking to Alec Potts the other day; he was in France for the finish in the summer and autumn of 1918 and his impressions were that it definitely was a rout; Germans shooting their officers and all the opposite of what Hitler has always tried to tell Germany.

Well, it seems much the same this time. The Germans apparently victorious on all fronts and unstoppable, but the Russians are supplying in five months, what the war of attrition from 1914 to 1918 supplied last time. In the East the Germans have got to go on, to maintain their reputation for invincibility, irrespective of what it costs them in lives or material losses. Any prospect of gain from their Russian campaign is already far outweighed by the immense sacrifice it has cost them, and a sacrifice from which they can never recover. If the Russians can hold out until the winter conditions preclude the prospects of active attack, if we can send in supplies to re-equip their reserves for a spring offensive, then we should be able to do an offensive in the West and in the East next spring[24] and I will be very surprised if that does not break the German resistance.

Neve's leave to Singapore was cancelled the day before he was due to go, due to the flap apropos of the change in Japanese Cabinet; rotten luck on him. Ralph has an idea of Mrs R coming here by ship and his joining her on the way down to Manila, where they spend a fortnight in Bagiou; I am all for the idea, but all Naval leave has been cancelled.

I hope your arrangements for a holiday at Christmas work out alright. You certainly deserve and should have a change and a bit of a rest if that is obtainable. Re finances, you are much to be congratulated on having managed so economically to date; I feel we are building up credit for a big reunion bust-up when we meet again.

---

24 There was a Russian offensive in January 1942, but the Germans held on until January 1943. Beevor, p. 399.

N. L. Smith is about to resign from the Govt. Services and go on pension and I gather it is not on account of age or illness. Rightly or wrongly the errors of the past year, Immigration Office, Evacuation and ARP have been laid at his door and his stewardship has been found wanting. I gather Maude was very upset about it all and wanted people to sign a petition, but why are you paid as top man if you are not responsible?

Have been playing a bit of DWB [Deep Water Bay] golf with UE, but his standard seems to be decreasing visibly. He seems rather run down and depressed these days and AE is a bit worried about it but I suppose he will cheer up in due course.

My position in *Cornflower* is still no clearer, as I have not been appointed First Lieutenant. Watson arrived back from Aden today (he as CO of the other tug) and I must say I was a bit jealous when he had a charming young wife to greet him, but I suppose I should not be as they only had about one and a half day's honeymoon poor things and he sailed about three days after they were married, so she can scarcely feel more than a fiancée.

I went to a cocktail party in *Tamar* last Monday, third anniversary of the MTB Flotilla; we must have made rather a row, as the Commodore [RN] has issued a rule against further parties in HM ships. Gandy who is at present in command of the MTB Flotilla, is shortly off home and very cheered about it.[25]

I don't know when you will get this letter but I will wish you very many happy returns for 26 November our fifth wedding anniversary. It will probably arrive too early, but then you will get at least one in time as I will repeat it at intervals. Incidentally, re a Christmas present (also a birthday one if you think fit) for HP, would you collect whatever you think suitable and try to kid him that it comes from me.

All the best, my love, and don't let yourself get low. We must look to the possibilities of the future, that is where our life lies, not in the inconveniences of the present.

To Therese   2 November

No letter from you this week and I hope that does not mean you have forgotten all about your little hubby in HK. Also it does not mean that you have been ill; probably neither is the case as I have seen no Australia mail in at all.

---

25 He did not go and retained his command until the surrender and then escaped to China in a MTB with the Chinese Admiral, Chan Chak aboard. Snow, p. 74.

Incidentally there was a notice in the papers a day or so ago to the effect that the military are taking over Deep Water Bay, the Clubhouse and the [Golf] course. No one seems to know what it is all about: estimates range from the idea that there is a further regiment coming here and they are going to build a camp on the course,[26] to a more fanciful idea that the course is to be used as a grazing ground for bullocks and sheep which have been imported against siege.

HK seems a very dead spot with you away and although I do not indulge in colossal jags, there is too much of a tendency to be constantly nipping at the bottle, it seems to be the only bright spot in an otherwise rather dull and pointless existence. All of which is leading up to the idea that I continue to miss my little wifey very badly. I think of you a tremendous amount, my love, and feel very lonely and lost without you. I long for you to be back here so that we can be together again but I must admit that, at the moment, I do not see any immediate prospect of that happening.

Master Chan seems to be getting into trouble; the Whites are moving out to Fanling for the winter and he does not want to go there. Then, on top of that, she gave me a harrowing story of how he was supposed to stand by to answer the telephone at their flat in Austin barracks and absented himself one night to Wanchai. I should think she is rather a trial to work for but all the same he should have stuck to the rules when jobs are so scarce. There is a prospect of getting him into *Cornflower* shortly as a cook or a mess boy and if he cannot hold his job down then I am going to wash my hands of him and cut off the unemployment pay.

I was listening to a broadcast of messages this evening from HK wives in Sydney, but their voices were almost indistinguishable. They did not seem to have picked any of the county families or Jardy-Jardy [Jardines] folk, in addition people spoke far too fast, so the mixture of accents, voices unsuitable for broadcasting[27] and hurried speech, was a bit over the odds and produced a most unsatisfactory result at this end.

UE seems to have gone off into a prolonged depression. I suppose it is delayed reaction to Jack's death, striking a not very resilient temperament, and there you have it. I try to be as bright and cheerful as possible, but I must admit that recently I have not altogether felt so.

---

26 It was kept very secret and was built for two Canadian battalions that arrived on 16 November.
27 Deeper voices were needed in the early days of radio.

Steel Perkin's romantic interludes are daily discussed at the ARP enquiry, while I hear there is another ripe one coming along. A rather hysterical Russian Dame came into the rooms of a fairly senior Naval Officer and said she had stabbed a man in her flat, close too. He, like a sap, went along with her to see and found it was true. He wakes up with a crack and realises he will be the chief witness in a case of attempted murder if the laddie lives, and murder if he dies. Nice work, but why did she come to him in her hour of need?

I still don't think the Japs will precipitate war at this end of things; possibly an expedition from Indo China to cut the Burma Road, but not a war against Britain, USA, Russia and the DEI[28] simultaneously. As far as one can make out the Japs are not in too happy a state of affairs at all and the present economic blockade is making them think pretty hard.

Peter to Jack Dulley   2 November

I am writing this in the hope that it will get to England in time to bring you my best wishes for Christmas, also to Betty and Jacqueline. I am not sending presents or Christmas cards this year, so my good wishes are all I have to offer.

While I was taking the tug to Aden, I was doing something interesting and absorbing, but back here as budding First Lieutenant of the Naval Volunteer Force, I have a shore organising job which gives me rather a pain and leaves me feeling a bit listless about life.

To my mind the Japanese menace is rather over-rated. Their army is bogged down in an unsuccessful war in China, and their industrial cities (mostly wooden frame houses) are terribly vulnerable to an air attack from Manila or Vladivostok. They know it too and are scared pink. By all means they have a strong navy but so have the Americans. Can the Japs afford to risk theirs with their army on the mainland and dependent on sea communications?[29]

Well, a very happy Christmas to all three of you, and may 1942 be a happier year for us all.

---

28 America, Britain, China and the Dutch East Indies (DEI) became known as the ABCD Powers. Wheeler, p. 325.
29 In the event the Japanese strategy was to knock out the American Pacific Fleet and invade Hong Kong and the Philippine Islands simultaneously on the 8 December 1941, thus eradicating the American threat. Beevor, pp. 250-2.

To Therese 9 November

It was very good to hear so much from you; I am so glad that your holiday in January at Lepstone[30] seems to be fixed up and I should think that Mary Williams and Doreen Ralph would be a very pleasant couple to go away with.

I was so glad to hear that HP is proving such a credit to the name of Dulley. The present may be dreary and the past full of memories of happier days, but in the future we apparently have a fine young son to look forward to and it is to this future we must look. Other directions are too tinged with unhappiness and self-pity and it does not help to dwell on that.

I am afraid from what I read in your letters, that you have been very lonely, forlorn and unhappy down in Sydney and my heart goes out to you my sweet. The knowledge of your general state of unhappiness, together with life's worries up here, has succeeded in driving me into a state of the deepest gloom I have experienced for many years. My worries are mainly the headaches of becoming First Lieut. in *Cornflower* and not having a proper job and any serious work to do until I am appointed as such. As you know, gloom is not exactly my mark, so when I go about with a low feeling in the pit of my stomach for days on end and knowing that I could burst into tears with the slightest provocation, then it would appear that something has struck your little spouse.

I think it is being back from the Aden trip with all the old associations to remind me of you. When you were first away in Baguio, I was so full of hopes that you would soon be back. Then after you got back and after you left for Australia in March, I did not seem to have time to settle down to gloom before the Aden trip came off. New places, new faces and the feeling that one was really doing something to help in the war effort. Back here again and at first all seemed good fun, seeing everyone one we knew. But after a week or so I started to feel lonely and depressed and to ache with the idea of seeing you and being with you again. It got worse and worse until towards the end of last week, I felt I was losing my nerve and in eminent danger of going to bits completely. However, I went out to Fanling with Sommerfelt yesterday afternoon and had a bit of golf. He is an extraordinarily nice, level headed and cheerful soul and he did me a power of good, with the result that I feel sane and almost cheerful today for the first time in nearly ten days.

I feel convinced that we will be more united and more one than ever before. After

---

30 In the light of events, Therese did not go.

all, marriage is for life, which being parted is only a year or two at the most, so we will win in the end as our present troubles over a short period will have the effect of ensuring and making more certain our future happiness when we are together again.

As regards the prospects of your coming back here, at the moment with the uncertainty of the Japanese,[31] I will be quite frank and say I don't think there is a hope in hell. But don't let that discourage you; for the time being, until things clear up here, I think you are much better off down in Australia. I don't agree with these lads who say it will be a long war. The difficulty here, even if you could get back, is over this billeting: most of the houses on the Peak have been requisitioned for the billeting of families of Chinese, ARP workers, volunteers, special police and so forth; No.168 and the E's included. If the gun were to go off a woman with no war job and a baby would be in a hell of a fix, as she might suddenly find herself turned out of house and home and with no claim on the issue of rations. I fancy all women are presumed to have jobs in the event of a crisis and those who have not would be just out of luck without a friend in the world. We would all be on rations with the shops shut, so I do not see how an unattached woman lives. The authorities have quite enough headaches sorting out their official schemes, without making provision for women who should not be here.

I gather Marjorie Fortescue has fixed for her infant to go to Mrs Van Wylick at Peak Mansions while she joins some hospital, but the idea does not strike me as too hot, as some authority may suddenly bob along and say he has requisitioned Peak Mansions. Mind you, I still don't think the Japs will attack here, but if they did or we went into a precautionary period on a war basis, this would be no spot for unattached women and children. I would be able to do absolutely nothing to help.

There you have the black side of things and I hope I have not been too depressing. I have just put things as I see them and I feel it is only fair to you that I should. The more cheerful side is that with the Military Cabinet in Japan things are more likely to come to a head; they have pledged themselves to do wonders but they fairly obviously do not want to have a war with the USA. I think China has taken a fairly heavy toll of their resources, so the thing to do is to fix that before they embark on adventures, the outcome of which will be pretty doubtful. I think they will try this expedition to cut the Burma Road and generally rev up the tempo of the China War, but I doubt

---

31 The invasion was in fact just under a month away.

whether they will have much success. Altogether I think the Japs are in about the same jam with the China War as the Germans are with their Russian Campaign[32] and I should not like to be directing the affairs of either nation. They have both missed the lens[33] and are wondering what the hell to do next, so I do not feel there is any case for us to be too gloomy and think we will not see each other for many years. Chins up, optimism and look forward to the good things, which the future holds for us, that is the line to follow, my sweet. I miss you terribly, more so as the days go by, but we must not let it get us down.

I saw the Lady Hamilton film and thought it was very fair; Vivien Leigh is certainly a good actress and easy to look at.

The papers here published the gist of the Australian news commentary on the evacuation and they read pretty fair sense to me. The whole thing is the most colossal muddle and inequality just stands out in chunks everywhere. Poor Jack Potts seems to be a bit down in the mouth about Antonia's trip not coming off; his late father's share broking firm is in a bit of a mess financially and I think he has nothing except his pay. He has sold his car, given up the flat and lives as a PG [paying guest] with a couple at Mountain View, who are not my cup of tea at all. He shortly gets going in a new tug and intends to live on board to economise, so there at least is one person with greater troubles than mine.

Well lovey, I must close, as I have to write a Christmas letter to my mother. This [letter] should arrive around 26th [November], so I wish you everything nice I can think of for that momentous date in my young life. We have never looked back since then and we never will. Further, I lay you long odds that we will have our next anniversary together.

All my love and look after yourself so that you can enjoy the good times, which are in store.

To Therese   15 November

No further news since I last wrote but I had three letters from you last week, so I could scarcely expect this one. In my last I am afraid I wrote in a mood of considerable

---

32 An interesting comparison, both countries taking on vast countries, with very large populations and plentiful resources.
33 Lost their vision.

depression and I hope I did not sound morbid; depression is not my line in the normal way and I think it came from having too little to do and too much time to sit around bathing in self pity. I have now been appointed First Lieut. of *Cornflower* and although the job is too full of headaches to be entirely to my liking, it certainly keeps me busy and I feel the better for it. The deep black depression has passed, thank goodness, but do not think I am happy about your being alone in Australia with me up here. That pang remains, and is likely to do so, until we can arrange things otherwise. It has suddenly occurred to me that I have committed one of the supreme 'faux pas', I wrote last week and the week before wishing you very happy returns of our wedding anniversary and I think I went and called the date 26th. Disgraceful on my part, I must have been mixing it up with your birthday. How could I have done it I don't know?[34]

But worse still I wrote to Townend shortly after my return here, asking him to send you some flowers and chocolates on the appropriate day and I have a suspicion I said the 26th.[35] Call me a worm by all means, but at least the right intention was there.

I had dinner last Wednesday at the Cook's. Gillespie[36] looking pale; his six weeks holiday to Vancouver got stalled at Manila as the weather was bad in the Pacific and they said they had to carry extra petrol and mail in the plane in place of Gillespie. The following planes were all booked with priority passages, so there seemed every prospect of his sitting in Manila until all was blue. He then cancelled the whole idea and came back to HK, after spending $800 on an abortive trip: pretty galling.

To Therese   23 November

I was very cheered to hear that your infant prodigy has started to walk. It does me good to hear what a fine young fellow he is. I feel that we, or rather you, have produced something that is really worthwhile and I have the highest hope of him turning out to be one out of the bag, a great improvement on his father, but a male replica of his mother.

Bish Lander's wife is down in Manila: he has hopes of getting down there periodically by plane, which now runs twice a week.

Petrie will be back with us in about a month or six weeks, as he has been given instructions to return here. It is not clear what happens about Vernall as all leave is at

---

34 In fact both dates were the 23rd, which indicates that despite his cheerful letters he was feeling deeply unsettled.
35 He did and Therese lovingly records their arrival in her diary on that date.
36 Gillespie wrote Therese a letter of condolence in 1943.

present cancelled, at any rate for the RNVR. I feel he should most certainly get a spell in Australia, as he has been out here for over five years and has had a pretty dirty run over the last two. If it had not been for him, the Naval Volunteers would probably have packed up[37] and he has been in his job seven days a week for over two years; he is far from well and should certainly have a holiday.

The *Cornflower* job does not appeal to me at all. Put in simple terms, we are trying to make bricks without straw and there will be a change of command if Petrie comes back.

Last Sunday went out to lunch with the Potters at Seko. On Monday UE and I dined with the Fortescues, Joan Armstrong and Pat Sedgwick also being there. I feel rather guilty about the Potters and Fortescues entertaining me and my doing nothing in reply, but possibly the occasion will arrive in the future.[38]

Today is our wedding anniversary and I thought about doing something to celebrate it, but Sunday is not easy for a party when you have not got your own house and I do not seem to have the bounce or initiative these days to plan ahead. I was on board *Cornflower* last night and this morning, so we drank your health in the wardroom today and I left it at that for formal stuff. However, I have thought of you a lot today, more than I usually do, and believe me sweetie, you mean far more to me than I can express in words. I think there is a lot in the term 'better half' as I know that I will not be complete and whole without you.

---

37 Presumably through lack of someone suitable to take command.
38 All three of the men would be dead by Christmas.

CHAPTER 16

The Japanese Threat
1936 to 1941

Peter made various statements about the possibility of a Japanese invasion in his letters. It is interesting to see how these views change over time, from actively trying to get Therese back to Hong Kong in late 1940, to a year later when he is not prepared even to consider acting on her pleas to return. However, it was in 1936 Peter foresaw the possibility of a Japanese invasion in a letter to Lizzie Blunt, to whom he had confided his thoughts on politics through the years.

To Lizzie Blunt   2 November 1936
Altogether this looks like being a very interesting part of the world during the next fifty years or so,[1] but I hope all sides manage to keep the peace,[2] because in the event of war we would be too much in the front row of the stalls for it to be exactly comfortable.

Then before the commencement of World War 2 he wrote:

To Lizzie Blunt 6 July 1939
Except in a streak of emergency madness, the Japs will not attack Hong Kong, because if she did she would be cut off from the Empire's raw materials and could not export to the Empire, which would blow her up [her economy] in about three to six months.

Then a year later following Therese's evacuation to the Philippine Islands there are all the letters to her of a more personal and practical nature. The whole focus of the correspondence is on how Therese could return to Hong Kong. At that stage the majority of the European population in the Colony were against the evacuation and Peter was keen to have his wife and son back with him.

---
1 Peter considers that China has great economic potential, with a stable Government, which proved to be the case.
2 This phrase was no doubt triggered by Japanese occupation of Manchuria in 1932.

To Therese   23 November 1940
I think the risk of anything going wrong here is slight, but it is always there and must be considered.

The family were finally reunited in Hong Kong in December 1940 but this joy was short-lived. When Therese was evacuated again in March 1941, she and Peter did not raise any objection. Perhaps because they knew they had done well and had broken the rules, which they had accepted when Therese returned to Hong Kong. There was then all the upheaval of Therese moving to Australia and Peter getting his tug and crew ready for the trip to Aden. Then in June 1941, Germany invaded Russia. Prior to this Japan had been concerned that Russia would interfere with its plans in China or the Far East. The German invasion changed all this and gave impetus to Japan's plans for expansion. Being out of touch he writes:

To Therese   10 August 1941
As regards the question of your return to HK, book straight off as soon as the ban has been raised and pay the fare yourself if necessary.

However when he returns to Hong Kong from Aden it is a very different story.

To Therese   3 October 1941
While on the question of money, if anything goes wrong up here, apply to Townend [in Sydney], who will pay you £30 per month.

To Therese   25 October 1941
The difficulty here, even if you could get back, is over this billeting: most of the houses on the Peak have been requisitioned for the billeting.

He goes on to say it would not be the place for a woman and a baby without a house and a claim on official rations.

To Therese   9 Novembers 1941
As regards the prospects of your coming back here, at the moment with the uncertainty of the Japanese, I will be quite frank and say I don't think there is a hope in hell [the

invasion was in fact just under a month away]. But don't let that discourage you; for the time being, until things clear up here, I think you are much better off down in Australia. I don't agree with these lads who say it will be a long war.

He returned to this theme twice over the last two weeks, which must have been because of pressure from Therese to return. He was clearly against this, as he feared an invasion and did not want Therese and HP caught up in it and to end up at best spending the rest of the war in a concentration camp.

As an employee of Jardine Matheson, Peter is likely to have reflected the views of this international trading company (see Appendix VIII). Those in the commercial world in the Far East traded with the Japanese and knew them and their economy well. They looked at the threat too logically; the Japanese lacked raw materials and as Peter had said would lose the not inconsiderable commercial income from the British Empire after an invasion. There was also the effect of ten years of war with China. Before World War 2 Peter records that Japanese civilians were suffering from lack of food and by the end of the war they were suffering from starvation. When it came to the point, the war required major industrial production. The Japanese could not match the industrial power of America and the British Empire.

Peter argued in all his letters to Therese that there would not be an invasion. The only direct insight to his thoughts should this actually happen are in a letter to his brother, Jack, where he states on the back of a photo of himself in his HKRNVR winter uniform:

To Jack   30 March 1940

Myself in uniform looking so serious. The Commander in Chief, Admiral Sir Percy Noble,[3] had just inspected us and I had not got over the 'Outposts of Empire' speech, which he made. (See photo on page 259.)

The logic of an outpost was to hold it for as long as possible but not to defend it permanently. This was the War Office's strategy i.e. Hong Kong would not get any outside military support if attacked. Churchill had famously said at the beginning of 1941 that there was 'not the slightest

---

3   The *Times*, 26 July 1955, extract from the obituary for Sir Percy Noble. He took over his post of Commander-in-Chief on the China Station in the early 1930s. During his time in Hong Kong, Japanese attitudes to the British were at their worst, but he managed to uphold British dignity with few resources and great strength of character. In July 1940 he returned to England to become Commander-in-Chief, Western Approaches.
http://1914-1918.invisionzone.com/forums/index.php?showtopic=111406. 2 November 2014.

chance' of defending Hong Kong and he went on to say 'or relieving it'.[4] Consequently at that stage he was against reinforcing the Colony. Under the new British plans in autumn 1941, in response to American encouragement, Hong Kong was to be reinforced. Selwyn-Clarke, Hong Kong's Director of Medical Services remarked that 'Hong Kong could not be held but it must be defended.'[5] Churchill in his mission to defeat the Axis Powers needed America to become an ally. The Americans had reinforced the Philippine Islands so Canadian troops were sent to add to the Hong Kong garrison. The tone of Peter's letters became less upbeat as he must also have realised that they were a comparatively small force, comprising of many units, races and volunteers, under-equipped and not ready for an aviation war; their opponents being battle hardened and experienced Japanese troops with an effective air force.

The reasons the Japanese went to war in 1941 have been covered by many. In the twentieth century Japan had modernised and modelled itself on the colonial powers in the Far East. Japan considered that following its role in World War 1, it should be accepted as an equal to the USA and Great Britain. This view was not, however, reciprocated by the great powers. Japanese ambitions were articulated in their plans for the Greater East Asia Co-Prosperity Sphere, basically a self-sufficient Far East.[6] This was influenced by their need for more space and raw materials in order to continue to expand their economy.

The training and tradition of the military was aggressive. As a result of this many of the incidents in the Sino-Japanese war were instigated by quite junior officers. Linked to this was loyalty to the Emperor, in whose name the Pacific War was declared, and the military's view that conquest in the Pacific was a divine mission. Add to this USA's and Great Britain's act of freezing trade with Japan and then the USA's 'Ten Point' document which stated that Japan should withdraw from Indo China and China and renounce the Axis pact. To the Japanese, military retreat would involve an impossible loss of face. They would rather risk a major loss of Japanese life than loss of face.[7]

General Tojo Hideki, the Minister for War, realised that taking on the USA with its industrial strength, was a major gamble. Admiral Yamamoto said that he could only be successful for six to twelve months and after that he did not to expect to be so.[8] It is frequently stated that they did not want a long war but this was inevitable given America's power and its desire to redress its humiliation at Pearl Harbor.

---

4 Snow, p. 41.
5 Snow, p. 41.
6 Keay, p. 161.
7 Beevor, p. 248
8 Beevor, p. 248.

Peter following the Outposts of the Empire speech.

In the first week of September 1941, Emperor Hirohito had reluctantly accepted the desire of his military cabinet to declare war. By 6 September, Japan decided to complete preparations for attacking the Americans, British and Dutch and on 6 November the Japanese Imperial Headquarters ordered the China Expeditionary Force to be ready to attack Hong Kong. The invasion was expected from the end of November. Although they negotiated with the USA at this time, the military had no intention of making major concessions.[9]

---
9 Beevor, p. 248

CHAPTER 17

The Invasion

December 1941

'All one hears of is killing, killing everywhere. When will it all end and what will be left and where will we both be?'

Extract from Peter's letter to Therese of 23 November 1940

Peter must have known that they were on the edge of war when he went to Fanling to play golf on 1 December. There would have been an obvious heightened level of activity, with troops at their posts. On return he wrote his last letter to Therese.

My Darling Therese

I received a letter from you last week but am stuck in *Cornflower* and so have not got it with me. Yesterday I fixed to go to Fanling to play golf with Griffiths and went down to *Cornflower* for divisions[1] at 9.30 and the new monthly Divine Service at 10.00, where incidentally I read the lesson. I left the ship at 10.45 and got out to Fanling at 13.15 [NB two and a half hours], only to find that all the army people had been called in and there was a phone message for me from *Cornflower*.

It took me a long while to get through on the phone and there seemed to be some flap on, so much to my disgust I packed up any ideas of golf and got a lift in.[2] Most annoying as it was my first day at Fanling for over a month. The answer seemed to be that the Army in Singapore had cancelled leave the day before, so the Army went onto four hours notice (we have been on that since the war started), then the Commodore decided we should do something, so he cancelled all leave from midnight.

We got a bit too enthusiastic about it and did a sort of test mobilisation and sent people out into the highways and byways to haul everyone back into the ship, including unmobilised officers. Today the flap has quietened considerably but they

---

1 The parade of the ship's company.
2 This amused Therese because despite all that was going on around him he should make this comment, but no doubt it was for her benefit to make light of events.

cannot say it was all a mistake, so they are easing the situation off quietly by granting leave to midnight. All of which brings me back to the start and explains why I am in the ship and cannot get hold of your letter.

The photos of HP arrived and I thought they were perfectly sweet; he looks the picture of health and that is one consolation, even if a small one, for your enforced stay in Australia; AE was most impressed with them. I think we have achieved a fine young lad for a son and he reflects much credit on you for your major part in bringing him into the world and looking after him after that.

Poor UE is still in the depths of depression and seems rather rattled.[3] I think he needs a holiday and on top of that is very worried as to what will happen to AE in her present state of ill health if there is a Japanese attack here and the house is taken for billeting. I agree it is a rather worrying process but I still think the Japs will climb down and that we will not have a war out here. In fact, with our advance in Libya and the Russians holding out, coupled with their recent success at Rostov,[4] I think the war looks better than it ever has done. There seems to be very definite evidence of the tide turning our way.

As regards your remittance of £5 per month, through the HK Treasury, I am arranging to have it increased to £50 by cable should anything go wrong here. You should apply at your end to make sure of it. Not that I think things are going wrong but it is silly not to make preparations. The Japanese situation seems to be coming up to one of its periodical crises but I am extremely doubtful whether the Japs will take the plunge. The situation is as adverse from their point of view as it has ever been, slightly more so in fact, as they have had four months of economic blockade, which I gather is hitting them fairly hard. The point which stands out to my mind is that they would not be doing all this talking if they wanted to scrap; they would be getting on and doing it.

Not much news from here. I seem to spend a lot of time mooching round in *Cornflower* and not getting very far on with anything. I saw Vines Gordon at a cocktail party given in the Ladies Lounge for the officers of the recently arrived Canadian regiments and passed on your messages about Marion.

---

3 Edgar Davidson had first-hand knowledge of the discussions on the Hong Kong Executive Council.
4 In late November the Germans pulled back at Rostov, following a Russian counter attack and realising they would not be able to make any progress until the following spring. Beevor, p. 239.

Well, this should get to you a bit before Christmas so I will wish you all the best for the festive season and may 1942 bring some better news than its predecessors; I think it will. I am afraid I have not bought a Christmas present for HP, partly because I seldom seem to be in the town to get any of those jobs done, and partly because I am rather chary of sending parcels around these days, using shipping space and giving everyone extra work. Can you buy him something from me down in Sydney, so he won't feel he has been forgotten by his father at Christmas.

My love, sweetie, and I feel in my bones that better days are just round the corner.

Peter

Peter's letter was signed off by the censor on 2 December, six days before the Japanese invaded the New Territories, thus the urgency of Peter's letter.

Hong Kong had a garrison of just over 12,000 Army, Navy and Air Force personnel[5] commanded by Major General C M Maltby. Defending the New Territories and the Island were six battalions, two Indian, two British, two Canadian and two supporting volunteer units, the HK Volunteer Defence Force, Hong Kong and Singapore Royal Artillery plus the engineers. There were also a few RN and HKRNVR ships and a very small RAF detachment. The Japanese were represented by the 23rd Army of some 60,000 troops, but only one division of 20,000 landed on the Island of whom 13,000 were part of the attacking force.[6]

When all the British forces retreated to the Island, the defence was divided between two brigades, East and West. Both brigades also employed artillery and volunteers, while the 1st Middlesex manned the pillboxes apart from on the north coast, where the attack was expected to come. Brigadier Wallis was in charge of East Brigade consisting of the 5/7th Rajputs and Royal Rifles of Canada. Brigadier Lawson of West Brigade commanded the 2/14th Punjabis, 2nd Royal Scots and the Winnipeg Grenadiers.[7]

The battle starts gradually to unfold:

1 December: 'The defences are prepared.'[8]

---

5 Banham, p.336.
6 Banham, p. 337.
7 Banham, p. 95.
8 Banham, p. 13. Plus references under 3, 4 and 5 December.

3 December:	Major General Maltby, following intelligence reports that Japanese troops had arrived at Sham Chun close to the border, visits the frontier to observe the enemy.
	Therese posts Peter's Christmas present and she then wrote to him on 7 and 12 December, with a photo of HP, and again on 18 December.
4 December:	HKVDC exercise stopped at Fanling near the Chinese border.
5 December:	All defences manned. 38th Division of the Japanese 23rd Army on other side of border.
8 December:	The Invasion of Hong Kong began. At about this time the Japanese were attacking Pearl Harbor, the Malaya Penninsula and the Philippine Islands.
	Great Britain and the United States of America declared war on Japan and Germany and Italy declared war on the United States as a result of the Axis alliance.
	There was a system of trenches and bunkers running across the New Territory to protect the harbour, but it was soon lost and the retreat to Kowloon began.[9]

In a letter from Eric Cox-Walker[E C-W][10] HKRNVR to Therese:

8 December:	*I'm afraid all I can tell you is the little I saw whilst serving under your husband in HKRNVR. First of all when the balloon finally did go up I and many others complained bitterly as to why they should have an air-raid practice at that time of the morning, but we soon realised it was the real thing, and the HKRNVR ships were in action right away. Later that morning they were all shifted round to Aberdeen.*
9 December:	*They were moored single line ahead and presented such a target that of course we had two raids the following day [9 December] with one or two near misses. After that all ships were transferred to Deep Water Bay with the 'Cornflower' as HQ, where your husband was. We managed to hold our own against the occasional planes which came over, then HQ transferred to a house ashore, one of those big houses overlooking Deep Water Bay on the Island Road just past the turn off to*

---

9 Keay, p. 180.
10 The letter was written sometime after the event and dated 14 December 1944, Bombay. He said contact was made through a meeting with Mrs Swable, who knew Mrs Ralph, who knew Therese: the benefit of the Hong Kong network.

Wanchegong Gap [Wong Nai Chung Gap]. *From then on your husband, as Second in Command, was ashore all the time organising defences and patrols, being in constant touch with Battle HQ by telephone.*

11 December: The evacuation of Kowloon commences. APV *Indira*, captained by Hindmarsh[11] ... was attacked causing the death of one crew member. She was sunk on 15 December. 'Japanese forces land on Lamma Island and attempted to cross to Aberdeen' but are driven back.[12]

'All available ships are ordered to assist in the evacuation of Kowloon.'[13]

13 December: Evacuation of Kowloon 'completed', leaving behind the bulk of the Kowloon Chinese population and a few Europeans.

15 December: E C-W: *The small auxiliaries were still doing patrol work in the Lamma Channel and so forth, where they did some grand work. There was one concentrated attack on 'Cornflower' but no hits were registered and her 2lb pom-pom did some useful work. There were several raids on Aberdeen Dockyard, especially when the one destroyer[14] was in dock there, when the Naval Tug 'Gatling' got a direct hit, many were killed and wounded. The days at the HQ house were spent in generally preparing defence with an occasional working party going to Aberdeen and later a guard party went over each night to assist at the Dock Yard in HK.*

16 December: Therese received Peter's letter of 1 December. Despite its low-key tone, she must have realised the seriousness of the situation now, and recorded in her diary 'HK State of Siege.'

18 December: At 21.00 the Japanese landed on the Island at North Point and Shau Kei Wou; their first wave, estimated at 7,500 men. 'They overwhelmed the initial defences they encounter, bypassing any significant points of resistance in their race to get to high ground, and approach Wong Nai Chung Gap.'[15]

19 December: E C-W: *I believe your husband was in one of those parties[16] but had returned and was at Deep Water Bay the night of 18/19 December. The Japs managed to make a landing that night under cover of a pall of smoke caused by the Petrol Installation at North Point being hot and going up in smoke. That was their third attempt, the*

---

11 Banham, p.30. Hindmarsh served under Peter on *St. Aubin* before it left for Aden.
12 Banham, p. 48.
13 Banham, p. 53.
14 HMS *Thracian*.
15 Banham, p. 97
16 Guard parties which assisted the guards at the HM Dockyard facing Kowloon.

Postbridge where Peter and others were killed during a Japanese attack

first one was broken up by 'Thracian' and the second by the MTBs. That night I was on board the 'Cornflower' but I heard later that when the Japs were forcing their way through Happy Valley and up to Wanchegong Gap your husband heard of some troubles at a house up there [Postbridge].

04.00	Brigadier Wallis, fearing that part of East Brigade will be cut off, orders troops to withdraw south to Stanley.[17]
04.30	Major Marsh of the Middlesex phones HKRNVR to ask for help in clearing Postbridge of suspected fifth columnists.[18]
05.20	Dulley takes a party of HKRNVR (Grenham [Lieut], Morahan [Lt.Cdr], McDouall [Lieut], Rutherford [Lieut], Cockle [Lieut], Price [Lieut], Blakeney [Lieut], Sommerfelt [Lt.Cdr], Mack [A.Lieut], Lamble [Cadet] and Castelton [Seaman Gunner]) on a lorry to Postbridge.[19]

---

17 Banham, p.126.
18 Banham, p. 126.
19 Banham, p. 126.

Peter as First Lieutenant would have been automatically the senior officer, but his party of twelve, including himself consisted of three Lieutenant Commanders and seven Lieutenants, ten officers in all. This was a seriously top heavy platoon, but was the result of the policy of not allowing the Chinese to have access to firearms, because the authorities did not feel they could be trusted. The Chinese population outnumbered the British and there was a history of uncertainty about the Chinese loyalty to the British cause.[20]

E C-W: *So he took a volunteer party up to investigate, there being one or two crews ashore by then, their ships having been badly damaged or sunk.... After that we received orders to scuttle all ships, so having done that we proceeded to Aberdeen Industrial School, where the HKRNVR were formed into a regular guard of the HQ [RN & RAF base] there.*

08.00 'Postbridge comes under fire.'[21]

10.00 Brigadier Lawson, killed as he and others abandoned West Brigades HQ.[22]

'Once ... the strategically important police station at the south of the Gap is captured, the fighting moves south along Repulse Bay Road. In 1941 it is relatively sparsely populated, thus the skirmishes on this and later days are generally named after the houses at or around which they occur.' Postbridge was the most northerly.[23]

The rest of the fighting at the Gap is a number of attempted counter attacks including one by members of HMS *Thracian's* crew. They all failed as there was no concerted plan of attack. The defenders at the Gap suffered from the loss of Lawson, who was not replaced for twenty-four hours, and East Brigade were not able to provide support as Wallis had decided to move back to Stanley on 18 December.[24] This all must have reduced the length of time the Island was able to hold out.

23.30 While at Postbridge Capt. Avery of the HKRSA dies of wounds and Major Crowe and Capt. Atkinson of the Royal Artillery are wounded. Mr G. G. Tinson, the owner of the house – who had won the MC in the World War 1

---

20 Snow, pp. 8/9.
21 Banham, p. 131.
22 Banham, p. 134.
23 Banham, p. 18.
24 Banham, p. 116.

– is also mortally wounded by a sniper. At midnight Lt. Cdr. Dulley is killed by a mortar[25] and buried in the garden at Postbridge.[26]

The parochial nature of the defence of the Island is demonstrated by the fact that George Tinson, as part of the HK Defence Force, was defending his own house. He left behind his wife, who was serving elsewhere on the Island as a hospital nurse; in captivity his death must have been a particularly harsh blow. It was a dire end to a year at Postbridge, when the year had started so well. No doubt like many before it, Mrs Tinson had given a cocktail party on New Year's Day, which Therese had attended, though Peter had missed it because he was out on patrol in *St. Aubin*.

---

19 December was 'by far the hardest day's fighting, with defenders incurring in twenty-four hours approximately one-third of their fatalities. Losses to attackers are probably in a similar ratio. By midnight although there are still pockets of resistance, the Gap and the majority of the road are in all practical terms in Japanese hands.'[27]

21 December:	There was a Churchillian response to the Governor's request to surrender. 'The eyes of the world are upon you. We expect you to resist to the end. The honour of the Empire is in your hands.'[28] Churchill was due to meet President Roosevelt soon and wanted to show that Britain could resist the Japanese forces.
20 to 26 December:	The Japanese move towards Wanchai and Mount Cameron is taken after a hard struggle; the invaders move further to the south west of the Island. The defenders are then encircled at Stanley Mound and Stone Hill, where there is strong fighting and East Brigade is forced down the Stanley Peninsula, which is held until they receive orders to surrender on 26th.[29] The formal surrender took place the previous day, Christmas Day. Some wag described it as a Black Christmas.

---

25 Barham, p. 143.
26 Constance Fairburn's letter of condolence dated 2 November 1943. See Appendix IX.
27 Banham, p. 18.
28 Keay, p. 181
29 Banham, p. 19.

The final estimated dead and wounded figures for the British forces are – dead 1,560[30] and seriously wounded 1,300.[31] The Japanese figures are harder to come by and the most likely figures are from the *Hong Kong News*, 29 December, although possibly high – 1,996 killed and 6,000 wounded; that latter figure does not state that they were seriously wounded and may not compare with the British figure.[32] This is a total of 7,996 Japanese killed and wounded, which is stated as high and is also a high proportion of the invasion force if correct. Following the invasion there were 9,000 POWs placed in camps and 4,000 civilian dead, most of whom were Chinese.[33]

In Tony Banham's view: 'General Maltby had been given an impossible task. He was charged with defending a small isolated island without armour or sea and air cover, against a numerically superior and battle-hardened enemy.'[33] Singapore would also fall in two months' time and there was the loss of the Philippine Islands and most of the American fleet at Pearl Harbor. Churchill is quoted as saying that he tossed and turned in his bed at night thinking about the total vulnerability of the Pacific and Indian Oceans. That said, there were still Australian divisions operating in the Mediterranean, despite the Australian's understandable pleas to Churchill for their return to bolster the limited defence of their own country.

In July 1946 *The London Gazette* announced awards: 'For distinguished services during the defence of Hong Kong and while Prisoner of War in enemy hands.' The first entry under 'Posthumous Mention in Dispatches', which would have covered those killed in battle or who died in a POW camp, was Peter as the most senior officer. Also mentioned in a different section, headed Mention in Despatches, was Cmdr. J. R. Vernall.

---

30   Banham, p. 317.
31   Morris, p. 247.
32   Banham, p. 318.
33   Morris, p. 247.
34   Banham, p. 290.

CHAPTER 18

Epilogue

In Sydney, Therese had been watching the events in Hong Kong with ever growing horror. In her diary she wrote:

25 December – 'Hong Kong fell.' Her Christmas lunch with Doreen Ralph was cancelled.
27 December – 'Heard Peter missing.'
2 January – 'Mrs Vernall [wife of Commander Vernall] to lunch.'
It would appear to be an opportunity for them both to provide each other with support, as Mrs Vernall may have been unaware that her husband was in a POW camp at that stage. Alternatively it may have been that Mrs Vernall had more news on Peter and that was the reason for her visit.

Therese had said over the evacuation to Australia, that she was heartbroken and miserable, but there is no diary entry as to when she heard of Peter's death. Her aunt Eva Davidson had sent a postcard to her in February saying that Peter was 'missing believed killed', but it may not have been until Eva's letter of 21 May that his death was confirmed as definite. It may well be that Therese heard this on the Hong Kong grapevine in Sydney before this date. At the beginning of the year Therese had a lunch or dinner most days with her girlfriends, in particular Kathleen Took. They were all in a similar situation, desperately anxious about their husbands in Hong Kong and they provided support for each other. Later Therese records the fall of Singapore on 15 February and the Japanese raid on Darwin on 19th and, if it had not been for a change in Japanese plans, Australia might also have been invaded,

Back in Hong Kong during the invasion Eva Davidson was at the Matilda Hospital, which managed to avoid any unfortunate incidents with Japanese troops. Edgar may have been in the Government Offices and thus among the first to hear of the surrender.

The Davidsons were placed in the Stanley concentration camp for the rest of the war. Edgar was a tall, thin man and suffered from the lack of food, diet and hygiene in the camp. Eva did her best for him by selling her jewellery to buy extra rations. The transactions were carried out through the camp fence possibly with their old Chinese servants; the result was

A later confirmation of the E's internment and an example of a standard cable

sometimes fresh eggs. Their means of buying these extras must have dwindled during the war, although those who were considered credit worthy could use IOUs. Eva also had her own health problems as she had just finished treatment in hospital prior to the invasion and had been fitted with a brass belt, which restricted her activities considerably but it was said she would be able to live a quiet life[!].[1]

---

[1] From Peter's letter of 1 December; this paragraph was not included in the full version on pp. 260–262.

Edgar (on the far right) and other survivors of Stanley Camp in August 1945

As early as 1942 news was coming out of Stanley Camp, as some prisoners were repatriated to their own countries. One letter was written by George C. Dankwerth on 4 August 1942 whilst en route to the United States. He sent it to Edgar's elder brother, Willie Davidson, in Liverpool with a copy to Therese. The letter gives positive news of the Davidsons. 'I am happy to inform you that your brother Edgar came safely through the Japanese attack on Hong Kong and when I left there on 29 June he was at Stanley Civilian Internment Camp. He was feeling very fit, in good mental spirits and was generally content with life, inasmuch as he was able to get sufficient smoking tobacco.' There is also a record of a conversation with Mr R. D. Gillespie, of the Imperial Chemical Industries, on his experiences as a prisoner in Japanese hands in Hong Kong dated autumn 1943. He was in Stanley Camp and provided considerable detail on life there and the Davidsons.[2]

Eva wrote to Therese on 21 May. Her letter is written in block capitals, except for the signature, and was on one side of airmail paper which was obviously to meet Japanese censorship regulations for letters to be short and clearly written. The number of letters sent was limited to one letter a month per couple.

---

2 Both documents are included in the Appendix IX.

EPILOGUE

MAY 21ST. CIVILIAN INTERNMENT CAMP STANLEY, BLOCK 13

DEAREST THERESE

HOPE YOU RECEIVED POSTCARD SENT IN FEBRUARY WITH BARE STATEMENT THAT PETER IS MISSING BELIEVED KILLED. THIS IS MY FIRST CHANCE TO WRITE. HAVE NOT MET ANYONE YET WHO WAS WITH PETER BUT FEAR NO DOUBT HE WAS KILLED DEFENDING GEORGE TINSON'S HOUSE DECEMBER 19TH. SOMMERFELT[3], NOW PRISONER OF WAR, TOLD JUDY GRAVE, WHO IS HERE, THAT PETER FOUGHT MAGNIFICENTLY, AND DIED HERO'S DEATH. HOPE ONE DAY SHALL GET FIRST HAND NEWS FOR YOU. YOUR HOUSE AND OURS BADLY DAMAGED. NO SPACE HERE TO EXPRESS OUR GRIEF AND SYMPATHY WE MOURN LOSS AS OF A SECOND SON, AND YOU ARE ALWAYS IN MY MIND AND HEART. JOHN POTTER MISSING – RUSTY FORSYTH KILLED, AND MANY OTHERS. WE ARE QUITE WELL, IF THIN. SHARING SMALL ROOM WITH POTTERS. HOPE YOU AND SON WELL. EVERYONE GRIEVES FOR PETER.

ALL OUR LOVE AND SYMPATHY

Eva Davidson

Therese received a number of other letters of condolence. Extracts from Eric Cox-Walker's letter have already appeared in the previous chapter and the full text is included in Appendix IX, together with a letter from Constance Fairburn dated 2 November 1943. Fairburn and Gillespie were both Canadian citizens and therefore able to seek repatriation. Franklin Gimson, who arrived the day before the invasion to take up his post as Colonial Secretary, resisted proposals for the repatriation for British prisoners, in order to ensure that there was a continuous Imperial presence in Hong Kong.[4]

For those in the services who survived the battle, some were massacred but the majority spent the rest of the war in bad conditions in Japanese POW camps mainly in Hong Kong, where many died. Among the POWs were Lt. Goodwin, who was subsequently moved to the Shamsuipo Camp where he shared a room with Lt. Glover of the *St. Aubin*, who he described as a close friend.[5] Maybe they whiled away some of the time reminiscing about their trip to Aden. Lt. Goodwin was previously in North Point Camp, where Cmdr. Vernall

---

3 Sommerfelt was in the party that went to Postbridge.
4 Welsh, pp. 418/419.
5 Goodwin, p. 12.

> May 21st Civilian Internment Camp
> Stanley Block 13
>
> Dearest Therese
>
> Hope you received postcard sent in February with bare statement that Peter is missing believed killed. This is my first chance to write. Have not met anyone yet who was with Peter but fear no doubt he was killed defending George Tinsons House December 19th. Sommerfelt, now prisoner of war, told Judy Grave, who is here, that Peter fought magnificently, and died hero's death. Hope one day shall get first hand news for you. Your house and ours badly damaged. No space here to express our grief and sympathy. We mourn loss as of a second son, and you are always in my mind and heart. John Potter missing — Rusty Forsyth killed, and many others. We are quite well, if thin. Sharing small room with Potters — Hope you and son well. Everyone grieves for Peter — all our love and sympathy.
>
> Eva Davidson
> (Eva Davidson)

Eva's original letter from Stanley Concentration Camp

Admiral Chen Chak and Chinese officers and the British officers and men who escaped from Hong Kong commanded by Lt. Cmdr. Gandy, seated 7th from left, wearing a white scarf.

Eric Cox-Walker, who wrote to Therese, is in the back row also 7th from left.

was held prisoner, the latter had an elicit radio secreted in his hut.[6] Lt. Goodwin escaped from Shamsuipo Camp in July 1944 and eventually arrived back in New Zealand only to return to Hong Kong a year later as part of the British relief force. J. J. Paterson[7] was also held there sharing a mess with Major General Maltby.[8] The previous reference comes from David Bosanquet in his book *Escape through China*. He does not appear in Peter's letters but he was in Jardines at the time and took over Roger Grieve's post while he was on leave in England. David Bosanquet took Joan Armstrong, Peter's personal assistant, to a ball on 30 November 1941. Next day he was at Fanling Golf Club earlier than Peter so he did manage to get a game of golf in before the mobilisation.

Few others attempted to escape through China to India, but among those who did were Cox-Walker, Gandy and Proulx. As can be seen many escapees were from the RN and HKRNVR, some of whom had the advantage of a boat for the first stage of their journey. Eric Cox-Walker in his letter to Therese said, 'I was fortunate and lucky enough at the time of the surrender to be actually on the launch that was requisitioned to join Admiral Chan Chak's[9] party and so I was one of the lucky ones who got away into China and so on into India.' The party was lead by Lt. Cmdr. G. H. Gandy RN (Retd.), who had been the Honorary Secretary of the Royal Hong Kong Yacht Club, so he would have known Peter through the Club and met him in November when Gandy was hoping to go on leave. What happened next was quite the reverse of this. He was in command of the MTBs manned by HKRNVR officers during the invasion, the MTBs saw heavy fighting in the harbour. He then took a party of sixty-two men over 3,000 miles through China and Burma.[10] The last of the escapees was Warrant Officer Benjamin Proulx HKRNVR who had met Peter through his mine watching duties and is mentioned in a letter in 1940 as his wife was getting around the evacuation by living in Macao. He escaped early in the occupation and wrote a book *Underground from Hong Kong*.[11]

Back in Australia Therese and HP set off on 27 February for Armidale, a country town about 250 miles north of Sydney as the crow flies. Their trunks and HP's toys were sent up after them. It may be that Therese waited in Sydney for news of Peter and on receiving

---

6 Goodwin, p. 25.
7 See reference to JJP in Paleraon's letter in Appendix IX.
8 Bosanquet, p. 57.
9 A Chinese Nationalist, raised in Hong Kong, who returned there to take charge of the underground. Snow, p. 48.
10 http://www.hongkongescape.org/HERO.htm. 12 February 2016.
11 Published by Dutton in New York in 1943.

Therese and HP in central Sydney

AE's postcard in February saying that Peter was missing believed killed, she decided they would escape Sydney for a change of scene in the country. Another factor may have been the Japanese attack on Darwin; the Australians believed that this must be the prelude to the invasion of Australia. Half of Darwin's population headed for the Adelaide River and the interior,[12] and some 'Sydneysiders' were moving out to places like the Blue Mountains.[13] Therese, sometime after her arrival in Armidale with HP, went to Port Macquarie and Coffs Harbour to enjoy the Australian beaches. She returned to Armidale on 19 December and had Christmas lunch with Mrs Woods and tea with Mrs Skinner.

Therese and HP returned to Sydney in the New Year and there are photos of both of them taken by street photographers, in the smart shopping areas in central Sydney. The photos would have been used to send to relatives back in England. It must have been a desperate time for Therese, arriving in a strange country back in March 1941 with a small baby. Initially she would have lived with the thought that Japan might invade Hong Kong. She clearly voiced her worries to Peter in her letters. He, however, followed a policy of being steadfastly optimistic and suggested that the war might be over by the end of 1941. Sadly the outcome proved to be very different and Therese bore the burden of widowhood without the support of any family but with a small close circle of friends. Although she and Peter had been married for five years, they were only together for just over three years.

The Far East that they had known had changed at a stroke under Japanese rule and would not revert to what it had been. The war had changed the balance of power in Hong Kong and there was considerable pressure from the Chinese for their fellow countrymen to have jobs opened up for them. It was certainly Jardines' policy subsequently to fill posts previously occupied by Europeans with Chinese staff unless they could not find someone with necessary skills locally. Fergie's[14] letter to Therese dated 27 October 1946, from The British School, Kowloon, underlines this:

> 'It seems like another life since we met and I miss all my old friends terribly. Three of my closest friends were killed and the other two are no longer in Hong Kong so it's a bit lonely. The place is not what it was either by a long way and never likely to be, but that is common to most places I suppose.'

The invasion was the end of an era, one hundred years after the British had first occupied Hong Kong.

Peter and Therese, like other residents of Hong Kong, lost all their belongings from the house, with one exception. Peter had had two oars painted to commemorate his wins at

---
12 Perry, p. 126.
13 Perry, p. 118.
14 Fergie had been Peter's best man.

HP (fifth from the left) and friends outside the flats at Rose Bay

Henley Royal Regatta and had taken them to Hong Kong. After the war they were found in their home and sent back to England. It was a mystery why they had survived, as all valuables and firewood were looted from the houses. A possible explanation was that the oars were crossed and considered to be a mystical symbol.

Returning to the war, in Europe 'Victory in Europe Day' took place on 9 May 1945. Fighting, however, continued in the Pacific until the dropping of the atomic bombs on Japan. Finally on 15 August 1945 the Emperor of Japan in a recorded radio message asked for all his forces to surrender. The formal surrender took place on 2 September on the battleship USS *Missouri* in Tokyo Bay off Yokohama.

There was great excitement in Sydney and particularly at the block of flats in Rosebay with the news that fathers would be coming home, but Hugh Peter knew his own father would not be returning.

As Peter had once predicted, the Japanese troops in China and Hong Kong became

HP on the 'Nestor' on the voyage to England

trapped there because of the new supremacy of the US Navy. Immediately after the Japanese surrender Rear Admiral Harcourt's 11th Carrier Squadron sailed from Sydney and arrived in Hong Kong on 30 August. There then followed a major operation to relieve Hong Kong. Edgar Davidson had to be taken home on a hospital ship, suffering from beriberi and dysentery, accompanied by Eva. On their return to England they joined Therese's mother, Nancy, in Tonbridge, Kent. They subsequently all moved to Somerset to be near Therese. Eva surprisingly enjoyed telling tales of camp life to the Women's Institutes in Somerset, suggesting that despite the tough life in camp, her extrovert nature had helped her survive. This is interesting as she came from a well-off, middle class family, throughout her life relying on servants.

In late 1945, when it was considered there were no rogue enemy submarines left at sea, Therese booked the trip home to England. The future was uncertain apart from the fact they could initially stay with Nancy in Tonbridge. When finally the time came to leave, Therese and HP went to the Sydney docks, beside the Harbour Bridge, and boarded the

SS *Nestor* of the Blue Funnel Line.[15] As the ship pulled away from the dockside and sailed down the harbour, Therese had her last glimpse of Sydney. Her thoughts must have gone back to the first time she had arrived in Hong Kong, with all the excitement and the beauty, and then meeting Peter. As the Harbour Bridge became more distant she said goodbye to Australia, her home for the last five years, and her Far Eastern dream, which had turned into a nightmare, and she looked forward to her new life in England.

On the voyage home Therese met Lieutenant Commander Peter Pudge RNVR.[16] They married shortly after returning to England and later produced a son, who was called Simon.

---

15 The SS *Nestor* was built for the Australia run. She had been a troopship for the Australian Expeditionary Force in World War 1 and was used to evacuate British children to Australia in World War 2.
linehttp://iancoombe.tripod.com/id25.html.15 August 2015.
16 Before the war, Peter Pudge (his Christian name was in fact James) worked in the Imperial Tobacco Company and trained in the RNVR in Bristol. After he was called up he became a gunnery officer and served in the North Atlantic convoys. He was then posted to India where he was offered promotion to Commander to take part in the final surrender of Japan, but his UK employer said that if he wanted his job back he needed to resign his commission and return home immediately. He decided to do the latter but took a break in Australia for a minor operation before he returned to England on the *Nestor*.

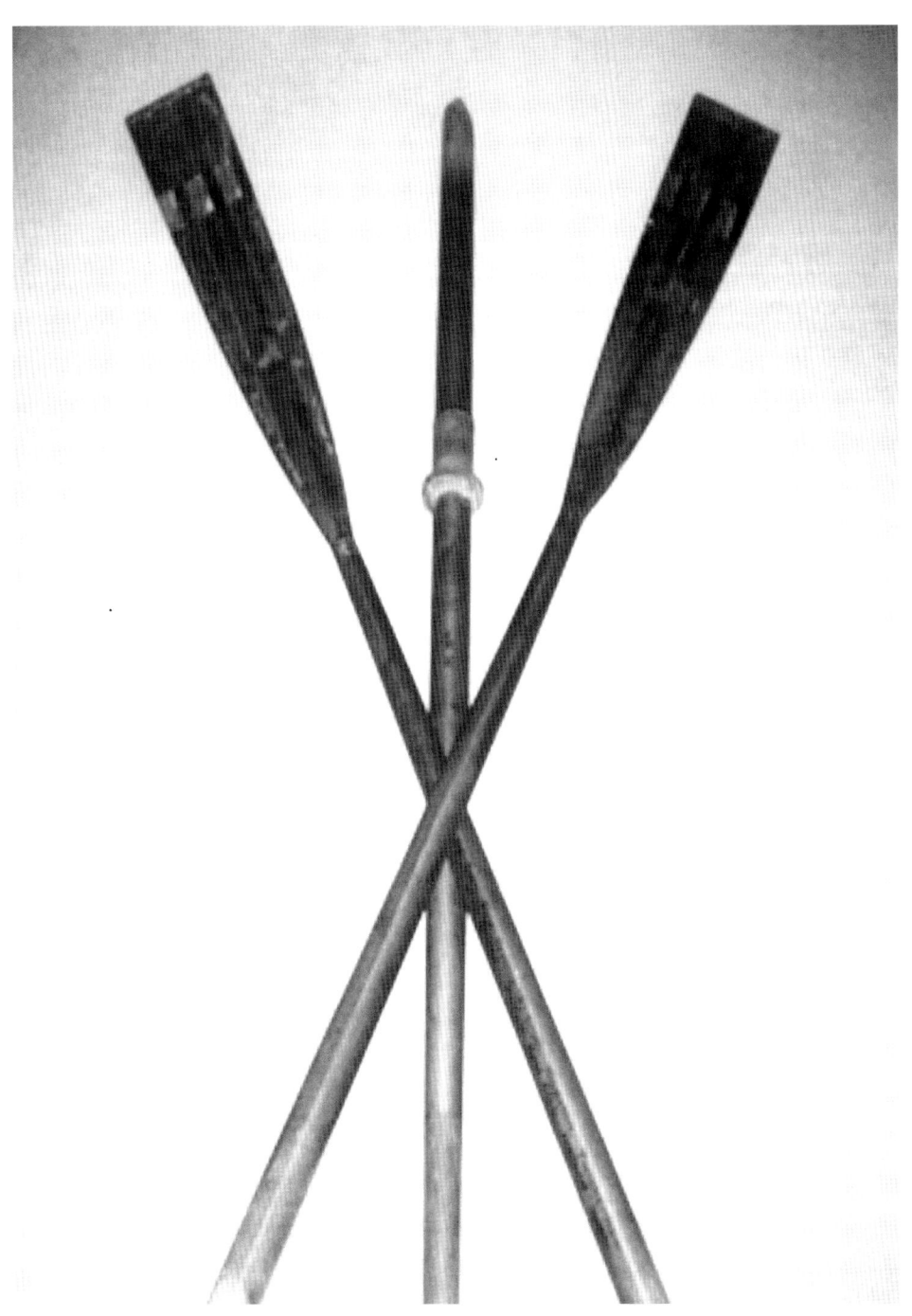

The Henley oars were the only salvageable item from Peter and Therese's home.

APPENDICES

APPENDIX I

The Glossary

Axis	A loose alliance between Germany, Italy and Japan.
ARP	Air Raid Precautions.
Amah	Chinese maidservant. There were a number of different types of amah e.g. baby care, washing and a general amah who did the cleaning.
B I	British India shipping line.
Boy	A male servant.
Coolie	A Chinese labourer paid on a daily basis.
Comprador	Chinese manager of a hong (business).
Lt.Cmdr/Cmdr	Lieutenant Commander or Commander.
DEI	Dutch East Indies.
DWB	Deep Water Bay, Hong Kong.
EWO	Chinese name for Jardines.
F M O	Fleet Mail Office.
Furlough	Leave of absence. In Jardines this was the six months every four years to enable staff to go home.
Gripps, The	Nickname given to the Hong Kong Hotel.
HMAPV	His Majesty's Auxiliary Patrol Vessel, part of the HKRNVR.
HMPS	His Majesty's Patrol Ship, part of the HKRNVR.
Huseliers/ Hughesiliers	Peter uses the former, most people use the latter, which is no doubt the correct version. Founded by Col A W Hughes and drawn from men over 55 in the commercial and professional world.
HKRNVR	Hong Kong Royal Naval Volunteer Reserve.
HKSRA	Hong Kong and Singapore Royal Artillery.
JCJL	A service from Java to China and Japan known as the Java China Japan Line subsidised by the Dutch Government.
JM	Jardine Matheson or as it was usually known Jardines.
M O	Medical Officer.

Monsoon	Seasonal wind blowing from SW across South China Sea from May to September and NE from November to February.
M T B	Motor Torpedo Boat.
N O I C	Naval Officer in Command.
P O	Petty Officer.
P O W	Prisoner of War.
P W D	Public Works Department.
RN	The British Royal Navy.
RNVR	Royal Naval Volunteer Reserve.
Taipan	European head of a hong (house of business or firm.)
Tiffin	Lunch.
Toot	To go out for a few drinks.
Typhoon	A tropical cyclone.
VAD	Variety and Amateur Dramatics.

APPENDIX II

Place Names Old and New and Abbreviations

Aden	Adan
Amoy	Xiamen
Bombay	Mumbai
Canton	Guangzhou
Chunking	Chongqing
Colombo	Capital of Ceylon, now Sri Lanka
Hunjao	Hongqiao
KL	Kuala Lumpa
Madras	Chennai
Nanking	Nanjing
Peking	Beijing
Persia	Iran
Philippine Islands (PI)	Philippines
S'hai	Shanghai
S'pore	Singapore

APPENDIX III

List of Names Mentioned in Letters

The criteria for inclusion in the List of Names, is being frequently mentioned in Peter's letters or importance to the story. The list provides the known names, some details of the person concerned and, where known, what happened to them after the invasion. As it was the practice to call people by their surnames, refer to them formally as Mr or Mrs or use nicknames, many forenames are not known. The list is compiled primarily from Peter's letters, photos and Therese's documents but there is also information from Tony Banham's book *Not the Slightest Chance* and other sources.

Surname	Forename	First Mentioned	Links to Peter and Therese and any other relevant information	What happened to them after the invasion
Ah Kung		Therese 3 January 1936	He was their 'boat boy' and was also a rating in HKRNVR in 1936.	There is no mention of him in the 1940 letters, probably because he was called up with the HKRNVR.
Armstrong	Joan	Therese's papers 1939	Invited to 1939 party. Worked in Insurance Dept. Jardines, probably as Secretary/PA to Peter.	Survived internment.
Barham	Mr & Mrs	18 June 1936	Dinner and advice on renting first flat. Resident of Garden Terrace.	Not known.
Blunt	Lizzie	13 June 1936	Loyal retainer of the Dulley family and mother figure to Peter.	Remained in England.
Bosanquet	David	Therese's papers 1939	Employed by Jardines. Invited to 1939 party.	Escaped from POW Camp and wrote a book on his escape (see Bibliography).
Boxer	Charles R.	19 October 1941	Major in intelligence. Friend of Peter and Therese, attended various parties at their house. Wife Ursula evacuated to Australia. He had an affair and child with Emily Hahn.	POW Shamsuipo Camp and then held in a Japanese prison. Survived the war.
Boxer	Ursula	7 October 1940	Wife of Charles and friend of AE.	She was evacuated to Australia.
Brown	(Rev) Cyril	Photograph HKRNVR 1937	HKRNVR chaplain and friend. Christened HP.	Believed to have survived the war.

LIST OF NAMES MENTIONED IN LETTERS

Surname	Forename	First Mentioned	Links to Peter and Therese and any other relevant information	What happened to them after the invasion
Burgess	C. B.	3 August 1940	Civil servant in the Colonial Office (Hong Kong). On the Evacuation Advisory Committee, known to Peter prior to meetings on Therese's return to Hong Kong.	Not known.
Cockle		Photograph HKRNVR 1937	RNVR group photo 1937. Was a Lieut. in the Postbridge party.	Not known.
Croucher	N.	Christmas Card to HP 1940	Invited to 1939 party. Owner of the yacht La Cigale 1.	Not known.
Davidson	Edgar (Known as UE)	Therese 3 January 1936	Uncle to Therese. Senior partner of Hastings & Co. Solicitors and a senior figure in Hong Kong, arrived about 1906.	Interned in Stanley Camp.
Davidson	Eva (known as AE)	Therese 3 January 1936	Aunt to Therese and important player in the Hong Kong social scene.	Interned in Stanley Camp.
Davidson	Jack	Chapter 1	Son to the E's. He went to Cambridge and planned to be a lawyer. He joined the RAF and trained pilots and then was in an operational squadron.	Killed in a flying accident in 1941 in England.
Davidson	Gerald	Chapter 1	Uncle to Therese. Escorted her out to Hong Kong in 1935. He was an architect and designed a number of buildings in Hong Kong.	Married and lived in England.
Dixon	Major & Mrs	20 August 1936	Friends who Peter took sailing.	Probably left Hong Kong before the war as they are not mentioned in later letters.
Dulley	Agnes Leonora	Chapter 1	Mother of Peter. Lived in Kensington, London.	Remained in England and stayed in her flat during air raids.
Dulley	Evelyn	Chapter 1	Peter's elder sister, who became a Mother Superior in a convent of the Order of Sion.	Remained in England.
Dulley	Jack (J. H. M.)	Chapter 1	Peter's elder brother. Worked in a bank in India until he contracted TB.	Was invalided out of the RAFVR, and remained in England.

APPENDICES

Surname	Forename	First Mentioned	Links to Peter and Therese and any other relevant information	What happened to them after the invasion
Dulley	H. W. M. Known as Peter		Third child of Agnes and Herbert Dulley.	Killed in action on 19 December 1941.
Dulley	Therese (Nee Sander)		Met Peter at a New Year's Eve party in 1935 and they married November 1936.	Evacuated to Sydney in March 1941 and returned to England after the war and married Peter Pudge and had a son Simon.
Dulley	Hugh (HP)		Son of Peter and Therese, born in the Philippine Islands on 26 July 1940. Referred to by Peter as HP.	Evacuated to Sydney, Australia in March 1941 with Therese and returned to England after the war.
The E's	UE & AE		See Davidson.	
Fairbairn	Tommy	11 October 1940	Friend/acquaintance with inside information on how to return to Hong Kong after the evacuation.	Unknown.
Fairburn	Constance	Fairburn's Letter of Condolence	Canadian nurse, who was a friend of Therese.	Released from Stanley Camp under an agreement between the Japanese and Canadian Governments.
Ferguson	G. P. (Known as Fergie)	14 July 1940	Great bachelor friend of Peter. The Dulley's best man and godfather to HP.	Survived the war and returned to Hong Kong as Headmaster at King's College, Hong Kong.
Forsyth	Henry R. (Rusty)	Chapter 18	Friend. Major HKVDC, commanded the Scottish Company of the HKVDC. Nominated for VC but it was not approved.	Killed in fighting at Stanley.
Fortescue	Mr	10 April 1941	Friend and golfer. Was a producer for the VAD's society [Variety and Amateur Dramatics].	Not known.
Fortescue	Marjorie	10 April 1941	Friend of Therese. She was in the Philippine Islands with Therese and was in Hong Kong during the invasion with her child.	Interned in Stanley Camp.
Gandy	G. H.	25 October 1941	Lt. Cmdr. (RN. Retd) responsible for the MTB Flotilla. Invited to 1939 party with his wife. Hon Sec of the RHKYC and helped to negotiate the Club's move to its present site, Kellett Island.	Lead an escape to China in a MTB.

LIST OF NAMES MENTIONED IN LETTERS

Surname	Forename	First Mentioned	Links to Peter and Therese and any other relevant information	What happened to them after the invasion
Geer	R.	3 July 1940	Took over 168, when the Dulleys left. Also in Jardines and invited to 1939 party.	Not known.
Gillespie	R. D.	15 September 1940	Worked for the Imperial Chemical Industries in Hong Kong. Was on the Exemption Committee for those appealing against evacuation with UE. Wrote a letter of condolence to Therese.	In 1943 he returned to Canada, where he was born.
Glover	H. C.	8 May 1941	Sub Lieut. HKRNVR on the *St. Aubin* on the voyage to Aden, previously in the Shanghai Police. At the invasion he was on HMAPV *Indira*.	Returned to Hong Kong directly after the Aden trip. Completed the war as a POW in the Shamsuipo Camp.
Goodwin	R. B.	20 June 1941	In the RNZNVR (Royal New Zealand Naval Volunteer Reserve) First Lieut. on the *St. Aubin* on the voyage to Aden.	Returned to Hong Kong directly after the Aden trip to serve on the MTBs. Was injured during the invasion. Escaped from Shamsuipo POW Camp 1944 and wrote a book about it (see bibliography) Returned to Hong Kong for the surrender in 1945.
Gompertz	Geoffrey (Gomp)	25 June 1936	Good friend of Peter and was at Westminster School with him. Worked in Jardines first in Hong Kong and then Shanghai. Father Chief Justice of the Federated Malay States.	Went to Shanghai as No.1 in Jardines in October 1940. Returned subsequently because of the Japanese incursions. Served in the HKVDF and became a POW when Hong Kong fell but survived the war.
Grieve	Roger	24 September 1936	Great friend of Peter's, sailed together and both were in Jardines and the HKRNVR.	Went on leave just prior to the war, and was called up to join the RNVR in Scotland.
Grieve	Frances (Nee Boullin)	24 September 1936	Wife of Roger Grieve, great friend of Therese. Had twins, James and Elizabeth.	Spent the war in Scotland.
Griffith	'Griff'	14 July 1940	A friend of Peter's. Shared bachelor 'Mess' with him in 1936.	Not known.
Grimble	Sir Arthur	16 July 1941	Peter met him on his voyage to Aden. British colonial governor of the Gilbert and Ellice Islands and the Seychelles and Windward Islands.	Not known.

Surname	Forename	First Mentioned	Links to Peter and Therese and any other relevant information	What happened to them after the invasion
Hahn	Emily	19 October 1941	An American journalist/writer. She was Major Boxer's lover and they had a child. Befriended by Eva Davidson after the birth of her child.	Managed to avoid internment due to Boxer's influence with the Japanese and her previous marriage to a Chinese man. Helped to provide additional food for those in Stanley Camp.
Hall	F. C.	28 May 1936	Peter's boss in Jardines. Lent them his house for 6m in the summer of 1936 and leased a house to them subsequently. They were invited to the 1939 party.	Not Known.
Hall	Mrs F. C.	23 July 1936	It was Mrs Hall who suggested that they should be married at the Peak Church and hold the reception at the Peak Club.	Not Known.
Highet	Mr	11 October 1940	Friend and golfer, worked for the 'Bank' (Hong Kong & Shanghai Bank) Invited to 1939 party.	Not Known.
Hindmarsh	Desmond	8 May 1941	Lt. HKRNVR. On the *St. Aubin* before voyage to Aden. During the invasion he commanded HMAPV *Indira*.	Not Known. His wife was evacuated to Australia shortly after they married.
Ho Tung	Sir Robert	29 September 1940	Millionaire and philanthropist. Lent a ship to HKRNVR which was renamed HMS *Cornflower*.	Left Hong Kong for Macao before the invasion.
HP	See Hugh Dulley			
Hung	Chan	8 May 1941	The Dulley's Chinese cook and No.1 Boy. From July 1940 Peter supported him either by helping get employment or by paying him some money.	Last known contact when he went to work for Col. & Mrs White at the Austin Barracks.
Keswick	Tony (William J.)	3 July 1936	Taipan, Jardines' Shanghai office.	He was still working in Shanghai in 1941, but was shot at a public meeting by the head of the Japanese community. He recovered and returned home subsequently.
Killery	Val	15 April 1941	Held senior post in Jardines.	Went to Singapore early 1941 to work for the Ministry of Economic Warfare.

LIST OF NAMES MENTIONED IN LETTERS

Surname	Forename	First Mentioned	Links to Peter and Therese and any other relevant information	What happened to them after the invasion
Killery	Peggy	21 May 1936	Cousin to Therese.	Did not follow her husband to Singapore initially. Left Hong Kong before the Japanese invasion.
Lander	'Bish'	20 October 1940	Fellow grass widower.	Was due to return to HK as No.2 to Bonzo Bonsfield in April 1941.
Le Fleming	Mr & Mrs	20 June 1936	Great friends of Peter and Therese. Lived in Kuala Lumpa. Peter visited them a number of times in his bachelor days.	They were on leave in autumn 1941 and hopefully did not return before the Japanese invasion.
McAvoy	D.	5 July 1940	Sub. Lieut.in HKRNVR in 1937 photograph. Friend of Peter's living in Manila in 1940.	Not known.
Macpherson (Aunt Helen)	H. G.	29 August 1941	Peter's favourite aunt, lived in France.	Stayed in France after the war.
Meeke	H. C.	11 May 1936	Sailed with Peter from 1930 and was in the HKRNVR. Helped to discover Dulley Rock. Early neighbours at the Garden Terrace flats. Came to 1939 party.	Not known.
Nicholson	'Gaswork'	11 May 1936	Lived and sailed in Hong Kong, and then moved to Colombo where Peter visited him in 1941.	Not known.
Paterson	J. J.	21 May 1936	Taipan, Jardines Hong Kong. Peter's ultimate boss. Major HKVDC valiantly defended the power station during the invasion.	POW Shamsuipo Camp, returned to Jardines after the war.
Paterson	Mrs J. J.	21 May 136	Wife of J. J. Very generously arranged a dinner party for the Dulley wedding party.	Probably interned in Stanley Camp.
Petrie	J.	12 October 1941	Commander HKRNVR. Invited to 1939 party with his wife.	Went to Australia on sick leave in 1941 and did not return before the invasion.
Potter	John	23 November 1941	Great friend. God father to HP. Became a Major in the HKVDC. Was an architect and designed the Yacht Club at Kellett Island, opened in 1941.	Killed on 25 December 1941, the final day of the invasion.

APPENDICES

Surname	Forename	First Mentioned	Links to Peter and Therese and any other relevant information	What happened to them after the invasion
Potts	Jack	25 June 1936	At party in 1939. Was in the HKRNVR, had not been in Hong Kong long.	Not known.
Potts	Antonia	12 October 1941	Antonia refused permit to visit Hong Kong October 1941.	She spent the war in Australia.
Proulx	Benjamin	16 May 1941	Warrant Officer HKRNVR, who was a mine watcher. Sent letter of condolence to Therese.	Early escapee from the Hong Kong POW camps. Wrote a book in 1943 *Underground from Hong Kong*.
Ralph	D. P.	30 March 1941	Came to the 1939 party with his wife, Doreen. In the 1937 RNVR photo and 1st Lieut. on *St. Aubin* in March 1941. Captain of HMAPV *Shun Wo* in December 1941.	Not known.
Ralph	Doreen	9 November 1941	As a fellow evacuee she became a close friend of Therese in Australia.	Spent the war in Australia and no doubt returned to England afterwards.
Samuel	Philip The Hon.	7 October 1940	Met with Peter and Gompertz. His father was the 1st Viscount Samuel. School friend of Jack Dulley and worked for the Kadoories. Served with the HKVDC.	He was a POW and was transferred to Japan to work in a factory. Survived the war.
Sander	Nancy	Therese 3 January 1936	Therese's mother. Separated from her German husband after he was interned in WW1. Lived in Tonbridge, Kent.	Remained in England.
Sander (Married name Stewart)	Agnes	11 September 1940	Therese's sister. Lived in Weybridge, Surrey during the war.	Remained in England.
Shewan	Ian and Mrs	7 July 1940	Friends. Invited to 1939 party. She helped Therese during the evacuation to P.I.	She was evacuated to Australia. What happened to Mr Shewan is not known.
Shields	A. L. The Hon.	HKRNVR Photo 1937	Was Commodore of the RHKYC in 1933. Subsequently founded the HKRNVR and became Commodore in 1937. In 1941 he was made a member of the Hong Kong Executive Council.	No doubt went to Stanley Camp.

LIST OF NAMES MENTIONED IN LETTERS

Surname	Forename	First Mentioned	Links to Peter and Therese and any other relevant information	What happened to them after the invasion
Smith	N. L. The Hon. (C. M. G.)	14 November 1940	The Colonial Secretary, Hong Kong. Peter met him while trying to get approval for Therese's return to Hong Kong in 1940. Resigned in 1941 as a result of two major government scandals.	Replaced as Colonial Secretary by F Gimson in December 1941. Probably returned to England before the invasion.
Sommerfelt	A.	9 November 1941	L.Cmdr HKRNVR. Cheered Peter up, when very depressed before the invasion. In party that went to defend Postbridge.	He became a POW.
Stewart	Robert	11 September 1940	Husband of Therese's sister Agnes. Research engineer, who worked on gun sights at Vickers and helped Barnes Wallis with developing the bouncing bomb for the Dam Busters.	Remained in England.
Tinson	George	Constance Fairburn's letter 2 November 1943	A WW1 veteran, who helped to defend his house, Postbridge, during the invasion. Peter was part of the army and navy units defending the house in the Wang Nai Chung Gap.	Killed defending 'Postbridge', Tinson's wife Eileen interned in Stanley Camp.
Townend	Mr	18 August 1940	Business friend of Peter's. Geo King & Co., Sydney.	Remained in Sydney.
Townend	Mrs	18 August 1940	Therese and HP initially stayed in their house in Sydney.	Remained in Sydney.
Vernall	Lt.Cmdr.	3 May 1941	Invited to 1939 party with his wife. Acting commanding officer HKRNVR in 1941 and promoted to Commander in October 1941.	POW Shamshuipo Camp. His wife was evacuated to Australia.
Watson	K. A.	3 July 1940	Captain of second tug taken to Aden. He married his wife, Florence just before sailing for Aden.	Not known.
Wilson	D. G.	11 October 1940	1st Lieut *St. Aubin* 1940. Left to become Acting Co. Secretary to Whampoa Dock.	At the invasion listed as 'unallocated RNVR'.

APPENDIX IV

Exchange Rates

29 June 1940

These are the rates of exchange that H. W. M. Dulley prepared for Therese when she was evacuated to the Philippine Islands.

1 Hong Kong $ = 40–45 Centavos Manila (Spanish American currency)
1 Manila Peso = 50 Cents USA (Fixed Rate)
1 English £ = Australian £1 5s 0d (One Australian pound and five shillings and no pence)
1 English £ = US $ 4.0 or thereabouts, the rate is very variable*
1 HK $ = Australian £0 1s 9d (One Australian shilling and six pence)

* The presence of the US $ in the Philippine Islands was due to America's influence there. America established the first Republic in the Philippine Islands in 1899 and then the Commonwealth of the Philippines in 1935, with a view to later independence. https://en.wikipedia.org/wiki/First_Philippine_Republic. 13 September 2015.

APPENDIX V

Press Statement on the Evacuation – October 1940

Statement issued by the Colonial Secretary and published in the *South China Morning Post* on 12 October 1940:

EVACUATION PLAN

The Government States The Position

PRESENT ACTION

The Colonial Secretary yesterday evening issued the following statement to the Press, giving in detail the Government's policy regarding evacuation of British women and children of European race from the Colony:

At the end of June instructions were received from the Secretary of State for the Colonies to the effect that certain classes of women and children were to be evacuated from the Colony. The implementation of those instructions is at present proceeding, and in order to remove any misconceptions as to the present position and Government's policy with regard to evacuation, the following statement has been drawn up for general information.

1. All British women and children of European race are required to leave the Colony unless exemption has been obtained from His Excellency the Officer Administering the Government.

2. No British women or children of European race will be allowed to enter or re-enter the Colony except in the most exceptional circumstances.

3. Women and children of American or European nationalities other than British will be allowed to remain in the Colony for the time being, but applications to enter or re-enter the Colony from persons in this class will be considered by Government individually and on their merits.

Notes on the above

4. Exemption from evacuation:

(a) Applications for exemption are considered in the first place by the Evacuation Advisory Committee who advise His Excellency the Officer Administering the Government on individual cases. Any person dissatisfied with a decision made by His Excellency the Officer Administering the Government with the advice of the Evacuation Advisory Committee for a hearing in person which will normally be held in public session.

(b) Permanent exemption from evacuation may be given to women who have no minor children in the Colony and who are willing to undertake, and are considered by His Excellency the Officer Administering the Government to be qualified to undertake work essential to the maintenance and security of the Colony. Such work will normally be with the Nursing Detachment of the Hongkong Volunteer Defence Corps or the Auxiliary Nursing Service or with the Air Raid Precautions Organisation. Women who are granted exemption on these grounds may be required to sign an undertaking to remain in the Colony and to perform their duties if the Colony should be subjected to investment or attack.

(c) Temporary exemption from evacuation my be given to women who have no minor children in the Colony and who are in active charge of their own businesses in the Colony, or who are considered by His Excellency the Officer Administering the Government to be essential members of the firm, organisation or Government Department in which they are employed. It is hoped that arrangements can be made for the evacuation of such women if the Colony should be subjected to investment or attack.

(d) Temporary exemption from evacuation may be given to women and children on medical or other grounds but such exemption will be limited to the most exceptional cases.

Re-Entry Qualification

5. Re-entry of British Women and Children:

(a) Applications for permission to re-enter the Colony will be considered by the Evacuation Advisory Committee as at 4(a) above.

(b) It cannot be emphases too strongly that permission to enter or re-enter the Colony will be given only in the most exceptional circumstances. Re-entry for the purpose of settling private matters, packing household effects or clothes will not be allowed.*

(c) Women who have qualifications which would enable them to undertake voluntary work as outlined in 4(b) above, except women with professional nursing qualifications, will not normally be given permission to re-enter the Colony on these grounds alone. This question may be subjected to review at a later date.

(d) Bona-fide transit passengers through the Colony will be allowed to enter the Colony. Their stay will be strictly limited to the least period of time in which it is possible to tranship and will, in any event, be limited to a maximum period of one week. Applications for transit facilities should be made to the Commissioner of the Police.*

Other Nationalities

6. Entry of Women and Children of other Nationalities other than British:

(a) Where there is a Consular representative in the Colony of the nation concerned, applications under this head will be considered by the Government in consultation with that representative. Permission for the entry of foreign children under 18 years of age will not normally be given.

(b) Where there is no Consular representative in the Colony of the nation concerned, or where applications are received from Stateless persons, the applications will be considered by the Evacuation Advisory Committee, who will advise Government as to the action to be taken.

Action Being Taken at Present

7. Government, through the Evacuation Advisory Committee, is at present considering the cases of British women and children who are in the Colony without previous exemption. As the public is aware Government has recently taken powers to enforce the evacuation of women and children whose presence in the Colony is unnecessary for its defence or the maintenance of its essential services.

8. At the same time Government, through the Evacuation Advisory Committee, is considering many applications to re-enter the Colony from women and children who are at present outside the Colony.

9. When these cases have been disposed of, it is proposed, in view of the public demand, to reconsider all previous exemptions and to review them in the light of the policy stated in the above paragraphs. Exemption from evacuation has hitherto been given "for the time being" or "until further notice". Those persons who hold such temporary exemptions and who are unable to satisfy Government, through the Evacuation Advisory Committee, that they possess grounds for exemption valid in the sense of the above paragraphs, will be required to leave with the Colony.

10. When this final stage of the review of exemption from evacuation has been completed, it is hoped to be able to publish a list of all women who have been granted exemption together with an indication of the grounds on which such exemption was approved.

11. Permission to re-enter the Colony may be given to exempted women who are at present in the Colony provided they shew good grounds for wishing to leave and to return.

GOVERNOR'S APPROVAL

Replies to Applications For Exemption Soon

Women who have not yet received replies to their written applications for exemption will be noticed of the Evacuation Advisory Committee's decision shortly, the Secretary, Mr. C. B. Burgess, said yesterday.

In the event of an adverse decision, women will be informed that they have the right to appeal for a public hearing at one of the Committee's sessions.

The Committee as yet can give no indication of the number of exemptions as all hearings take time and have to be approved by H. E. the Acting Governor.

Until the number is ascertained arrangements for departure are held up.

Tribunal's Next Session

It is notified for general information that a public session of the Evacuation Advisory Committee will be held on Tuesday, October 15, at 9 a.m. in the Council Chamber, Colonial Secretariat.

Only the cases of women who have applied to the Committee for a hearing in person, and have been requested to attend the meeting, will be considered.

On the original newspaper article Peter put a comment that these two sections seemed a bit contradictory.

APPENDIX VI

H. W. M. Dulley's Ships

1939–1941

Ship	Dates in Command	Details	Armament	Fate
Perla HMPS	Commissioned August 1939 – December 1939	35 tons, steam powered. Photo in 1939 Christmas card	1 x 6 pounder 1 x Bren gun	Scuttled by HKRNVR during invasion
Britannia* Governor's Launch	December 1939 – early February 1940	Used for the 'longest beat' to a minefield that had 'come rather badly unstuck'	Not known	Not known
Edith* ?	Early to end Feb 40	50 ton tug	Not known	Not known
St. Aubin HMAPV	Took command March 1940. Ship commissioned July 1940. Voyage to Aden June – July 1941	468 tons, steam powered. Used for patrol work and minesweeping until taken to Aden	1 x 12 pounder 2 x Lewis guns	She was laid up in 1943 as had become out of date. Sold in 1946. Sunk off Taiwan in 1950 during Chinese civil war
Cornflower HMS	First Lieutenant November–December 1941 HKRNVR HQ	The ship (SS *Tai Hing*) was donated by Sir Robert Ho Tung for the duration of the war to replace the previous *Cornflower*	2lb Pom-pom	Scuttled by HKRNVR during invasion

*The names, dates and details are from a letter to Jack Dulley dated 30 March 1940.

APPENDIX VII

The Crew of *St. Aubin*

Peter stated that the crew of *St. Aubin* totalled thirty-five; it is assumed that it is most probable that Peter was referring to the whole crew including officers. This breakdown of the crew is based on Peter's letters and Lt Cmdr Collingwood-Selby book *In Times of War*. The latter's ship was HMS *Redstart*, a minelayer, based in Hong Kong and built for ocean travel. The large crew for a relatively small ship will be due to the naval duties and sailing for 24 hours a day. RN ships had a largely white crew, the HKRNVR had Chinese crews apart from the officers. A possible breakdown of the *St. Aubin* crew is therefore:

Wardroom
Captain
First Lieutenant
2 Lieutenants
1 CERA*

Chinese Crew's Mess
Engine Room
2 ERA*
3 Leading stokers
6 Stokers
Deckhands
1 Boatswain
2 Quartermasters
3 Leading Seaman
8 Able Seamen
Galley
1 Head cook
1 Cook
1 Cabin boy
2 Wireless operators   (they may have had bunks in the wireless room)
TOTAL CREW   35

* Chief Engine Room Artificer and Engine Room Artificer

APPENDIX VIII

The Jardine Matheson Archive
University of Cambridge

This is a short extract from the notes taken by Hugh Dulley in January 2016 while researching Jardines' Archives at University of Cambridge to ascertain the company's view on the threatened Japanese invasion of Hong Kong.

The Japanese occupied Manchuria in 1932 but it was not until much later that they spread to other parts of China and came into contact with Europeans. The following extracts from an exchange of letters between the Jardine Taipans in Hong Kong, Shanghai and London and a further letter from the Foreign Office, all reflect the escalating situation:

> W. J. Keswick, Shanghai to J. J. Paterson, Hong Kong   24 July 1940
> 'The Japanese pressure has increased lately as was to be expected. Terrorism is more rampant than ever and the situation can but be described as distressing…'

As early as the beginning of 1941 the Foreign Office considered that there was a strong possibility of war with Japan.

> R. A. Butler[1] Foreign Office to McGowan   17 February 1941
> 'The Head Offices of firms concerned should be warned of the risks in the present situation and told that, unless they give early instructions for the withdrawal of their staff, the staff risk being caught in Japan at the outbreak of war and being obliged to remain there for the duration of hostilities.'

The Japanese threat to Hong Kong had existed for some time and increased over the years. Jardines' decision to remain in Hong Kong was made before May 1941, and the period researched, as Peter[2] stated in a letter dated 27 May to Therese:

---

1 R. A. Butler became a Cabinet Minister in 1941.
2 The Jardine Insurance files dated 6 February 1933, stated that Peter should remain in the Head Office as 'the Companies Funds now require a special man to supervise them. He should be given early opportunity of spending a couple of months in Shanghai in order to make himself conversant with conditions of accountancy there.' So his trip to Shanghai was planned all along.

'…'C'est la guerre' and everyone must take his chance. The Union weren't willing and moved to Sydney in order to avoid just these same troubles, but we are sitting pat and chancing our hand.'

The reason behind this decision is no doubt summed up in the following extract:

B. D. F. Beith London to J. J. Paterson Hong Kong 21 February 1941
'If you shut up shop you may never be able to open it again – although actual hostilities never occur.'

Later in the year, the senior executive with J. J. Paterson, Taffy Landale, who had been in Hong Kong before enlisting wrote:

Taffy Landale to B. D. F. Beith London   14 September 1941
'How are they all in Hong Kong. I am afraid they must be feeling a little marooned at the moment. …. it is difficult to guess what is going to happen. What does Tony, who I presume is still in Shanghai, make of it all?'

The following letter is written just over a month before the invasion of Hong Kong:

B. D. F. Beith London to J. J. Paterson Hong Kong   5 November 1941
'…the Foreign Office consider that, in view of the present tense situation vis-a-vis Japan, all non-essential people should leave Shanghai, that there is no panic in this notification and that the Foreign Office had no intention of disturbing active trading. He asked that you encouraged non-essential people to clear out of Shanghai whilst there was a chance of doing so.'

Finally there is the slightly despairing but accurate statement from the London Office:

B. D. F. Beith London to J. J. Paterson Hong Kong   12 November 1941
'Surely no reliance can be placed on anything based on logic today.'

APPENDIX IX

Letters from Internees of the Japanese Camps in Hong Kong

The letters are from, with two exceptions, former prisoners in camps in Hong Kong. The civilians were released, as they were not British, and the military escaped.

There are excerpts from these letters in Chapter 17:

Eric Cox-Walker	14 December 1944
Constance Fairburn	2 November 1943

Other letters:

Marjorie Paleraon	1 May 1942
George C. Dankworth	4 August 1942
(Letters to Therese and W A Davidson)	
Benjamin A Proulx	10 April 1942
J. W. Hurst	June? 1942
Colonial Office	22 February 1946

The dates of the letters are spread over a number of years, which are explained in the letters. The letters have been placed in order according to the information they provide.

Eric Cox-Walker to Therese Dulley

14 December 1944   c/o Jardine Matheson & Co. Ltd. Bombay, India

Dear Mrs Dulley,
I really must apologise for being so slow in answering your air-letter, and the only excuse I can give you is that I have been so busy. As regards giving you news of what happened in H-K I'm afraid all I can tell you is the little I saw whilst serving under

your husband in HKRNVR. First of all when the balloon finally did go up I and many others complained bitterly as to why they should have an Air-Raid Practice at that time of the morning, but we soon realised it was the real thing, and the HKRNVR ships were in action right away. Later that morning they were all shifted round to Aberdeen where they were moored single line ahead and presented such a target that of course we had two raids the following day with one or two near misses. After that all ships were transferred to Deep Water Bay with the *Cornflower* as H.Q., where your husband was. We managed to hold our own against the occasional planes which came over, then H.Q. transferred to a house ashore, one of those big houses overlooking Deep Water Bay on the Island Road just passed [sic] the turn off to Wanchegong [sic] Gap. From then on your husband, as second in command, was ashore all the time organising defences and patrols, being in constant touch with Battle H.Q. by telephone. The small auxiliaries were still doing patrol work in Lama Channel and so forth, where they did some grand work. There was one concentrated attack on *Cornflower* but no hits were registered and her 2lb pomp-pomp did some useful work. There were several raids on Aberdeen Dock Yard, especially when the one destroyer was in dock there when the Naval Tug 'Gatling' got a direct hit and so many Indo-China officers were killed and wounded. The days at the H.Q. house were spent in generally preparing defence with an occasional working party going to Aberdeen and later a guard party went over each night to assist at the Dock Yard in H-K. I believe your husband was in one of those parties but had returned and was at Deep Water Bay the night of 18/19 Dec. The Japs managed to make a landing that night under cover of a pall of smoke caused by the Petrol Installation at North Point being hot and going up in smoke. That was their third attempt, the first one was broken up by the 'Thracian' and the second by the M.T.Bs. that night I was aboard the *Cornflower* but I heard later that when the Japs were forcing their way through Happy Valley and up to Wanchegong [sic] Gap, your husband heard of some troubles at a house up there so he took a volunteer party up to investigate, there being one or two crews ashore by then, their ships having been badly damaged or sunk. It was apparently whilst investigating at Tinson's house that your husband was so unfortunately killed, but I am afraid I cannot give you any more details as I was not there myself. After that we received orders to scuttle all ships, so having done that we proceeded to Aberdeen Industrial School, where the HKRNVR were formed into a regular guard of the H.Q.

there, and I was fortunate and lucky enough at the time of the surrender to be actually on the launch that was requisitioned to join Admiral Chan Chak's party and so I was one of the lucky ones who got away into China and so on into India by way of the Burma Road and the Haukwang Valley.

It was very extraordinary my meeting Mrs Swabie on the ship when I was returning from leave and so getting in touch with Mrs Ralph. I hope you are keeping quite fit and getting on all right in Aussie, I see you give your address as George King's so give my regards to Mason when you see him. Here's wishing you all the very best of luck & the best compliments of the season. I didn't see I was getting to the end of the page so please excuse squash in finishing off.

Yours truly,

Eric Cox-Walker

E Cox-Walker HKRNVR (23/11/1901 – 06/08/1983) who had been employed by Jardines in Hong Kong, escaped from Aberdeen on Christmas Day.

Constance Fairburn to Therese Dulley

2 November 1943   Motorship Gripsholm

My Dear Therese

I can hardly yet believe I am on my way to freedom – being Canadian I got a chance to be repatriated and I took it.

Therese dear I thought you might want to know that Peter was killed in the Tinson's house & he is now buried in the garden. The war for Hong Kong was a terrible thing – it seemed to cost so much & accomplish so little – we did hear that defending it saved Australia & so I suppose it's worth any amount of sacrifices.

Tom seems well & cheerful – he is in Argyle Street camp & was allowed to write to me before I left – which made my leaving so much easier as he was very keen on having me get back to Vancouver and look after Angela.

Stanley is absolute hell – I expect every internment is pretty awful but I think Stanley is worse than any other in the FAR EAST. We have people on board from every camp. China, Japan, Manila, Saigon – & none of them were ever hungry – &

people in Stanley are literally starving. We were thankful to see thousands of tons of red Cross supplies being loaded in the Teia Maru for HK & only hope it won't be too many months before reaching Hong Kong.

Before I left Eileen Tinson & I had tea with your uncle and aunt – they both sent you their fondest love & said to tell you they think you have been wonderfully brave – it's rather difficult for them to write to you as we are only allowed one letter or one card per month & only one from husband or wife – that isn't very much when one has two families to write to. Mrs Davidson has been quite ill several times but this summer she was in hospital & really was very ill with dysentery – she is still terribly thin but says she feels better. Mr Davidson has been much better this last summer but thin too – I think most men in the camp have lost 40-50pounds – it's really very grim. Mr & Mrs Davidson have a room to themselves & next door live Mr & Mrs Pritchard & PAM so they have congenial companions. I lived also in the Indian quarters in one room with Mrs Simpson Margen [Margaret?] & Mrs Tinson & we were a very happy home. We got as much fun & happiness as one possibly could under such grim circumstances. We were known to be the happiest mess in Stanley – so you see I was very fortunate – I simply loathed leaving all my friends behind – but couldn't miss this opportunity of getting away – it would have been very foolish – & I hope before very long they too will be repatriated. We do not hear any news in this ship – but arrive [at] Port Elizabeth tonight & perhaps might hear definite news about their leaving Stanley – I am sure Mr & Mrs Davidson will be in the first ship as they will take women children old & infirm. We are all very bitter about women & children who stayed behind – the children get more & better food than the men & have done so ever since the beginning – it's hard to see men fading before your eyes & all the Chinese & Eurasian children looking blooming & bursting with health.

I am sure you will be surprised to hear our friend Robert Minnitt got married in Camp – he married a girl called Peggy Sharp – her father is in Wireless & Cables. I felt sorry to see him get married under such sordid conditions but it's their business after all & they seem to be very happy. Robert has been very ill – he looks perfectly ghastly. Worse I believe than many other men. As a matter of fact everyone looks ghastly, at the moment saved by a marvellous TAN – but that soon fades. I must admit that the saving grace of Stanley was its climate & lovely outlook. One spends hours sitting on the hillside gazing out to sea! During the summer the swimming was lovely – you almost forgot you were in prison.

About 55 Canadians left Hong Kong – among them Frances Dodds & Mr Gillespie & Gladys Collard (a nursing sister) we 4 play bridge & drink beer together – the rest of the ship is composed of missionaries, nuns and all kinds of Americans – mostly pretty awful. This ship is lovely, all but our cabins & needless to say the 200 Canadians were given the worst accommodation! But we don't spend much time in our cabins – and really Therese after the terrible ship Teia Maru this seems like heaven. It was the old Line Aramis built for about 600 passengers and not 1500! I shall certainly be glad when I reach New York and can begin to live a more or less normal life again – the thought of having a room to one's self seems to be like heaven.

Good bye now my dear – if you see Tiné Garrard give her my love also Stamp [?] & tell her I shall write. Please tell Doreen Ralph that the Blakes hear from him frequently & they received 5 yen from him just before I left H.K.

Write to me Therese c/o Canadian Bank of Commerce, Robson District Bank, Vancouver.

Lots of love

Constance Fairburn

Marjorie Paleraon (?) to Therese Dulley

1st May 1942   2373 Washington Street, San Francisco, California

Dear Therese,

Ever since I received a letter from Mrs Dodwell and then from Dorothy Cavanuagh telling me that you had received word that Peter was reported missing, I have thought of you many times and deeply sympathized with you in your anxiety. The uncertainty must be terrible for you and I only hope that you will receive word that he is a prisoner in some camp. You know for long time young Bosanquet was reported as being missing and probably killed, yet he turned up in the same prison camp as J. J. The news seemed to be so authentic that it was carried in one of the circular letters which is being gotten out by Mr Lennox, who is in New York, and the good news that he actually is alive came out months later.

Both Dorothy and Mrs Dodwell say that your little Hugh is adorable. What a comfort he must be to you. I am sorry for the evacuee' and refugee wives who have no children because they must feel so useless. At least we can feel that we are doing the thing which our husbands care about most – that is, bringing up their children properly.

I suppose you have heard that J. J. is in the Argyle Street prison camp in Kowloon. I never thought the day would come when I should worry he should not have enough to eat! I only hope the very fact that he gains weight so easily on a very small quantity of food will stand him in good stead now. At first when I heard he had been taken prisoner I was tremendously relieved because that meant that at least he had lived through the fighting, and I truly believed that the Japs would be decent to their prisoners, but that does not seem to be the case and I am awfully worried about him. It must be simply ghastly in an overcrowded prison camp.

I only wish that J. J. could have the fun of watching Nancie grow up. She has changed tremendously in the last few months. She is almost as tall as I am, but very slim and her hair has grown very curly. She is just completing her second year in the Dominican Convent in San Rafael. It is a wonderful school – extremely progressive – and the nuns know how to handle each individual child. They have done so much to give Nancie self-assurance and confidence. She was quite shy when she first went there because she was not accustomed to doing class work since she had always had a governess. For the past three terms she has been on the Honour Roll every month. She is my great joy and comfort, as I know your little Hugh must be to you.

Are the Davidsons still in Hong Kong? If so, I suppose that means they are interned in Stanley. At least the buildings are new. Well do I remember when the so-called 'Good and Great' of Hong Kong went to an afternoon reception at the prison when it was opened. I remember the Governor got burned on the new steam-cookers. Peggie Newbegging received word through John Keswick in Chungking that Buggins is at Stanley and she imagines he has charge of distributing what food is available, since his job during the war was that of food controller.

None of the British wives are here in San Francisco, but there are lots of Americans. Mrs Southard, the American Consul-General's wife is here. She has been seedy for a long time. I think she is very lucky to have a husband who will probably be exchanged before the war is over, but she worries awfully about him nevertheless. I see the Jimmie Taggarts quite often as they live near us. They have a beautiful apartment commanding a gorgeous view of San Francisco Bay.

Ever since December 17th I have had a job in the Navy. I wanted to do something which would be so difficult and exacting that I simply couldn't worry as much as I otherwise would. It really kept me sane during the awful days of the Battle of Hong Kong. It has been excellent discipline for me. However, Nancie's three months' holiday this summer will complicate matters so my plans are a bit uncertain.

It is encouraging to realize that America is awake at long last. Even the labor unions are getting into line and I do feel that the weight of American production will soon make itself felt.

If you ever have time to write me a letter, I should love to hear from you. Mrs Dodwell and Dorothy say that your courage is magnificent, but I know what a ghastly strain you are under and I want to know that I am holding the thought that you will be rewarded with good news.

Affectionately,

Marjorie Paleraon

George C Dankworth to Therese Dulley

4 August 1942　　　　　　　　　　MS Gripsholm, en route to the United States

Dear Mrs Dulley,

It is with deep regret that I have to inform you of the death of your husband at Hong Kong. I understand from Mr Edgar Davidson that he was killed in action near Wong Nei Chong gap. I have written to Mr W. A. Davidson in England and enclose a copy of my letter to him. The brave boys who gave their lives for the defence of Hong Kong were more than heroes as they did not have an even chance against the enemy. There was not a single military plane or warship to support the land forces and the enemy outnumbered them eight to one. It is estimated that three thousand defenders lost their lives, but that losses of eighteen thousand were inflicted on the Japanese.

Mr. Edgar Davidson sends you his love and sympathy, and may I add my condolences to you in your loss.

Sincerely,

Geo. C. Duckworth

4 Mt. Nord Fayetteville, Arkansas, U.S.A. Original: airmail Copy: steamer mail

George C Dankworth to W. A. Davidson (Brother of Edgar Davidson, known as UE, and Uncle to Therese)

4 August 1942　　　　　　　　　　　M. S. Gripsholm, en route to the United States

W. A. Davidson, Esq.,
57 Cable Road
Hoylake, Cheshire
England

Dear Mr Davidson:

I am happy to inform you that your brother Edgar came safely through the Japanese attack on Hong Kong and when I left there on June 29 he was at Stanley Civilian Internment Camp. He was feeling very fit, in good mental spirits and was generally content with life, inasmuch as he was able to get sufficient smoking tobacco. Unfortunately, Peter Dulley was killed in action at Wong Nei Chong Gap and I am writing Mrs Dulley in Sydney, and enclosing a copy of this letter.

The internment camp at Stanley is partly in the grounds of Hong Kong Prison and in the adjoining St. Stephen's' College property. In 24 flats, three rooms, kitchen and bath, with servants' room and bath, 760 British are quartered – men, women and children – twelve or more in a room of moderate size. This is situated on an elevation. Your brother, however, is in the quarters formerly occupied by the Indian guards, down in the hollow, but conditions are not too bad, as there only are four in a small room. All of the Peak residents are in the lower buildings – probably as punishment for having been the business and social leaders of the Colony. Even Sir Atholl MacGregor, the chief justice, lives in the Indian quarters.

I am with Marsman Investments Limited in Manila and was caught in Hong Kong when the war broke out, after having attended a shareholders' meeting of Marsman Hongkong China, Ltd., for which your brother's firm has acted as counsel since the company was organized in 1936. Mr Marsman was also trapped by the war, but managed to escape and has written up his experiences in an article entitled 'I escaped from Hongkong' which appears in the Saturday Evening Post for June 6,13 and 20.

The rations at Stanley which the authorities furnish are decidedly on the short

side, and lack variety. Your brother, however, receives parcels each week, containing foodstuffs, tobacco and clothing, from friends and employees and manages very nicely.
With best wishes, I am
Yours faithfully,
Geo. C. Dankwerth
4 Mt. Nord
Fayetteville, Arkansas, U.S.A.

Original: airmail
Copy: steamer mail
Copy: airmail to Mrs Dulley, Sydney
Copy: steamer mail to Mrs Dulley

Benjamin A. Proulx (Warrant Officer HKRNVR) of the American Volunteer Group wrote from Calcutta on 10th April 1942.

Original lost; excerpts from it transcribed and a synopsis made by Jack Dulley.

Dorothy Coates' husband was alive and safe, but held at North Point Japanese Military Prison. Mr Proulx escaped the night of 27 January and got away to Calcutta by walking, paddling and motor trucks covering 3,500 miles in 59 days through Waichow, Kukong & Kweiang.

Of 'Tiny' Coates, Mr Proulx said:

> ...he is honestly well and cheerful as ever. I went through the war with him and believe me did some good work all over the shop, no fooling. Was on the same watch with him at Lamma and we ended up in the mountains with rifles, fighting like hillbillies, especially good ones too. 'Tiny' was away from me for a few days around Stanley, where he put in good work under Forthsythe, who was killed; then he came back to us. We were seven of us who stuck together in prison, first at Shamshuipo [Camp], then at North Point, where we were transferred on 24th January. The seven in our group were 'Tiny', Jupp, Harrison, Westwood, self, Worrall and Evans of the B.A.I. Tell Mrs Irene Evans that her husband is O.K. (Bill Evans' wife is Beryl George's first cousin, both parents in Shanghai with Beryl's in laws).

I can't remember the names of all of them but some who were killed are: Gregory, Dulley (of Jardines), Ian Pearce, George Tinson, Rogers the American Exchange Broker, Des Voeux the broker, Vine[s] Gordon Fielding, Forsythe, Mackinley and Winter-Blythe, from Deacons, Johnny Hearn the jockey, and there are a great many more.

Of the B.A.I. men I saw O'Grady, Sullivan, Merritt, and one other whose name I cannot remember are O.K. Merritt is in civilian camp.

I got away taking two Dutch submarine officers; none of the boys in our little mess would come. Between two camps about 15 have escaped. I saw many of the homes on my way crawling through Hong Kong to Shekko and they are in a mess, looted etc. Peak Mansions where you had your flat was badly shelled and the flats are all looted. We all lost our personal belongings.

Merritt is being expatriated.

END

B. A. Proulx wrote about his escape in 'Underground from Hong Kong' 1943.

J. W. Hurst to an unknown recipient, possibly Jack Dulley (who transcribed the letter)

June (?) 1942   Stonehenge, 118 Newcastle Road, Sunderland

Dear Sir,

In reply to your enquiry, I am afraid there is very little information I can really give you.

In the case of Dulley (HWM) he was killed when a party of men were trapped in a house. I understand they put up a good show, but the odds were too heavy and they were all more or less blown out of it. In regards to the other people (Edgar & Eva Davidson) I was not acquainted with them, but I should imagine they will be interned in the civilian camp in the houses around Stanley. There was very little damage done to the peak or even Hong Kong itself. Most of the damage was centred around military objectives and landing places. As I spent over a month in two military camps before my escape, I can't give you any information as to the treatment accorded to the civilian camps, though I should imagine they would be better off than we were. From my own experience while a prisoner, apart from the feeding conditions and general living conditions, there was nothing really which we could complain of. There was no interference from the Japs in any way and no brutalities committed towards prisoners. Atrocities of course were committed during the fighting when both sides are abnormal. After the surrender everything was conducted in an orderly manner and I do not doubt that by this time things have improved.

Trusting that this news though small, will relieve your feelings.

Yours sincerely,

J. W. Hurst

The Colonial Office to 'A. L. Dulley Esq'

22 February 1946   Colonial Office (Enquiries and Casualties) 2, Park Street, W1

Sir,

I am directed to inform you that after careful consideration of the available evidence, and in view of the absence of any favourable news of your son, Lieutenant Commander H W M Dulley since the cessation of hostilities and subsequent liberation of prisoners of war and internees in the Far East, the Secretary of State has reluctantly and with deep regret, reached the conclusion that there can no longer be any hope of his survival.

It is consequently being officially recorded that Lieutenant Commander Hugh William Macpherson Dulley of the HKRNVR is presumed to have been killed in action between the 7th and 25th of December, 1941.

The Secretary of State desires me to convey to you an expression of his very deep sympathy with you in your bereavement.

I am. Sir,

Your obedient servant,

[sgd] M. G. Willis

Bibliography

Allen, Charles *Tales from the South China Seas,* 1984, Futura Publications, London.
Banham, Tony *Not the Slightest Chance: The Defence of Hong Kong, 1941,* 2003, Hong Kong University Press, Hong Kong.
Beevor, Anthony *The Second World War*, 2012, Weidenfeld & Nicolson, paperback edition 2013 Phoenix, imprint of Orion Books, London.
Bosanquet, David *Escape Through China*, 1983, Robin Hale, London.
Brice, Martin *The Royal Navy and the Sino-Japanese Incident 1937–41*, 1973, Ian Allan, London.
Chambers, Gillian *Eastern Waters-Eastern Winds: History of the Royal Hong Kong Yacht Club*, 1993, printed by Everbest Printing, Hong Kong.
Collingwood-Selby, Henry and Others *In Time of War*, 2013, Proverse, Hong Kong.
Deakes, C. and Stanley, T *A Century of Sea Travel*, 2010 Seaforth, Barnsley, UK.
Goodwin, R. B. *Hong Kong Escape*, 1953 Arthur Barker, London. Republished in 2015 by Pen & Sword Books, Barnsley, South Yorkshire.
Harland, Kathleen *The Royal Navy in Hong Kong since 1841*. No date, Maritime Books, Cornwall, England.
Heywood, G. S. P. *Rambles in Hong Kong*, 1938, The South China Morning Post, Hong Kong.
Keay, John *Last Post: The End of the Empire in the Far East*, 1997, John Murray, London.
Kerr, J. L. and Granville, W *The RNVR: a Record of Achievement*, 1957, George G Harrap, London.
Keswick, Maggie (Editor) *The Thistle and the Jade: A Celebration of 150 Years of Jardine, Matheson, & Co*, 1982, Octopus Books, London.
Lavery, Brian *In Which They Served*, 2008, Conway, London.
Lindsay, Oliver *The Battle for Hong Kong 1941– 45: Hostage to Fortune*, 2005, Spellmount, Stroud, England.
McCart, N. *HMS Hermes: 1923 & 1959*, 2001, Fan Publications, Cheltenham, England.
Melson, P. J. *White Ensign – Red Dragon: The History of the Royal Navy in Hong Kong 1841–1997*, 1997, Edinburgh Financial Publishing (Asia), Hong Kong.
Morris, Jan *Hong Kong*, 1993, Second Edition Penguin, London.
Perry, Roland *Pacific 360: Australia's Battle for Survival in World War 2*, 2012, Hatchette, Sydney, Australia.
Roberts, Andrew *Letters from the Front*, 2012, Osprey Publishing, Oxford.
Snow, Philip *The Fall of Hong Kong: Britain, China and the Japanese Occupation*, 2003, Yale University Press, Newhaven & London.
Spence, Jonathan D. *The Search for Modern China*, 1990, Hutchinson, London.
Thorbecke, Ellen *Hong Kong* (1930s) Kelly & Walsh, Hong Kong.
Tsang, Steve *A Modern History of Hong Kong*, 2004, Tauris, London.
Welsh, Frank *A History of Hong Kong*, 1993, Harper Collins Publishers, Glasgow.
Wheeler, Harold *The Peoples History of the Second World War: January–December 1941* (Page with date missing) Odhams Press Ltd, Long Acre, London.
Woolf, B. S. *Chips of China*, 1930, Kelly & Walsh, Hong Kong.

Other Reference Sources:

The Imperial War Museum, London
The Jardine Matheson Archive, Cambridge University
The National Archive, Kew, London
The Times newspaper, London
Various internet websites as indicated in footnotes

Index

Locators refer to page numbers; those with the suffix 'n.' also refer to information in the notes. Page numbers with suffix 'app.' relate to information in the Appendixes, and those with 'g.' will be found in the glossary in Appendix 1. For names of people, the information is found under the persons' surname. Cross-references are shown for nicknames used within the text. Any references to 'war' in the index are for World War 2.

The following abbreviations are used in the index:
HK = Hong Kong
PI = Philippine Islands
HP = Hugh Peter (Dulley)
P&T = Peter and Therese (Dulley)

Aden, Peter's trip to (1941)
    censorship of details 197, 199, 200
    leaving HK for 198–201
    map of *18–19*
    return journey to HK 227–35
    stay in 216–27, *218*
    stop-overs en route
        Padang 207–11
        Seychelles 211–15
        Singapore 202–07
'AE' *see* Davidson, Eva ('AE')
Ah Kung (boat boy) 43, 53, *57*, 287*app.*
airmail 48, 83*n.*, 178, 213
air travel, commercial 38–40
Amah 102–03, 284*g.*
    recruited in HK 146, *168*, 175–6
    recruited in PI 142
Amoy 188*n.*–190
Armstrong, Joan 140, 144, 165, 287*app.*
Australia
    censorship in 116
    evacuation of women and children to 123, 136, 148, 150
    Therese, evacuation plans 127, 140, 142, 147, 154, 162, 171
    involvement in war 186*n.*, 204*n.*, 222*n.*, 238*n.*
    Japanese attack on Darwin 277–8
    Sydney, evacuation of Therese and HP to 171, 181, 183, 186, 243*n.*
    contingency plans for 127, 140, 146
    after Peter's death 269, 276–8, 277, 279, 280–1
    tax rules in 196
    White Australia Policy 146*n.*
axis, Germany, Japan and Italy 120*n.*, 156–7, 193

Baguio, Philippines
    Notre Dame de Lourdes Hospital *139*
    P&T honeymoon in 99, 100
    plans for 74, 81, 91
    Therese evacuated to 123, 126, 127, 158, 170
    see also Philippine Islands (PI)
'Balkan Campaign' 178, 187, 191
Beijing (Peking) 32
Blunt, Lizzie 28, 89, 287*app.*
    letters from Peter
        1930s 66–7, 72, 95–6, 101, 107–11, 255
        1940s 119–22, 180–1
Bosanquet, David 276, 287*app.*
Boxer, Major Charles R. 49, 238, 243, 287*app.*
Britain *see* Great Britain, role in war
bungalow *see* Peak, The, No. 168, P&T's home on
Burma Road 128*n.*, 134, 136, 155, 157

cables (communication) 40, 48, *270*
Camp John Hay, PI 123, *144*, 145, 149, 152
Canada, troops in HK 248, 258, 262
Canton 67
    Chinese governance of 77, 95
    Japanese occupation of 32, 110
Cantonese (language) 33
car, Austin 10 (EOF) 104, 107, 173, *174*
censorship
    of Aden trip 197, 199, 200
    of mail 115–16, *208*, 271
    of Peter's letters 156, 160*n*, 208*n.*, 209–10
    of photographs 195
Ceylon *see* Colombo, Sri Lanka (Ceylon)
Chan Chak, Admiral 247*n.*, 274–5, 276
Chennai (Madras), India 230, 231, 232–3
children, separated from, in England 46–7
children *see* evacuation of women and children, from HK
Chile 23
China
    ancient traditions of 28–30
    Burma Road 128*n.*, 134, 136, 155, 157
    governance over Canton 77, 95
    historical ties with HK 30–1, 32–3
    imperial history of 31
    Japanese invasion and occupation of 34, 67, 110–11, 157, 237
    following surrender of Japanese 279–80
    'Manchurian incident' 32, 113–14, 255*n.*

INDEX

occupation of China 32, 67n, 95, 110–11, 115, 120
   threats of invasion 134, 236, 237–8, 301–02app.
   maps of 16–17, 22
   restrictions of subjects entering Australia 146n.
   see also Hong Kong; Shanghai
Chitral (ship) 199n.
Churchill, Sir Winston 123, 169
   addresses Japanese aggression in China 227, 267
   references to HK and Far East 257–8, 268
Colombo, Sri Lanka (Ceylon) 230
   return journey from Aden 227–32, *228*
communication, systems of 40, 48–9
   cables 40, 48, *270*
   mail, delivery of 48, 178, 213
Communism, in China 31–2
concentration and POW camps 268, 269, 272
   letters from internees 303–13app.
   Stanley camp 269, 271, *271*, 305–06app., 310–11app.
constitutional reform, calls for, in HK 33
cook boy 101–03
coolie 103, 186, 188n., 284g.
Cornflower see HMS *Cornflower*
Cox-Walker, Eric 274–5, 276
   letter to Therese, 1944 263–6, 303–05app.

Darwin, Japanese attack on 277–8
Davidson, Edgar ('UE') 50–1, 53, 56, *109*, *129*, *172*
   death of son 179, 248
   during wartime and occupation in HK 173, 280
   in concentration camp 269–70, *270*, *271*, 306app.
   friendship with Peter 61
   positions in HK 126n., 153, 163–4n.
   on Executive Council 236, 261n., 269
   social activities in HK 195, 236, 242
Davidson, Eva ('AE') 50–1, 53, 55, *109*, *129*, *172*
   during wartime and occupation in HK 173, 192, 280
   in concentration camp 269–70, *270*, 306app.
   evacuation, refusal of 125, 126n., 130n.
   friendship with P&T 61, 68, 129
   involvement in wedding 78, 85, 96
   letters
      from Peter 206–07
      to Therese 107, 272, 273
   relationship with and death of son 47–8, 153, 158, 179, 183, 195
Davidson, Gerald 51, 56, 288app.
Davidson, Jack 47–8, *106*, 153, 158, 288app.
   death of 171, 179, 195
Davidson, Willie 271
dead reckoning 189n.

Deep Water Bay see Postbridge, Deep Water Bay, HK
DEI see Dutch East Indies (DEI)
Dixon, Major & Mrs. 78, 81–3, 89, 288app.
drinking culture 36–7, 49
Dulley, Agnes Leonora (mother) 27, 28, 61, 71, 132n., 181
   letters from Peter 197, 199, 200–1
   on trip to Aden 207–08, 210–13, 216–18
   from Aden 221–2
   on trip from Aden to HK 229, 231–2, 235
Dulley, Evelyn (sister) 27, 28, 66, 74, 181
   letters from Peter 210–11
Dulley, Herbert (father) 27, 28, 48
Dulley, Hugh Peter (HP)
   Therese's pregnancy 118, 122
   birth of 123, 127–8, 139, 141
   returns to HK (1940) 168
   Christening of 171, *172*
   sent to Australia 171
   evacuation in Sydney 239, *239*, 247
   after Peter's death 276–8, *277*, *279*, *280*
   returns to England 280–1
Dulley, JHM (Jack) (brother) 26, 28, 76
   letters, from Peter 116–19, 131–2, 226, 249, 257
   reactions to Peter's engagement 61, 71
   role in RAFVR 181, 192, 222
Dulley, Hugh William Macpherson (Peter) 53, 56–9
   rowing, Peter's talent for 28, *29*, 40–3, 44
   arrival in HK 1930s 23
   engagement and marriage to Therese 51, 55–9, 61, 97
   arrangements for 78, 85, 88, 93, 96
   honeymoon arrangements 74, 81, 88, 91, 99–100
   return to London (1938) 104, *105*, *106*
   work with Jardine Matheson & Co. 23, 71, 88, 118, 155
   socialising, during wartime 160, 166, 170, 186, 188
   during Aden trip 209–10, 230–1, 236
   sailing, Peter's love of 36, 40–4, 53, 68
   sickness 196, 205, 220n.
   depression 236, 250, 253
   sea-sickness 189, 195, 202
   naval duties 43, 112, 115, 116, *249*, 257
   on HMAPV *St Aubin* 125, 128, 135, 141
   HKRNVR duties 151, 154, 158, 163, 167, 175, 180
      action with HKRNVR 263–7, 303–04app.
   navigation 177, 178–9, 187, 189
      on trip to Aden 203, 234–5
      pilotage 190, 209, 240
      see also sextant (navigation tool)
   death and burial 267, 269, 272
   letters regarding 304app., 309app., 312app., 313app.
   mentioned in despatches 268

316

letters
    to Agnes (mother) 197, 199, 200–1
    on trip to Aden 207–08, 210–13, 216–18
    from Aden 221–2
    on trip from Aden to HK 229, 231–2, 235
    to Eva Davidson 206–07
    to Evelyn (sister) 210n.–11
    to Jack (brother) 116–19, 131–2, 226, 249, 257
    to Lizzie Blunt
      1930s 66–7, 72, 95–6, 101, 107–11, 255
      1940s 119–22, 180–1
    to Nancy (mother-in-law) 124, 126–8
    to Therese
      during engagement 61–6, 67–72, 74–94, 255–7
      during evacuation
        in PI 124–6, 128–31, 132–46, 255–7
        in Sydney 171–80, 181–2, 183–97, 198–99
      on journey to Aden 203–06, 207–11, 213–18
      from Aden 219–21, 222–5
      on journey from Aden to HK 227–31, 232–5
      from HK post-Aden 236–49, 250–4
      just before the invasion of HK 260–2
Dulley, Therese née Sander (wife)
  engagement and marriage to Peter 49–50, 51, 55–9, 61, 97
    arrangements for 78, 85, 88, 93, 96
    honeymoon arrangements 74, 81, 88, 91, 99–100
  journey back to England (1936) 60–2
  returns to HK (1936) 84, 87, 90
  return to London (1938) 104, 105, *106*
  pregnancy 118, 122
  evacuation, to PI 123, 125
  birth of son 139, 141
  planned return to HK (1940) 143, 147, 158, 161, 162, 163
  return to HK (1940) *168*, 170, 171
  evacuation to Sydney 171, 181, 183, 186, 243n.
  after Peter's death 269, 276–8, *277*, 279, 280–1
  return to England (1945) 280–1
  letters
    from Agnes Dulley 104
    from Constance Fairburn 305–07app.
    from Eric Cox-Walker (HKRNVR) 263–6, 303–05app.
    from Eva Davidson 272, 273
    from Peter
      during engagement 61–6, 67–72, 74–94, 255–7
      during evacuation
        in PI 124–6, 128–31, 132–46, 255–7
        in Sydney 171–80, 181–2, 183–97, 198–99
      on journey to Aden 203–06, 207–11, 213–18
      from Aden 219–21, 222–5
      on journey from Aden to HK 227–31, 232–5
      from HK post-Aden 236–49, 250–4
      following invasion of HK 260–2
    to her mother 53–9, 96–101
Dulley Rock 43, *44*
Dutch East Indies (DEI) 164, 212n., 249n.

Eastern front *see* 'Russian Campaign'
Empress of Japan 50, 127n.
England *see* Great Britain, role in war
EOF *see* car, Austin 10 (EOF)
E's *see* Davidson, Edgar ('UE'); Davidson, Eva ('AE')
evacuation of women and children, from HK 123–4, 127n., 162, 296–98app.
  criticism of 136n., 140, 142, 150, 163, 180
  Evacuations Exemption Committee 153, 161
  legal cases against 162, 164–5, 171
  of Kowloon 264
  rules of 126n., 133, 151, 155, 244
EWO *see* Jardine Matheson & Co.
exchange rates 295app.

Fairburn, Constance 272, 289app., 305–07app.
Ferguson, G. P. (Fergie) 93, 172, 278, 289app.
  sharing house with Peter 60, 61, 75
finances 65, 225
  taxes 63, 163–4, 196
  Therese's, upon marriage 56, 63, 91, 246
flat *see* Peak, The, No. 168, P&T's home on
France 123, 204n.
  see also Battle of Oran (1940)

Gandy, Lt. Cmdr. G. H. 247, 274–5, 276, 289app.
Geer, R. (Bobby) 128, 133, 191, 192, 289app.
George V, King 50
Germany 112, 263
  Balkans Campaign 178, 187
  invasion of Low Countries and France 123
  invasion of Norway 122n.
  pacts with Japan and Italy 120n., 156–7, 193
  Peter's opinions on 117, 131–2, 190
  preparation for war 104n.
  'Russian Campaign' 194, 223, 240, 246n., 256, 261n.
  German losses in 225, 237
  see also Hitler, Adolf
Gibbs & Co., Chile 23
Gillespie, R. D. 253, 271, 290app.
Glover, Lt. H. C. 195, 206, 219, 272, 290app.
Gompertz, Geoffrey (Gomp) 75, 93, 159, 290app.
Goodwin, Lt. R. B. 206, 209, 240, 272–6, 290app.
Great Britain, role in WW2
  attacks on, by Germany 156, 193n.
  death toll from invasion of HK 268

INDEX

Japan
  declaration of war on 263
  relationship with 257n., 258
  sovereignty of HK 30–1
  threat of war in 107, 131, 150
Greece, war in 178, 186–7
Grieve, Roger 39, 53, 40–3, 44 290*app.*
Griffiths (Griff) 60, 75, 93
Guangzhou *see* Canton

Hahn, Emily 243, 291*app.*
Hall, FC 65, 84, 145, 244, 291*app.*
Hall, Mrs 145, 291*app.*
Helen, Aunt (Macpherson) 75, 92, 292*app.*
Hideki, General Tojo 236, 258
Hindmarsh, Desmond 191, 194–5, 264n.
Hirohito, Emperor Sh wa 259
Hitler, Adolf 117, 169n., 193–4
  see also Germany
HK Defence Force 267
HMAPV *St. Aubin* 118, 119, 299*app.*, 300*app.*
  Peter's duties on 125, 128, 135
  see also Aden, Peter's trip to (1941)
HMPS *Perla* 112, 115, 211, 299*app.*
HMS *Barnet* 45, 47, 75
HMS *Cornflower* 175, 241, 263, 264, 299*app.*
  Peter as First Lieutenant of 240, 242, 253
HMS *Cornwall* 227n.
HMS *Hermes* 43, 216n., 216, 217n.
HMS *Tamar* 45
Ho Tung, Sir Robert 32, 155, 291*app.*
Hong Kong 30, 34–6, 110, 123–4, 185n.
  climate in 24, 67
  governance of, by China and Great Britain
  constitutional reform, calls for, in HK 33
  historical ties with HK 30–1, 32–3
  harbour 24, 73
  maps of 16–17, 22
  Peter's arrival in, 1930s 23, 28–9, 34
  return journey from Aden 235, 236
  refugee camps in 107n., 124
  war between China and Japan
  attempted attack by Japan (1940) 119–20
  change in threat of invasion (1941) 256–7
  invasion and occupation 262–4, 267–8, 278
  following surrender of Japanese 279–80
  see also Kowloon, Hong Kong
  members escape HK following invasion 276
  Peter's duties with 43, 112, 115, 116, 249, 257
  see also HMPS *Perla*; HMS *Cornflower*; Royal Naval Volunteer Reserves (RNVR)
Hong Kong Club 35, 35
Hong Kong Royal Naval Volunteer Reserve (HKRNVR) 43, 45–6
  see also Royal Naval Volunteer Reserve (RNVR)
hotels, in HK 34–5

Imperial Airways 38–40
Italy, role in war 123, 156, 169n., 263

Japan
  air attacks on Singapore 167n.
  and Burma Road 128n., 134, 136, 155, 157
  China, war with 134, 171, 157, 258, 262
  attempted attack on HK by Japan (1940) 119–20
  invasion and occupation of HK 34, 256–7, 262–4, 267–8, 278
  occupation of 32, 67n, 95, 110–11, 115, 120
  surrender of Japan 279–80
  threats of invasion in 134, 236, 237–8, 301–02*app.*
  death toll, from HK invasion 268
  embargoes placed on, by USA 155, 221n., 238n., 258
  'Manchurian incident' 32, 113–14, 255n.
  pacts with Germany and Italy 120n., 156–7, 193
Japanese concentration camps *see* concentration and POW camps
Jardine Matheson & Co. 34, 35, 71, 241n., 278
  archives of 301–02*app.*
  Peter's work with 23, 71, 88, 118, 155
Joseph, Sister Marie *see* Dulley, Evelyn (sister)
journeys, between London to HK 24–5, 38, 40

Keswick, William Johnstone (Tony) 34, 62, 65, 291*app.*
  see also Jardine Matheson & Co.
Killery, Peggy 55, 62, 292*app.*
Killery, Val 185, 291*app.*
Kowloon, Hong Kong 30, 46, 49, 263, 264

languages 33
leisure activities, in HK 49
  see also sailing, Peter's love of

Macpherson, Agnes Leonora *see* Dulley, Agnes Leonora (mother)
Macpherson, Helen G. (Aunt) 75, 92, 292*app.*
Madras, India 230, 231, 232–3
mail
  delivery of 48, 178, 213
  censorship of 115–16, 208, 271
Maltby, Major General 262, 268, 276
'Manchurian incident' 32, 113–14, 255n.
marriage *see also* Dulley, Hugh William Macpherson (Peter), engagement of
  Chinese traditions of 62n
  discouragement of, by companies 23–4

318

minesweeping 75, 112*n*., 118
Ministry of Economic Warfare 185*n*.
Monsoon (yacht) *41*, 43, 80
   entered in races 89, 93
   sale of 159, 169
monsoons 189, 284*g*.
Morgan family 154, 222
Mussolini, Benito 123, 169*n*.

Nanking (Nanjing) 32, 67, 77, 95, 115
navigation, Peter's skill at 177, 178–9, 187, 189
   on trip to Aden 203, 234–5
   pilotage 190, 209, 240
   see also sextant (navigation tool)
Nazi regime *see* Hitler, Adolf
Nellore (ship) 171, *173*, 174, 176, 181
Neptuna (ship) 147, 161, 165–6, 167–9, 171
Netherlands 211
   Dutch East Indies (DEI) 164, 212*n*., 249*n*.
   involvement in war 123
   loyalties of Dutch 210, 212
New Zealand, involvement in war 186*n*.
Noble, Sir Percy 227*n*., 257*n*.
Norfolk Broads 105, *106*
North Africa, war in 131*n*., 191, 238*n*.
Norway, invasion of, by Germany 122*n*.

Olympic Games, Paris (1924) 28
Opium Wars 30
Oran, Battle of (1940) 131, 217

pacts *see* axis
Padang, Indonesia 208–212
Paris Olympics *see* Olympic Games, Paris (1924)
Paterson, J.J. 159*n*., 276, 301, 302
Peak, The 37, 40, 53, 67, *73*, *99*, *184–5*
   Army, use of 46
   drying rooms 145
   No. 168, P&T's home on 100–03, 110, 120, *121*
   after evacuation 124, 128–9, 135, 169, 177
   oars salvaged from 278–9, *282*
   see also Geer, R. (Bobby)
   No. 191, Edgar and Eva Davidson's home on *129*
   Peak Church *97*, 101
Pearl Harbour, Battle of 258, 268
Peking 32
Penang, Malaysia 28, 232, 233
Peninsular & Orient Steam Navigation Company (P&O) 25
Perla see HMPS *Perla*
Petrie, J. 133, 134, 242, 253, 292*app*.
Philippine Islands (PI) 258, 263, 268, 295*n.app*.
   P&T honeymoon in 74, 81, 88, 91, 99–100

   evacuation to *see* evacuation of women and children, from HK
   see also Baguio, Philippines
pilotage 190, 209, 240 *see also* navigation
place names (pre–1945 usage) 286*app*.
Postbridge, Deep Water Bay, HK 265–6, *265*, 304*app*.
Potter, John 272, 292*app*.
Potts, Antonia 244, 293*app*.
POW camps *see* concentration and POW camps
Proulx, Benjamin 193*n*., 276, 293*app*., 311–12*app*.
Pudge, Lt. Cmdr. James (Peter) 281*n*.

raiders (German ships) 207*n*., 233*n*.
Ralph, Doreen 182, 263*n*., 293*app*.
Rawalpindi see SS *Rawalpindi*
recruitment, in the Far East 23–4
Repulse Bay Hotel, HK 34, *93*, 193*n*.
Richlieu (French battleship) 217*n*.
Rocky Island Bay 32
Roosevelt 66*n*., 165
rowing, Peter's talent for 28, *29*, 40–3, 44
Royal Hong Kong Yacht Club 35, 40–3
Royal Naval Volunteer Reserves (RNVR) 45, *46*, 47, 113
   disregard for, by Royal Navy 190, 197, 199, 205, 219, 234–5
   Peter's role in 45, 120
   see also HMS *Cornflower*, Hong Kong Royal Naval Volunteer Reserve (HKRNVR)
Royal Navy (RN), in HK 44–6, 112–13, 262
'Russian Campaign' 194, 223, 240, 246*n*., 256, 261*n*.
   German losses in 225, 237

sailing, Peter's love of 36, 40–4, 68
   described by Therese 53
   see also rowing; ship travel
Sander, Agnes Helen (Nancy) (mother-in-law) 51, 63, 74, *108*, 200
   letters & messages 174–5
   from Peter 124, 126–8
   from Therese 53–9, 96–101
   planned visit to HK (1939) 110, 112, 122
Sander, Agnes (sister-in-law) 80, 99, 108
Sander, Therese *see* Dulley, Therese née Sander (wife)
sea-sickness 189, 195, 202
Sea Transport Officer 229
servants *see* staff (servants)
sextant (navigation tool) 177, 187, 203, 207
Seychelles, trip to Aden via 213–217
   Peters opinions of 214–15
Shanghai
   Peters trip to (1936) 65, 69, 70, 71–2, 301–02*n.app*.
   attacks on, by Japan 110, 115, 119–20
Shewan, Mrs 126–7, 132, 134, 139, 293*app*.

shipping companies 25
ship travel 24–6, 50, 71n
silver purchase programme 66n
Singapore
    Japanese invasion of 193n., 268
    trip to Aden via 202, 203, 204, 207, 232–3
Sirdhana (ship) *see* SS *Sirdhana*
Smith, N.L. 165–6, 247, 294*app.*
social activities 35–6, 49
social status, in HK 85, 88
social barriers, between Europeans and Chinese 33
Sommerfelt, A. 265, 272, 294*app.*
Sri Lanka *see* Colombo, Sri Lanka (Ceylon)
SS *Nestor* 280, 281n.
SS *Rawalpindi* 23
SS *Sirdhana* 189n.
St. Aubin *see* HMAPV *St. Aubin*
staff (servants) 34, 49, 65, 101–03, 124
    see also Ah Kung (boat boy); Amah; coolie
Stanley concentration camp 269, 271, *271*, 305–06*app.*, 310–11*app.*
Suez Canal, attacks on 190–91, 193
Sumatra, invasion by Japan 211n.
Sydney, Australia
    evacuation to 171, 181, 183, 186, 243n.
    after Peter's death 269, 276–8, *277*, 279, 280–1
    contingency plans for 127, 140, 146
Syria, war in 204n.

taxes 63, 163–4, 196
    see also finances
telegrams 215
Thames Rowing Club 28, *29*
Tientsin, China 111, 119–20
Tinson, George 266–7, 294*app.*
Tjinegara (ship) 167–9, *170*
Townend, Mr. & Mrs. 145, 146, 186, 196, 240–1, 294*app.*
train travel
    on honeymoon 100
    return journey from Aden 230, 231, 232
travel 38–40
    between London to HK 24–5, 38, 40
    ship travel 24–6, 50, 71n
Treaty of Nanking (1842) 30
Turkey 187n., 191
typhoons 77, 78–80, *79*, 81, *82*, 85

UE *see* Davidson, Edgar ('UE')
United States of America (USA), role in war 154, 157, 158, 165
    embargoes against Japan 155, 221n., 238n., 258
    war declared on Japan 263

Vernall, Cmdr. J. R. 188, 199, 242, 272–6

'wash girl' 123
watch system 138n.
Watson, Lt. K. A. 197, *198*, 224, 247
Wavy Navy 45
weather systems
    monsoons 189, 284*g.*
    typhoons 77, 78–80, *79*, 81, *82*, 85
Wellingborough, Northampton 28
Westminster School, London 28
wires (communication) 40, 48, *270*
White Australia Policy 146n.
women, in HK 37, 130–1, 251
    travelling alone 71, 71n
    see also evacuation of women and children, from HK

Xiamen (Amoy) 188n.–190

yachting, Peter's love of 36, 40–4, 68
    described by Therese 53
    see also Monsoon (yacht)
Yamamoto, Admiral Isoroku 258

Zander, Agnes Helen *see* Sander, Agnes Helen (Nancy) (mother-in-law)
Zander, Max (father-in-law) 51